WOMEN
IN MUSIC

An Anthology of Source Readings

from the Middle Ages to the Present

Edited by Carol Neuls-Bates

HARPER TORCHBOOKS
Harper & Row, Publishers
New York, Cambridge, Philadelphia, San Francisco, Washington, London
Mexico City, São Paulo, Singapore, Sydney

1817

First HARPER TORCHBOOKS edition published 1986.

Designer: Sidney Feinberg

Library of Congress Cataloging-in-Publication Data

Neuls-Bates, Carol.
  Women in music.

  "Harper torchbooks."
  Bibliography: p.
  Includes index.
  1. Women musicians. 2. Women composers. I. Title.
ML82.N48   1986   780′.88042   81-48045
ISBN 0-06-132060-9 (pbk.)

86 87 88 89 6 5 4 3 2

Contents

Introduction   *xi*

MIDDLE AGES

1 Women as Singers in Christian Antiquity   3
2 Music in an Early Community of Women   6
3 Life at a Twelfth-Century Benedictine Convent   11
4 Hildegard of Bingen: Abbess and Composer   14
5 Three Women Troubadours   21
6 Women Among the Minstrels and as Amateur
   Musicians   28

RENAISSANCE

7 The Renaissance Lady   37
8 Vocal and Instrumental Music Performance at an
   Italian Convent   43
9 The Rise of Women as Virtuoso Singers   50

BAROQUE

10 Francesca Caccini: Singer-Composer   55
11 Elisabeth-Claude Jacquet de La Guerre: Composer
    and Harpsichordist   62
12 The Venetian Conservatories   65

CLASSIC PERIOD

13 Music as an Accomplishment   73
14 Marianne von Martinez: Composer and Singer   80
15 Maria Theresia von Paradis: Pianist on Tour   85

16 Corona Schröter and Julie Candeille:
    Two Composers Speak Out   87

    1820–1920

    Women as Concert Artists and in Opera

17 Clara Schumann: Pianist   91
18 Amy Fay: Pianist   109
19 Lillian Nordica: Operatic Soprano   122
20 Margaret Blake-Alverson: Contralto   131
21 Sissieretta Jones: Soprano   135

    Four Composers

22 Fanny Mendelssohn Hensel   143
23 Clara Schumann   153
24 Ethel Smyth   156
25 Luise Adolpha Le Beau   167

    A Composer's Wife

26 Cosima Wagner   175

    *Women as Amateur Performers, Music Teachers,
    and Music Patrons*

27 The Female Amateur: From Accomplishment
    to Achievement   179
28 Women as Teachers   184
29 Women as Patrons in the Club Movement   188

    Women as Orchestral Musicians

30 The Vienna Damen Orchester in New York, 1871   192
31 Caroline B. Nichols and the Boston Fadette
    Lady Orchestra   194
32 Camilla Urso on Professional Equity
    for Women Violinists, 1893   198

33   Should Women Perform in the Same
     Orchestra with Men?   202

     The "Woman Composer Question"

34   George Upton: A Classic Formulation of
     Women's Inferiority   206
35   Helen J. Clarke: Regarding Unequal Education
     in the Past   211
36   Mr. Meadows-White: Regarding the "Great Composer"
     Aspect of the Question   214
37   Amy Fay: Women Have Too Well Aided Men   217
38   Mabel Daniels: Fighting Generalizations
     About Women   219
39   A Corollary to the Question: Sexual Aesthetics
     in Music Criticism   223

     1920–1981

     A Patron and an Educator

40   Elizabeth Sprague Coolidge: Patron of Chamber
     Music   231
41   Nadia Boulanger: Teacher of Composers   239

     *Women in the Orchestral Field from the 1920s
     to the 1940s*

42   Women's Symphony Orchestras   247
43   American Women Demand "Mixed" Orchestras   251
44   Three Musicians Recall Their Careers: Antonia Brico,
     Frederique Petrides, and Jeannette Scheerer   253

     An American Pioneer for Minorities

45   Marian Anderson: Contralto   273

     The "Woman Composer Question" Revisited

46   Ethel Smyth: "Female Pipings in Eden"   278
47   Carl E. Seashore: "Why No Great Women
     Composers?"   297

Three Composers

48   Ruth Crawford-Seeger   303
49   Elisabeth Lutyens   312
50   Nancy Van de Vate   323

     Selected Bibliography   *333*

     Index   *339*

Illustrations

page

12   *Nunnery Officials and Procession*, from a manuscript dated ca. 1300. (The British Library)

15   *Hildegard of Bingen*, from a twelfth-century manuscript. (Hessische Landesbibliothek, Wiesbaden)

23   *The Countess of Dia.* (Bibliothèque Nationale, Paris)

23   *Castelloza.* (Bibliothèque Nationale, Paris)

29   *Women in a Procession Singing and Playing Handbells and Small Drums*, from a late-fourteenth-century manuscript. (Österreichische Nationalbibliothek, Vienna)

30   *A Jongleresse with Handbells*, from a late-tenth-century manuscript. (Bibliothèque Nationale, Paris)

31   *Sappho with a Harp*, from a Boccaccio manuscript, ca. 1470. (The New York Public Library at Lincoln Center)

32   *The Lady at the Positive Organ*, from *The Woman with the Unicorn* tapestries, late fifteenth century. (Musée de Cluny, Paris)

33   *Music Making at the Court of Duke René II of Lorraine.* (Bibliothèque Nationale, Paris)

40   *April: The Group of Lovers*, Francesco del Cosa, 1470. (Civico Gabinetto Fotografico, Ferrara)

41   *Three Young Women Performing Claudin de Sermissy's Chanson "Jouyssance vous donneray,"* ca. 1530. (Schloss Rohrau, Vienna)

42   *Woman Playing a Viol*, Tobias Stimmer, 1570s(?). (The New York Public Library)

57   *Lady Playing the Virginals*, Wenceslaus Holler, 1635. (The New York Public Library)

58   *The Sense of Hearing*, Abraham Bosse, 1636. (The Metropolitan Museum of Art)

59   *Woman with a Lute*, Joannes Vermeer, ca. 1664. (The Metropolitan Museum of Art)

67   *Gala Concert in the Casino Filharmonico*, Francesco Guardi, eighteenth century. (Alte Pinakothek, Munich)

page

75   *The Song*, Francesco Bartolozzi, after H. Bunbury, late eighteenth century. (The New York Public Library)

76   *Lady with a Harp: Elizabeth Ridgely*, Thomas Sully, 1818. (The Metropolitan Museum of Art)

82   *Mme. Favart*, François Hubert Drouais, 1757. (National Gallery of Art, Washington)

102   *Clara Schumann and Joseph Joachim*, Adolph Friedrich Menzel, 1854. (F. Bruckmann, Munich)

124   Lillian Nordica as Elsa in *Lohengrin*. (Robert Tuggle)

137   Sissieretta Jones. (The New York Public Library)

145   *Fanny Mendelssohn Hensel.* (The New York Public Library)

158   *Ethel Smyth at the Piano and Singing*, John Singer Sargent, 1901. (National Portrait Gallery, London)

238   Elizabeth Sprague Coolidge. (The New York Public Library at Lincoln Center)

241   Nadia Boulanger. (The New York Public Library at Lincoln Center)

260   Frederique Petrides and the Orchestrette of New York. (Frederique Petrides)

275   Marian Anderson. (The New York Public Library at Lincoln Center)

306   Ruth Crawford-Seeger. (Library of Congress)

Introduction

This anthology of source readings concerns the work of women in Western art music: chiefly as composers and performers, and to a lesser extent as patrons and educators. Many readings feature notable women, whereas others focus on lesser-known figures and on the collective activity of women in informal music making, as performers in convents, conservatories, and orchestras and as composers. The anthology does not pretend to trace the entire history of women in music, but it does outline parts of the history and charts the progress achieved by women in the professional arena. For although women have always made music, they have been subject to limitations and prescriptions; historically they have been encouraged as amateurs but not as professionals.

There are three broad purposes to the book. The first is to present vivid, contemporary accounts of women musicians, most often told in the words of the women themselves. A second aim is to call attention to the ways in which particular women have been able to obtain the encouragement, training, and opportunities necessary for a professional career, these advantages having been far less accessible to women in the past than to men. And third, the anthology seeks to illuminate women's experience by presenting examples of the prescriptive literature that has advised women at earlier times about their proper roles in music.

A few readings portray the female amateur, but the majority are about the professional or aspiring professional, and of these the major share date from the nineteenth and twentieth centuries. This imbalance reflects not only the availability of materials but also the increased participation of women in the field, made possible chiefly by the introduction of conservatory training. Indeed, before the rise of conservatories in Europe and the United States in the late eighteenth and nineteenth centuries, women musicians typically came from a limited number of backgrounds: the convent; the aristocracy, in which case women could command education, although in many instances only with men's consent; and finally, those families of musicians who nurtured their daughters' talents as well as their sons.' But even if a solid education in music could be obtained, there were additional obstacles facing women as professional performers and composers, and at the risk of creating a bleak mood in an introduction to a book that is overwhelmingly positive about what women have been able to achieve, it is only fitting that the restrictions against women should be reviewed here briefly.

The initial obstacle was the exclusion of women as singers from the church, beginning in the fourth century, in keeping with the Pauline injunction *Mulier in ecclesia taceat.*[1] As some compensation, women could and did make music in their separate convents, but these institutions hardly offered a scope of activities comparable to those available to male musicians in the church at large. Second, when women did establish themselves as professional singers in the mainstream in Italy late in the sixteenth century, thereby creating a demand for their high sound, the Catholic Church—in the throes of the Counter Reformation—advanced the castrato.[2]

In church castrati sang the treble parts that traditionally had been entrusted to falsettists and boys. Their real triumph, however, was in the new Baroque genre of *opera seria*, where they sang heroic male roles and were rivaled in popularity *only* by the female soprano. And since women were banned from the stage in parts of Italy and also north of the Alps, in fear for their respectability, castrati sang women's roles too, both in *opera seria* and comic opera.[3] Only with the decline of the castrati late in the eighteenth century did women achieve their rightful place in all opera. Concurrently they were accepted as solo artists in the expanding concert life of the time, but not until the nineteenth century could they generally participate in choruses and

1. Let women keep silence in church.
2. Owen Jander, "Singing," *The New Grove Dictionary of Music and Musicians*, ed. Stanley Sadie (London: Macmillan, 1980), vol. 17, pp. 341–42.
3. Thomas Walker, "Castrato," *The New Grove Dictionary*, vol. 3, pp. 875–76. The castrato was not accepted in France, and women as solo singers were prized.

church choirs, with the exception of the Catholic and some Anglican churches.

As instrumentalists women in the past faced restrictions because of the sexual stereotyping of instruments that began during the Renaissance with the rise of instrumental music. Women were expected to cultivate "feminine" instruments—instruments requiring no alteration in facial expression or physical demeanor. Accordingly, keyboard instruments such as the harpsichord and the piano were deemed especially desirable, all the more because they could be played at home. Other "feminine" instruments included the viol and the lute in the Renaissance and the Baroque eras, and the harp and the guitar in the Classic and Romantic periods.

By contrast, "masculine" instruments were more numerous: winds, brass, percussion, the larger strings, and also—for more than the first two hundred years of its existence—the violin. Not all women, of course, observed these prescriptions, and in unique circumstances such as Italian convents late in the Renaissance and in the Venetian conservatories for women during the seventeenth and eighteenth centuries, described in Readings 8 and 12, women played a great variety of instruments. But for women in general, the psychological pressure to conform was considerable. Only with the second half of the nineteenth century did the choice of instrument among women widen significantly, and even today the effects of sexual stereotyping linger.

Regarding professional opportunities for women instrumentalists in early periods, women were active among the minstrels of the High and Late Middle Ages, and also in Renaissance convents as noted above; elsewhere in the Church, however, at courts, or in theater orchestras in the Baroque era, opportunities were not open to them. As concert artists, women keyboard players and violinists found acceptance beginning in the eighteenth century, thereby gaining recognition for women of their fine interpretive powers as instrumentalists. Nevertheless, orchestras and other ensembles remained closed, all-male affairs, in part because as solidified groups they could easily resist change. Subsequently the all-female orchestras and chamber ensembles of the late nineteenth and twentieth centuries proved positive ways in which women players and conductors reacted to their exclusion and found experience and employment by advancing their own institutions.

Women's work in composition in the past was directly related to the restrictions placed on them as singers and instrumentalists, for it must be remembered that until the nineteenth century the roles of composer and performer were totally intertwined. Women accordingly came to composition through the convent in the Middle Ages and Renaissance, as secular singers beginning in the second half of the sixteenth century, and as keyboard players and violinists beginning in the seventeenth and eighteenth centuries, respectively. Typically these women wrote the kinds of music that fit into their professional situations, which were more limited than men's. They did compose large works but not in the same proportion as men, simply because they did not hold the prestigious positions that offered optimum opportunities for performance as well as crucial on-the-job training. In short, women were not *maestri di capella* at courts and churches; they did not head opera companies and orchestras.

Because of male domination in the composition field and the age-old association of musical creativity with masculinity, naturally some women composers in the past—particularly the earliest-known women—were hesitant about advancing their work. Maddalena Casulana, for instance, in the mid-sixteenth century and Barbara Strozzi in the mid-seventeenth both wrote in the dedications of their earliest publications about the humility they felt as women. A similar hesitancy does not seem to have affected Francesca Caccini or Elisabeth-Claude Jacquet de la Guerre, who are among the earliest composers represented in the anthology, but the theme certainly surfaces a number of times in later readings.

With the proliferation of conservatories in the nineteenth century, the number of women who were able to train for professional careers increased dramatically. At first female conservatory students were accepted only in performance, but by the end of the century, as a result of the efforts of many a pioneer, women could enroll in theory and composition classes at most institutions. As a consequence of their increasing numbers, and also in response to the momentum generated by the first wave of the women's movement as a whole, women in music in the years 1880–1920 were more widely active than ever before. Among solo artists, many women reigned supreme as singers, pianists, and violinists of international stature. More and more women aspired to careers in composition, thus drawing attention to their presence in the field and generating the "woman composer question." The activity of women instrumentalists as players of an increasing variety of instruments and their interest in performing in orchestras and other groups has already been mentioned. Finally, there were two other major developments: the emergence of women as music teachers, typically as private teachers of weekly pupils, and the work of women as music patrons in the club movement.

Since 1920 women have continued to press for acceptance in the musical mainstream as performers, composers, and educators, and with the growth of the modern music industry they have also figured importantly as managers and administrators and in related capacities. In the United States the greatest gains have been the integration of all orchestras, which began during World War II, the acceptance of minority women performers, and the strides made by women conductors and composers in recent years, aided by the new wave of the women's movement. Once again women and their supporters have focused attention on the inequities women still face and have sought to dispel remaining prejudices. And as with the earlier wave, the women's movement today has created a strong interest in determining women's experience in history. It is to be hoped that the voices in this anthology will enable us to achieve a better understanding of the past as well as of the present position of women in music.

Some statements about the decisions I made as editor in assembling the anthology seem in order. In choosing the selections I was motivated to represent a variety of experiences among women over time, and naturally, since this was to be a reader of firsthand accounts, there were some notable women I would have liked to represent but couldn't because of the lack of suitable materials. For similar reasons there are some time gaps. A number of selections are being newly published, whereas others are appearing in English translation for the first time. Within the 1820–1920 and 1920–1981 categories, multiple readings on similar topics have been grouped together, and hence the order throughout the entire two categories is not always strictly chronological.

In the interests of authenticity I have retained the punctuation, grammar, and all other aspects of the original texts, except for inserting umlauts in German words for publications that originated in England and conforming *Leipsic* to *Leipzig*. Regarding women's names, I have tried to use the forms they preferred or prefer. Generally I dislike referring to women, or men, in print by their first names, but in the case of annotations for readings where families of musicians were involved, it was frequently *less* confusing and cumbersome to use first names alone to distinguish women from their male relatives.

Specific works of music in the readings have been identified in all but ambiguous situations, and first names have been supplied for less well-known musicians and other figures in the past, with the exception of a few cases in which the people could not be identified with certainty. Similarly I have defined specialized musical terms, although a basic familiarity with music has been taken for granted. Naturally there are many topical allusions in the texts, but I felt I needed to explain only those that might be obscure.

Many people have aided me in compiling this anthology, and I wish I had the space to thank them all by name. Special thanks to Jane Bowers, Barbara L. Grant, Judith E. Olson, Judith Tick, and Gretchen Wheelock.

MIDDLE AGES

1   WOMEN AS SINGERS IN CHRISTIAN ANTIQUITY

Although early Christians preached the spiritual equality of all people, they denied women full participation in religious life, initially excluding them from the priesthood. Women were important as singers, however, both as members of the congregation and in choirs through the fourth century. After the legalization of Christianity in the Roman Empire with the Edict of Milan in A.D. 313, the Church began to perfect its organization and standardize practices. Congregational singing was gradually abandoned, beginning in the second half of the fourth century, and all musical portions of services were entrusted to professional choirs of men and boys. Two accounts here describe the participation of women as singers before they were officially silenced. The first is by Philo, Judaeus, dating from the first century, about religious song and dance among the Therapeutae, a community of Jews in Egypt who had become partially Christianized.

The vigil is conducted on this wise. They all stand up in a crowd, and in the midst of the symposium first of all two choirs are formed, one of men, and one of women, and for each, one most honoured and skilled in song is chosen as a leader and director. Then they sing hymns composed to the praise of God, in many metres, and to various melodies, in one singing together in unison, and in another antiphonal harmonies, moving their hands in time and dancing; and being transported with divine enthusiasm, they perform one while lyric measures, and at another

John Julian, ed., *Dictionary of Hymnology* (London: John Murray, 1925), p. 206.

tragic plainsong, strophes and antistrophes, as need requires. Then
when each chorus, the men separately, and the women separately,
had partaken of food by itself, as in the feasts of Bacchus, and
quaffed the pure God-loving wine, they mingle together and become one choir out of two—the mimetic representation of that
of yore standing on the shore of the Red Sea on account of the
miracles wrought there. To this (the singing of the Son of Moses)
the chorus of the male and female *Therapeutae* afforded a most
perfect resemblance with its variant and concordant melodies;
and the sharp searching tone of the women together with the
baritone sound of the men effected a harmony both symphonious
and altogether musical. Perfectly beautiful are their motions, perfectly beautiful their discourse; grave and solemn are these carol-
lers; and the final aim of their motions, their discourse, and their
choral dances is piety.

*The Spanish Abbess Egeria made a lengthy pilgrimage to the
Holy Places in the East late in the fourth—or possibly early
fifth—century, about which she wrote a richly detailed account.
Egeria clearly was a woman of stature: she traveled with a retinue
of her own, and she met with abundant hospitality wherever
she went. Her description of a service in Jerusalem at daybreak
notes the involvement of women as singers together with men.*

Each day before cockcrow, all the doors of the Anastasis [the
Church of the Resurrection with the Holy Sepulchre] are opened;
and all the monks and virgins come down—the *monazontes* and
the *parthene* as they are called here—and not only they, but
laymen as well, men and women who wish to rise very early.
From this hour until dawn, hymns are sung, and responses are
made to the psalms, and likewise to the antiphons;[1] and after

---

George E. Gingras, ed. and trans., *Egeria: Diary of a Pilgrimage,* Ancient Christian
Writers: The Work of the Fathers in Translation, no. 38 (New York: Newman
Press, 1970), p. 89.
  1. While Egeria makes an early distinction here between psalm and antiphon,
Gingras, as translator, indicates that her exact meaning is not clear. The later,
standard use of the antiphon to frame a psalm is not implied.

each hymn a prayer is said. Priests in groups of two and three, and a like number of deacons, take turns on successive days in coming at the same time as the monks, and after each hymn or antiphon they recite prayers. At the time when it begins to grow light, they start singing the morning hymns. Then you see the bishop come in with his clergy. He immediately goes into the grotto, and from within the railings he recites first a prayer for all the people; then he himself mentions the names of those whom he wishes to commemorate, and he blesses the catechumens. Then, after he has said a prayer and blessed the faithful, the bishop comes out of the grotto sanctuary, whereupon all present come forth to kiss his hand, and he blesses each of them in turn as he goes out. And so the dismissal is given, and by now it is daylight.

2   MUSIC IN AN EARLY COMMUNITY
OF WOMEN

*While women were forbidden to sing in the Church at
large, they pursued music within their own religious institutions—the convents. As refuges of worship and peace, these
female communities offered women an opportunity for self-expression and some scope in leadership and education. Saint Gregory of Nyssa's* The Life of Saint Macrina *from the fourth century
attests to the importance of music in an early convent that
Macrina, Gregory's sister, headed in Asia Minor. Macrina was
the eldest of nine children of a family that also included Saint
Basil, and Gregory credits Macrina with having great influence
over her brothers' education and choice of a religious vocation.*

*In Gregory's account he visits Macrina on his return from a
synod of bishops in Antioch. He has had a radiant vision in
his sleep, which he does not fully understand, and as he approaches the convent he is informed of Macrina's illness. A
monastic community of men lived nearby the convent, as was
typical.*

As I made my way (rumor had announced my presence beforehand to the community), a line of men streamed toward us. It
was customary for them to welcome guests by coming out to
meet them. However, a group of women from the convent waited
modestly at the entrance of the church for us.

When the prayer and blessing were finished and the women
had responded to the blessing by bowing their heads, they removed themselves from our presence and went off to their own

Saint Gregory of Nyssa, *The Life of Saint Macrina*, trans. Virginia Woods Callahan,
Fathers of the Church, vol. 58 (Washington, D.C.: Catholic University of America
Press, 1967), pp. 174–75, 182–83, 186–87. Reprinted by permission of the pub-
lisher.

quarters. Since not one of them remained with me, I correctly surmised that their Superior was not among them. An attendant led me to the house where the Superior was and opened the door, and I entered that sacred place. She was already very ill, but she was not resting on a couch or bed, but upon the ground; there was a board covered with a coarse cloth, and another board supported her head, designed to be used instead of a pillow, supporting the sinews of her neck slantwise and conveniently supporting the neck. When she saw me standing at the door, she raised herself on her elbow; her strength was already so wasted by fever that she was not able to come towards me, but she fixed her hands on the floor and, stretching as far forward as she could, she paid me the honor of a bow. I ran to her and, lifting her bowed head, I put her back in her accustomed reclining position. But she stretched out her hand to God and said: 'You have granted me this favor, O God, and have not deprived me of my desire, since you have impelled your servant to visit your handmaid.' And in order not to disturb me, she tried to cover up her groans and to conceal somehow the difficulty she had in breathing, and through it all, she adjusted herself to the brighter side. She initiated suitable topics of conversation and gave me an opportunity to speak by asking me questions. As we spoke, we recalled the memory of the great Basil and my soul was afflicted and my face fell and tears poured from my eyes. But she was so far from being downcast by our sorrow that she made the mentioning of the saint a starting point towards the higher philosophy. She rehearsed such arguments, explaining the human situation through natural principles and disclosing the divine plan hidden in misfortune, and she spoke of certain aspects of the future life as if she was inspired by the Holy Spirit, so that my soul almost seemed to be lifted up out of its human sphere by what she said and, under the direction of her discourse, take its stand in the heavenly sanctuaries.

Soon after, Macrina died:

My soul was disquieted for two reasons, because of what I saw and because I heard the weeping of the virgins. Until now, they had controlled themselves and kept in check the grief in their souls and they had choked down the impulse to cry out for fear of her, as if they were afraid of the reproach of her voice already silent; lest, contrary to her order, a sound should break forth from them and their teacher be troubled by it. But when their suffering could no longer be controlled in silence (their grief was affecting their souls like a consuming fire within them), suddenly, a bitter, unrestrained cry broke forth, so that my reason no longer maintained itself, but, like a mountain stream overflowing, it was overwhelmed below the surface by my suffering and, disregarding the tasks at hand, I gave myself over wholly to lamentation. The cause of the maidens' grief seemed to me to be just and reasonable. They were not bewailing the deprivation of some ordinary bond or carnal attraction or any other such thing for which one mourns. But, as if they were torn away from their hope in God or the salvation of their souls, they cried out and loudly bewailed as follows:

'The lamp of our life has been extinguished; the light that directed the path of our souls has been taken away; the safety of our lives has been destroyed; the seal of our incorruptibility has been removed; the bond of our union has been demolished; the support of the feeble has been shattered; the care of the weak taken away. With you even our night was illuminated like day by the pure life, but now even the day is turned into darkness.' The ones who called her mother and nurse were more seriously distraught than the rest. These were those she had nursed and reared after finding them prostrate along the highway at the moment of starvation and she led them to the pure and uncorrupted life.

But when I recalled my soul from the depths, gazing intently at the holy head, and, as if I were rebuked for the disorderly conduct of the women, I said: 'Look at her,' shouting at the maidens in a loud voice, 'and be mindful of the instructions she gave you for order and graciousness in everything. Her divine soul sanctioned one moment of tears for us, commanding us to weep at the moment of prayer. This command we can obey by changing the wailing of our lamentation into a united singing of psalms.'

I said this with a loud voice to drown out the noise of the wailing. Then, I bade them withdraw a little to their quarters nearby and to leave behind a few of those whose services she accepted during her lifetime.

Gregory describes the preparation of the body and the funeral procession:

When our work was finished and the body was adorned with what we had, the deaconess spoke again and said that it was not fitting that Macrina should be seen by the maidens dressed as a bride. She said: 'I have a dark mantle of your mother's which I think we should put over her, so that this holy beauty should not be made splendid by the extraneous adornment of the robe.' Her opinion prevailed and the mantle was put over her. But even in the dark, the body glowed, the divine power adding such grace to her body that, as in the vision of my dream, rays seemed to be shining forth from her loveliness.

While we were engaged in these activities and the maidens' psalm-singing, mingled with lamentation, resounded through the place, in some way the report spread about on all sides and all the people of the area began to rush in so that the vestibule was not large enough to hold them. There was an all night vigil with hymn-singing as is the custom in the case of the praise of martyrs, and, when it was finished and day dawned, a crowd of those who had hurried in from the entire countryside, men and women both, broke in on the psalmody with their cries of grief. Although my soul was distressed by my misfortune, I kept thinking, nevertheless, how it should be possible not to leave undone anything suitable for such an occasion. Separating the flow of people according to sex, I put the women with the choir of nuns and the men in the ranks of the monks. I arranged for the singing to come rhythmically and harmoniously from the group, blended well as in choral singing with the common responses of all. But as the day was advancing and the place was overcrowded by the multitude of people, the bishop of the region, whose name was Araxius (he was present with the full company of his priests), ordered the bier to be brought forward immediately, on the grounds that there was quite a distance to be covered and the crowd would prevent the swift movement of the funeral procession. At the same time, he ordered all the priests who were with him to escort the bier themselves.

When this was decided upon and the activity begun, I went to one side of the bier and called him to the other, and two of the others, distinguished in rank, took their position at the opposite end. I led the way slowly, as was fitting, and we proceeded at a moderate rate. The people crowded around the bier and could not get enough of that holy sight, so it was not easy for us to pass. There was a row of deacons and attendants on each side of the funeral train, all holding wax candles; it was a kind of mystical procession, the psalmody continuing from beginning to end harmoniously, as is sung in the hymnody of the three boys.[1] It was a distance of seven or eight stadia from the monastery to the House of the Holy Martyrs, where the bodies of our parents were at rest. We completed the journey with difficulty throughout most of the day, for the accompanying crowd and those who were always being added to our number did not allow us to proceed according to our estimate. When we were inside the gate of the House, we first put down the bier and turned to prayer, but the prayer was the starting point of lamentation for the people. When there was a lull in the psalm-singing and the maidens were looking at the holy face, as the tomb of our parents was being opened in which she was to be placed, one of them cried out saying that no longer would we look upon her divine face. The rest of the maidens joined her in her outburst and confusion drowned out the orderly and sacred singing. Everyone wept in response to the wailing of the maidens. We nodded for silence and the leader guided them to prayer by intoning the usual prayers of the Church and the people came to attention.

1. Daniel 3:51.

3   LIFE AT A TWELFTH-CENTURY BENEDICTINE CONVENT

With the development of the Benedictine and other rules that formally divided the day between labor and divine service, liturgical singing became the primary community activity in most convents. Nuns, like monks, were trained in singing by their elders, and they met to sing eight times a day to observe the Office Hours at three-hour intervals, and in addition for Mass. Some nuns also wrote music for their choirs—both chant and polyphony—which became incorporated in the largely anonymous repertory of the Middle Ages. This contemporary description of life in a twelfth-century nunnery was written by Wilbert of Gembloux about the convent of Abbess Hildegard in Rupertsberg, near Bingen, on the Rhine River in Germany, where Wilbert spent three years as Hildegard's secretary. The life and work of Hildegard of Bingen are considered in Reading 4.

It is so wonderful to observe here the contest in striving for virtue, with what affection the mother loves her daughters and with what respect the daughters submit to the mother! It is impossible to say whether the mother or the daughters excel. For these holy handmaids of God are so eager to serve God, to guard themselves, to honor and obey one another that one can easily see in them how with the help of Christ the weaker sex has conquered over self, the world and the devil.

On feast days the nuns sit quietly in the cloister and practice reading or singing. On work days they are busy in the workshops,

Stephanus Hilpisch, *The History of Benedictine Nuns,* trans. M. Joanne Moggli (Collegeville, Minn.: St. John's Abbey Press, 1958), pp. 44–45.

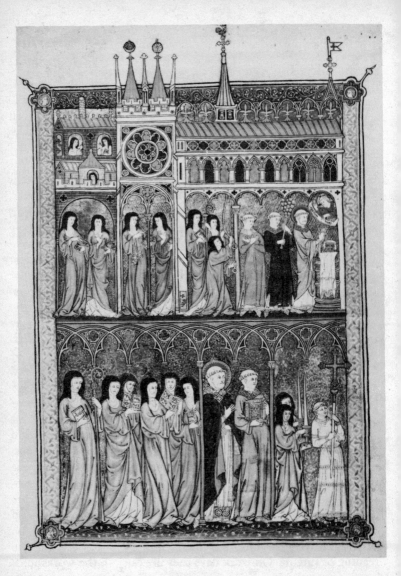

Nunnery Officials and Procession, from a manuscript dated ca. 1300. Top row, at right: Priests preside at the altar; behind them the sacristan pulls the bell rope; next, the abbess with her staff and the cellaress with her keys. Bottom row: Nuns in procession.

in copying books, in weaving clothing or doing other manual work.

The convent is rich in religious zeal and also in income. It has no tall buildings, but all the rooms are large, beautiful and monastic. All the workshops have running water and are well equipped. The convent supports 50 nuns, also many guests, who are never lacking, and a number of servants. The mother is kind to all, gives good advice to everyone who asks for it, resolves the most difficult problems presented to her, writes books, instructs her sisters, leads sinners back to the right path and is always fully occupied.

4   HILDEGARD OF BINGEN:
ABBESS AND COMPOSER

Abbess Hildegard of Bingen (1098–1179) is the lone woman composer of sacred music from the Middle Ages for whom a significant body of plainchant remains extant. She is further unique in that she was active also as a mystic, a writer of visionary and scientific works, an adviser to heads of state, and a teacher. Between 1151 and 1158 Hildegard collected seventy-seven of her chants—or songs, to use Hildegard's terminology—into a cycle as Symphonia armonie celestium revelationum (Symphony of the Harmony of the Heavenly Relations) *and gave them that name because, like the visions she experienced, "they are revealed to me and give musical forms to divine mysteries."*[1] *This repertory was intended mainly for use within her own convent, whose members all had trained voices.*

Hildegard wrote both the texts and the music for her liturgical songs, and likewise for her morality play Ordo virtutum (Play of the Virtues). *A large number of the songs are addressed to two women: thirteen to Saint Ursula and fifteen to the Virgin Mary, of which the text of Song 71, below, is an especially fine example. It has no designation as to liturgical function. Songs 38 and 39 extol women religious as a group. An antiphon is sung before and after a psalm, while a responsory is a musical postlude to a lesson.*

Barbara L. Grant, "Five Liturgical Songs by Hildegard von Bingen (1098–1179)," *Signs* 5/3 (spring 1980), pp. 566–67. © 1980 by the University of Chicago. Reprinted by permission of the University of Chicago Press.

1. Barbara L. Grant, "An Interview with the Sybil of the Rhine: Hildegard von Bingen (1098–1179)," *Heresies* 3/2 (summer 1980): 7.

ad exponen
dum ea dic
nıſ. nec ſcdín
inuentionıb
ne compoſ
çeleſtıbˀ deſuy
aıſ. ea ſıc edi
dum ı aud
enſ. ea ſcdín
lente. oſtend
ǧ ı tu ó hoı
be ea non ſ
nem ſ: ſecuı
tıſ ı diſpon
rıouın ſuoı
de çelo muc
hec. ı ſcrıbe
actun
quadr
ıncarnatıon
annoɥ ſep

Ecce quadra
geſimo tercıo

Hildegard of Bingen, from a twelfth-century manuscript of her *Scivias*. Hildegard, receiving a vision, prepares to record her revelations on a wax tablet with a stylus, while a monk waits to make a parchment copy.

SONG 71
ABOUT THE BLESSED VIRGIN MARY

Greetings, greenest branch
Who came forth on a spirit-filled
Quest for knowledge of all that is holy.

Since this is the time
When you have flourished in your branches,
Let there be greetings to you,
Greetings
Because the moist, vital heat of the sun has sweated into you
Like the pungent odor of balsam.

For in you has blossomed the beautiful flower
Which has given fragrance to all the spices
Which were dry.
And they have appeared all in full greenness.

Because of you the heavens gifted the meadow with dew
And every land has been made abundant,
Since your womb has brought forth wheat
And since the birds of heaven have made their nests in you.

At last is there food made for humanity
And great joy for the banqueters.

Therefore in you, sweet Virgin,
Every joy is in abundance
Also these Eve disparaged.
Now let there be praise to the Most High!

SONGS 38 AND 39
ANTIPHON AND RESPONSORY ABOUT THE VIRGINS
       Antiphon

You beautiful faces
Beholding God and building in the dawn
How noble you are.

In whom the King reflected himself
When he showed forth in you all the heavenly jewels;
And as you are also redolent with the odor of all those jewels
You are also the sweetest garden.

Responsory

You most glorious greenness,
You take root in the sun,
And in clear day-brightness
You shine forth in a wheel
Which no earthly excellence comprehends;
You are encircled
By the embraces of the divine mysteries.

Hildegard's most passionate beliefs about music are elaborated in a letter written to the prelates of Mainz circa 1178, when she was nearly eighty years old. Because of her refusal to exhume the body of a youth who had been excommunicated and was buried in the convent's cemetery, the prelates of Mainz—acting in behalf of the absent archbishop—imposed an interdict on Hildegard's community, banning the celebration of the Office Hours. Hildegard may have known that the youth had long since been given absolution, but in any event she keenly felt her authority and judgment had been violated, as her reply to the interdict makes clear.

In this reply Hildegard builds a reasoned theological argument that all sacred music, instrumental as well as vocal, functioned as a bridge for humanity to life, before the Fall. The key to the argument is the "spiraculo" of Genesis 2, the breath of life that God breathed into the body of the first human being. The same breath is used to sing and play in praise of God. In the course of establishing the biblical foundation for her argument, Hildegard sets forth her own brief history of liturgical music.

Jacques Paul Migne, ed., *S. Hildegardis, abbatissae: Opera omnia*, vol. 197 of *Patrologiae curcus completus . . . Series prima* [Latin] (Paris: Petit-Montrouge, 1855), "Epistola XLVII," cols. 219–21. This selection was chosen and translated by Barbara L. Grant and is introduced by her.

In order not to live as disobedients separated from the whole, we have left off singing the chants of the Divine Offices exactly according to the interdict, and we have abstained from participation in the Body of our Lord, whereas we celebrated it together every single month according to our general custom. So that above all for this reason, while I as well as all of my sisters was struck down with such great bitterness, held back by such monstrous harshness, and suppressed at length by such tremendous weight of authority, I heard these words in a vision. . . . And I heard the voice which comes from the living light bringing forth the different forms of praise, about which David sang in the psalms: "Praise Him in the sound of the trumpet; praise Him in the psalterium and cithra" etc., to which was added: "Let every spirit praise the Lord" (Psalm 150). In these words we are instructed about the interior life through exterior things: namely, just how to give form to the Offices serving the interior of human beings and direct them as much as possible towards the praises of the Creator, whether according to the setting of the texts or the nature of the instruments. . . .

The holy prophets, mindful of that divine sweetness and praise through which Adam rejoiced in God before the Fall, but not in his exile, wanted also to be aroused to these things themselves. So these prophets, taught by the very spirit they had received, composed not only psalms and canticles which were sung in order to kindle the devotion of the listeners, but also they created various instruments for the art of music. In this way they were able to bring forth a whole variety of sounds as much from the structure and properties of each instrument, as well as from the sense of the words. . . .

Clearly in imitation of the holy prophets, the studious and wise, through this same art, invented several kinds of instruments so that what they wanted to sing they could sing to the delight of their souls, by joining their hands while bending with the modulations of their voices. In this way can they also recall Adam (formed by the hand of God which is the Holy Spirit), in whose voice was the tone of every melody and the sweetness of the totality of musical arts before he transgressed and would have remained, were he still in the state in which he was created. . . .

Moreover, when that deceiver, the Devil, heard that man began to sing through the inspiration of God, and that in this way he was summoned to practice again the sweetness of the chants of the heavenly fatherland . . . then even in the heart of the Church and wherever he [i.e., the Devil] was able, whether through dissension and scandal or unjust oppression, he continually disrupted the manifestation and beauty of the psalms and hymns. . . .

It is necessary that you pay attention to this[2] so that you are drawn to this same devotion to the justice of God without the desire for punishment and revenge that comes from indignation or an unjust feeling of the heart, and it is always necessary to beware that in your judgments you are not possessed by Satan, who took man away from the heavenly music and from the delights of paradise. Therefore consider carefully that just as the body of Christ was born of the Holy Spirit from the integrity of the Virgin Mary, just so is the song of praise according to the heavenly music radiated by the Holy Spirit in the Church. The body is truly the garment of the soul, which has a living voice; for that reason it is fitting that the body simultaneously with the soul repeatedly sing praises to God through the voice.

In accordance with this meaning the prophetic spirit orders that God be praised with cymbals of jubilation and with the rest of the musical instruments which the wise and studious have created, since all of the arts (whose purpose is to fill uses and needs of man) are brought to life by that breath of life which God breathed into the body of man: and therefore it is just that God be praised in all things. . . . The prophecy in the psalm . . . exhorts us to confess ourselves to God in the cithara as we sing psalms with the ten-string harp; desiring to restore ourselves, let sound the cithara whose purpose on earth is to train the body; let sound the psalterium which gives back the sound from the heavenly realm above for expanding the spirit; let sound the ten-

2. "This" refers to the role of the Devil in obstructing the making of music, just as the prelates of Mainz were obstructing music performance at Hildegard's convent.

string harp for contemplation of the law. Therefore, those of the Church who have imposed silence on the singing of the chants for the praise of God without well-considered weight of reason so that they have unjustly stripped God of the grace and comeliness of His own praise, unless they will have freed themselves from their errors here on earth, will be without the company of the angelic songs of praise in heaven.

5   THREE WOMEN TROUBADOURS

In the secular realm the work of more than twenty women troubadours has survived from southern France from the twelfth and early thirteenth centuries, and since the Provençal language includes a designation for the female troubadour as trobaritz, *in contrast to the male* trobador, *undoubtedly numerous other women were active. Special circumstances permitted these women to flourish, chiefly their noble birth and their ability to inherit land under a legal system that was more favorable to women than those elsewhere in Europe. Also, during the Crusades of this period many aristocratic women governed fiefdoms during their husbands' absence, and while this situation prevailed throughout Europe, it was especially in effect in Provence and adjoining regions.*[1] *Together, then, these factors enhanced the position of women in the south of France and encouraged some women to find their voices as troubadours.*

Troubadour poetry takes its vocabulary from the economic and political system of vassalage in the Middle Ages. Just as the vassal paid homage to his powerful lord by swearing loyalty, so the troubadour in his poems pays homage to his lady. Similarly, the female troubadours address their men, but their poems tend to break away from the ritualized aesthetic of courtly love that is characteristic of the male troubadours, substituting instead a remarkable candidness, immediacy, and charm.[2]

Very little is known about the three women who are represented here, each with a single poem. The Countess of Dia (b.

Meg Bogin, *The Women Troubadours* (New York: Paddington Press, 1976), pp. 85, 87, 95, 97, 119, 121. Translations courtesy of the author. © 1976 Paddington Press Ltd.

  1. Bogin, pp. 29–36.
  2. Ibid., pp. 63–69.

*ca. 1140), probably from Die, and Castelloza (b. circa 1200),
of the Auvergne region, were aristocrats, while Azlais de Porcairages (b. ca. 1140), from a town near Béziers, appears to have
moved in courtly circles. The music for all the poems by the
women troubadours is lost, with the exception of the Countess
of Dia's striking "A chantar."*

Countess of Dia:
"A chantar m'er de so qu'ieu non volria"

Of things I'd rather keep in silence I must sing:
so bitter do I feel toward him
whom I love more than anything.
With him my mercy and fine manners are in vain,
my beauty, virtue and intelligence.
For I've been tricked and cheated
as if I were completely loathsome.

There's one thing, though, that brings me recompense:
I've never wronged you under any circumstance,
and I love you more than Seguin loved Valensa.[3]
At least in love I have my victory,
since I surpass the worthiest of men.
With me you always act so cold,
but with everyone else you're so charming.

I have good reason to lament
when I feel your heart turn adamant
toward me, friend: it's not right another love
take you away from me, no matter what she says.
Remember how it was with us in the beginning
of our love! May God not bring to pass
that I should be the one to bring it to an end.

The great renown that in your heart resides
and your great worth disquiet me,

3. Hero and heroine, respectively, of a lost romance.

The Countess of Dia.

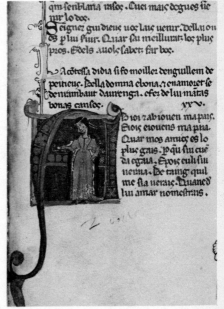

Castelloza.

for there's no woman near or far
who wouldn't fall for you if love were on her mind.
But you, my friend, should have the acumen
to tell which one stands out above the rest.
And don't forget the stanzas we exchanged.

My worth and noble birth should have some weight,
my beauty and especially my noble thoughts;
so I send you, there on your estate,
this song as messenger and delegate.
I want to know, my handsome noble friend,
why I deserve so savage and so cruel a fate.
I can't tell whether it's pride or malice you intend.

But above all, messenger, make him comprehend
that too much pride has undone many men.

Azalais de Porcairages: "Ar em al freg temps vengut"

Now we are come to the cold time
when the ice and the snow and the mud
and the birds' beaks are mute
(for not one inclines to sing);
and the hedge-branches are dry—
no leaf nor bud sprouts up,
nor cries the nightingale
whose song awakens me in May.[4]

My heart is so disordered
that I'm rude to everyone;
I know it's easier to lose
than gain; still, though I be blamed
I'll tell the truth:
my pain comes from Orange.[5]

4. This line recalls the May songs of the popular tradition.
5. Perhaps a reference to Raimbaut d'Orange, a great troubadour.

That's why I stand gaping,
for I've lost the joy of solace.

A lady's love is badly placed
who argues with a wealthy man,
one above the rank of vassal:
she who does it is a fool.
For the people of Vélay[6]
say love and money do not mix,
and the woman money chooses
they say has lost her honor.

I have a friend of great repute
who towers above all other men,
and his heart toward me is not un-
true, for he offers me his love.
And I tell you I reciprocate,
and whoever says I don't,
God curse his luck—
as for myself, I know I'm safe.

Handsome friend, I'd gladly stay
forever in your service—
such noble mien and such fine looks—
so long as you don't ask too much;
we'll soon come to the test,
for I'll put myself in your hands:
you swore me your fidelity,
now don't ask me to transgress.

To God I commend Bel Esgar
and the city of Orange,
and Gloriet' and the Caslar,
and the lord of all Provence,
and all those there who wish me well,

6. Corresponds to the southern part of the Auvergne region.

and the arch where the attacks are shown.[7]
I've lost the man who owns my life,
and I shall never be consoled.

Joglar,[8] you of merry heart,
carry my song down to Narbonne,
with its *tornada* made for her[9]
whose guides are youth and joy.

Castelloza: "Amics, s'ie.us trobes avinen"

Friend, if you had shown consideration,
meekness, candor and humanity,
I'd have loved you without hesitation;
but you were mean and sly and villainous.
Still, I make this song to spread your praises
wide, for I can't bare to let your name
go on unsung and unrenowned,
no matter how much worse you treat me now.

I won't consider you a decent man
nor love you fully nor with trust
until I see if it would help me more
to make my heart turn mean or treacherous.
But I don't want to give you an excuse
for saying I was ever devious with you;
something you could keep in store
in case I never did you wrong.

It greatly pleases me
when people say that it's unseemly

---

7. The Roman arch of Orange was one of the outstanding monuments of medieval Provence. The other references in the stanza are to now unknown landmarks, presumably also in the area of Orange.

8. The *joglar* (*jongleur* in northern French) was the court performer who sang and accompanied the troubadour's composition by embellishment.

9. Probably the Viscountess Ermengarda of Narbonne, a major political and cultural figure over a period of fifty years. *Tornada* refers to the closing of the piece.

for a lady to approach a man she likes
and hold him deep in conversation;
but whoever says that isn't very bright,
and I want to prove before you let me die
that courting brings me great relief
when I court the man who's brought me grief.

Whoever blames my love for you's
a fool, for it greatly pleases me,
and whoever says that doesn't know me;
I don't see you now at all the way I did
the time you said I shouldn't worry,
since at any moment I might
rediscover reason to rejoice:
from words alone my heart is full of joy.

All other love's worth naught,
and every joy is meaningless to me
but yours, which gladdens and restores me,
in which there's not a trace of pain or of distress;
and I think I'll be glad always and rejoice
always in you, friend, for I can't convert;
nor have I any joy, nor do I find relief,
but what little solace comes to me in sleep.

I don't know why you're always on my mind,
for I've searched and searched from good to evil
your hard heart, and yet my own's unswerving.
I don't send you this; no, I tell you myself:
if you don't want me to enjoy
the slightest happiness, then I shall die;
and if you let me die, you'll be a guilty man;
I'll be in my grave, and you'll be cruelly blamed.

6 WOMEN AMONG THE MINSTRELS AND AS AMATEUR MUSICIANS

Specialized terms in languages, literary sources, and iconography all attest to the activity of women as professional musicians among the minstrels and in amateur music making during the High and Late Middle Ages. Just as Provençal makes the distinction between the trobador *and* trobaritz, *Old English differentiates between the male musician as* gligmann *and the female as* gliewmeden. *Similarly, the famous incorporation of minstrels in Paris in 1321 states that the agreement is between the city officials and the* menstreus *and* menestrelles, *the* jongleurs *and* jongleresses.

That women played an important part in informal music making is implied by the French literary romances of the twelfth through the fourteenth centuries, which are rich with descriptions of medieval courtly life.[1] La clef d'amors *prescribes singing as a "noble and beautiful thing, especially for a young woman," who should "sing with a melodious, simple, pleasant, and gracious voice."*[2] *Typically the amateur females in the romances are singers, but they also play stringed instruments such as the psaltery, fiddle, lyre, and harp. Fresne, in* Galeran de Bretagne, *for instance, plays the harp and knows "lais and songs . . . all the Saracen tunes, Gascon and French songs, songs from Lorraine [and] Breton lais."*[3] *The heroine of Chrétien de Troy-*

1. Yvonne Roxseth, "Les femmes musiciennes du XII° au XIV° siècle," *Romania* 61 (1935): 464–80; Maria Vedder Fowler, "Women Musicians in Medieval France," in *Women Making Music: Studies in the Social History of Women Musicians and Composers,* ed. Jane Bowers and Judith Tick (Berkeley, Calif.: University of California Press, 1982).

2. *La clef d'amors,* ed. Auguste Doutrepont, *Bibliotheca Normannica* V (Halle: Max Niemeyer, 1890), lines 2589–90, 2601–62.

3. Jean Renart, *Galeran de Bretagne,* ed. Lucien Foulet (Paris: Édouard Champion, 1925), pp. 1168–71.

es's Philomena *is skilled in playing the psaltry, lyre, and rebec (fiddle), and in making verses.*[4] *Finally, the romances abound in references to groups of young women singing and dancing.*

The five illustrations of women making music that appear on the following pages constitute this "reading."

Women in a Procession Singing and Playing Handbells and Small Drums, from a late-fourteenth-century manuscript.

4. Chrétien de Troyes, *Philomena: Conte raconté d'après Ovide,* ed. C. de Boer (Paris: Paul Geuthner, 1909), lines 197–200.

A Jongleresse with Handbells, from a late-tenth-century manuscript.

Sappho with a Harp, from a manuscript of Boccaccio's *De claris mulieribus (Concerning Famous Women),* ca. 1470. The Greek poet appears dressed as a woman of the fifteenth century.

The Lady at the Positive Organ, from *The Woman with the Unicorn* tapestries, late fifteenth century.

Music Making at the Court of Duke René II of Lorraine; detail of women playing the dulcimer, shawm, and portative organ.

RENAISSANCE

7 THE RENAISSANCE LADY

A highly influential image of the Renaissance lady was set forth by Baldesar Castiglione in The Book of the Courtier, *a handbook for gentlemen and women about the social and cultural functions of the Renaissance court. First published in 1528 in Venice, the work became widely read throughout Europe. In describing the attributes of the lady, Castiglione creates a paradox. The lady has the same virtues of mind as the courtier and the same education in letters, music, painting, dancing, and so on. "Culture," to quote Joan Kelly-Gadol on* The Courtier, *"is an accomplishment for noblemen and women alike, used to charm others as much as to develop the self. But for the woman charm becomes the primary occupation and aim."* [1] *While the courtier's chief task is the profession of arms, and he hunts and engages in many sports, the lady is assigned a decorative role, entertaining men with her gracious conversation, charm, and modesty.*

In the cultivation of music there is a similar disparity between the amateur courtier and the amateur lady. Music ranks high on the list of Castiglione's attainments, and a courtier should be able to read music and to play several instruments. A lady, however, should sing or choose her instrument in accordance with the ideal of feminine gracefulness. Giuliano de' Medici speaks about the lady, and Lodovico Pia about the courtier in the following excerpts.

Baldesar Castiglione, *The Book of the Courtier*, trans. George Bull (New York: Penguin Books, 1967), pp. 212, 94, 215. Copyright © 1967 by George Bull. Reprinted by permission of Penguin Books Ltd.

1. Joan Kelly-Gadol, "Did Women Have a Renaissance?," in *Becoming Visible: Women in European History*, ed. Renate Bridenthal and Claudia Koonz (Boston: Houghton Mifflin, 1977), p. 150.

Regarding the chief attribute of the lady:

Leaving aside, therefore, those virtues of the mind which she must have in common with the courtier, such as prudence, magnanimity, continence and many others besides, and also the qualities that are common to all kinds of women, such as goodness and discretion, the ability to take good care, if she is married, of her husband's belongings and house and children, and the virtues of being a good mother, I say that the lady who is at Court should properly have, before all else, a certain pleasing affability whereby she will know how to entertain graciously every kind of man with charming and honest conversation, suited to the time and the place and the rank of the person with whom she is talking. And her serene and modest behavior, and the candour that ought to inform all her actions, should be accompanied by a quick and vivacious spirit by which she shows her freedom from boorishness; but with such a virtuous manner that she makes herself thought no less chaste, prudent, and benign than she is pleasing, witty, and discreet.

About music and the courtier:

Gentlemen, I must tell you that I am not satisfied with our courtier unless he is also a musician and unless as well as understanding and being able to read music he can play several instruments. For, when we think of it, during our leisure time we can find nothing more worthy or commendable to help our bodies relax and our spirits recuperate, especially at Court where, besides the way in which music helps everyone to forget his troubles, many things are done to please the ladies, whose tender and gentle souls are very susceptible to harmony and sweetness. So it is no wonder that both in ancient times and today they have always been extremely fond of musicians and have welcomed music as true refreshment for the spirit.

About feminine gracefulness, music, and the lady:

Since I may fashion this lady my own way, I do not want her to indulge in these robust and manly exertions [e.g., handling weapons, riding, hunting, and nearly all sports] and moreover, even those that are suited to a woman I should like her to practise very circumspectly and with the gentle delicacy we have said is appropriate to her. For example, when she is dancing I should not wish to see her use movements that are too forceful and energetic, nor, when she is singing or playing a musical instrument, to use those abrupt and frequent *diminuendos* that are ingenious but not beautiful. And I suggest that she should choose instruments suited to her purpose. Imagine what an ungainly sight it would be to have a woman playing drums, fifes, trumpets, or other instruments of that sort; and this is simply because their stridency buries and destroys the sweet gentleness which embellishes everything a woman does. So when she is about to dance or make music of any kind, she should first have to be coaxed a little, and should begin with a certain shyness, suggesting the dignified modesty that brazen women cannot understand. She should always dress herself correctly, and wear clothes that do not make her seem vain and frivolous. But since women are permitted to pay more attention to beauty than men, as indeed they should, and since there are various kinds of beauty, this lady of ours ought to be able to judge what kind of garments enhance her grace and are most appropriate for whatever she intends to undertake, and then make her choice.

April: The Group of Lovers, **from** the Schifanoia Months at Ferrara, Francesco del Cosa, 1470. Some of the women hold lutes and recorders.

Three Young Women Performing Claudin de Sermissy's Chanson "Jouyssance vous donneray," Master of the Three-Quarter Figures, ca. 1530. The two instrumentalists play a wooden flute and the lute, while the third performer appears poised to sing.

Woman Playing a Viol, Tobias Stimmer, 1570s(?).

Late in the sixteenth century a number of Italian convents were distinguished for their fine musical establishments, among them the convent of San Vito in Ferrara. The large influx into these orders of young women from wealthy families—some of whom had already trained in music—was partially responsible for an increase in activity. This influx in turn occasioned a considerable growth in the performance of polyphonic music and sparked the work of certain women as composers.[1] In his 1594 treatise on instrumental performance practice, Hercole Bottrigari provides an account of the nuns' ensemble at San Vito, which is the subject of this reading. Although the ensemble included singers, it was considered especially remarkable because of its instrumentalists.

Bottrigari reports twenty-three members in the San Vito ensemble, including cornetti and trombone players. In 1600 Giovanni Maria Artusi listed the entire composition of the group as cornetti, trombones, violins, viole bastarde (*lyra-viols*), *double harps, lutes,* cornamuses (*bagpipes*), *recorders, harpsichords, and voices.[2] Soon afterward, however, because of restrictions that were placed on Italian convents in the wake of the Counter*

Hercole Bottrigari, *Il Desiderio or Concerning the Playing Together of Various Musical Instruments,* trans. Carol McClintock (Rome: American Institute of Musicology, 1962), pp. 56–60. Reprinted by permission of Hänssler-Verlag.

1. Jane Bowers, "The Emergence of Women Composers in Italy, 1566–1700," in *Women Making Music: Studies in the Social History of Women Musicians and Composers,* ed. Jane Bowers and Judith Tick (Berkeley, Calif.: University of California Press, 1982).

2. Ibid.

Reformation, the ensemble at San Vito and others like it declined.[3]

Bottrigari's treatise is cast in the form of a dialogue between Alemanno Benelli, an anagram of the name of Bottrigari's friend Annibale Melone, who instigated the work, and Gratioso Desiderio. The maestra's wand described by Benelli is an early instance of the baton, which only became traditional with conductors in the nineteenth century.

Al. Now to that humble lay congregation which we have just mentioned,[4] it pleases me to add a most noble and high example of the musical concerts into which all sorts and divers kinds of instruments enter in the highest degree of perfection which human and earthly imperfection can achieve. . . .

Gr. And whatever concert can this be? It must certainly be of a marvelous excellence; and if it isn't the Philharmonic[5] I would never be able to guess.

Al. Indeed, it must be of a stupendous, if not marvelous excellence, as I can affirm, do affirm and confirm that it truly is, because I have had the good fortune not only to have been able to hear it but also to see it being assembled and effectively concerted together, both the first of the many occasions I was shown such a particular favor and on at least one other occasion. It appeared to me that the persons who ordinarily participated in this concert were not human, bodily creatures, but were truly angelic spirits. Nor must you imagine that I refer to the beauty of face and richness of garments and clothing, for you would err greatly, since one sees only the most modest grace and pleasing dress and humble deportment in them.

3. Ibid. Stricter claustration and curbs on the cultivation of polyphonic music were put into effect.
4. The Rivaruoli of Bologna, a group that gathered every evening for song.
5. The Accademia Filarmonica of Verona, a private organization of men especially devoted to madrigal singing.

Gr. You are making me so dizzy with your ambiguous speech, my mind responds to your will; however I should like to see if I could imagine which Concert that might be. But I can't come to any conclusion because if I think of the Philharmonic I feel that they do not fit your words very well for you have used the feminine gender; I cannot apply them to the three most noble ladies of the Duchess Serenissima of Ferrara for her private music,[6] since there is no great diversity of instruments, nor great number of them employed in their concerto; they almost always use their most sweet and sonorous voices in singing:—I don't know what to decide.

Al. As you can assure yourself, since I have never heard nor seen the concerts of the Philharmonic Academy, even though I believe because of the great fame of their worth that they might correspond to their academic name, which signifies lovers of harmony, I could not speak of them in any such way, and you may be certain that this concert is not theirs. Also, I would have had to use words of the masculine gender which, however, even though proffered under the feminine gender nonetheless relate to another, and have in themselves masculine force. Likewise you may be certain that I do not speak of the concert of those three Ladies, rather those three true and living images of the Graces—even though I can testify as to them, because I have been conceded more than once (thanks to the great kindness and generosity of their Serene Highnesses) the grace of both seeing and hearing them. Such concerts are not of that kind, as indeed you have said, in which a great variety of instruments are assembled and about which you have asked me to speak.

Gr. What then may this Concert be?

Al. Don't weary yourself any more, Sig. Gratioso; and if you so distress yourself only because you wish to guess what concert this might be, how you would melt away when you see them convene and play together with so much beauty and grace, and such quietness! You would certainly think

6. See Reading 9.

you were either dreaming or seeing one of those imagined incantations of the Sorceress Alcina; or perhaps one of those German dolls which by means of tempered steel springs move along the table playing instruments which have been made by their ingenious fabricators.

Gr. Good Lord, what kind of women are these?

Al. —And then finally when you hear the most sweet harmony which resounds in those angelic voices, and those instruments played with such judgment and discretion—

Gr. These are women, indeed?

Al. They are indubitably women; and when you watch them come in (for I will say "come" rather than "go," since I seem to be present there now) to the place where a long table has been prepared, at one end of which is found a large clavicembalo,[7] you would see them enter one by one, quietly bringing their instruments, either stringed or wind. They all enter quietly and approach the table without making the least noise and place themselves in their proper place, and some sit, who must do so in order to use their instruments, and others remain standing. Finally the Maestra of the concert sits down at one end of the table and with a long, slender and well-polished wand (which was placed there ready for her, because I saw it), and when all the other sisters clearly are ready, gives them without noise several signs to begin, and then continues by beating the measure of the time which they must obey in singing and playing. And at this point I am certain you would say, as also in such a moment I say, what the great Mantuan poet says repeatedly in his great poem:

Pandite nunc Elicona Deae Cantusque Movete. [Now, Goddesses of Song, fling Helicona wide.][8]

And you would certainly hear such harmony that it would seem to you either that you were carried off to Helicona or that Helicona together with all the chorus of the Muses

7. Harpsichord.
8. Vergil's *Aeneid*, books VII and X. Helicon is a mountain in Greece.

singing and playing had been transported to that place.

Gr. You told me not to distress myself, and yet you give me the greatest cause. I suffer to know at once where this Helicona may be, and who are these Muses; tell me now, if you don't want me to endure more agonies.

Al. Well then! Ferrara will be Parnassus; Helicona, the holy Church of San Vito; and the sacred Muses the reverend Nuns.

Gr. Then the Nuns of S. Vito in Ferrara make such concerts?

Al. That is the unvarnished truth. And if you had paid attention to the words I said in the beginning of my report, you would have known these women could only have been nuns. And if you should ever speak about this with [Giaches de] Wert, [Bartolomeo] Spontone, the Reverend Father [Costanzo] Porta, or [Claudio] Merulo of Correggio—musicians properly reputed to be the principal ones of our modern music—and several others who were in Ferrara in the same time I was there, I am most certain that they would tell you the same thing and perhaps even vouch for it more fully.

Gr. It seems strange that I have never before heard of this. But it is perhaps something new, and a work of [Hippolito] Fiorino and Luzzasco [Luzzaschi],[9] since they know how to do it considering their great concerto.

Al. What do you mean, a new thing? It is not at all new. If I were to speak of tens and twenties of years I would not be mistaken. Because of this, in great part, can one understand how the great perfection of their concordance comes about. Neither Fiorino nor Luzzasco, though both are held in great honor by them, nor any other musician or living man, has had any part either in their work or in advising them; and so it is all the more marvelous, even stupendous, to everyone who delights in music.

Gr. That's all right as to the general effect of their concerto. But what about the particulars of their learning to sing, and even more, to play instruments, particularly those of wind, which it is almost impossible to learn without maestri.

9. See Reading 9.

Being women they cannot easily manipulate Cornetti and
Trombones, which are the most difficult of musical instruments.

Al. Those instruments are nearly always used doubled in the
music which they play ordinarily on all the Feast days of
the year. And they play them with such grace, and with
such a nice manner, and such sonorous and just intonation
of the notes that even people who are esteemed most excellent in the profession confess that it is incredible to anyone
who does not actually see and hear it. And their passagework
is not of the kind that is chopped up, furious, and continuous,
such that it spoils and distorts the principal air, which the
skillful composer worked ingeniously to give to the *can-
tilena*;[10] but at times and in certain places there are such
light, vivacious embellishments that they enhance the music
and give it the greatest spirit.

Gr. I am stupefied; I am truly amazed. But, after all, who instructed them in the beginning? It must be necessary if one
wishes to maintain, if not to increase the bright splendor
of musical concerts, that there be someone who looks after
it, and is intelligent and expert enough to instruct, so that
it may be done so carefully and dextrously.

Al. That same nun who is the director of the concerto is also
Maestra of all the beginners both in singing and in playing;
and with such decorum and gravity of bearing has she always
proceeded and continued in this office that her equals, as
they are, are glad to acknowledge her and esteem her for
their superior, loving and obeying her, fearing and honoring
her completely.

Gr. She must have a rare and noble intellect to direct and instruct
in the profession of music those other honest and learned
persons, especially if they are numerous.

Al. If I remember rightly, there are twenty-three of them now
participating in this great concerto, which they perform only
at certain times—for most solemn feasts of the Church, or

10. Lyrical melody.

to honor the Princes, their Serene Highnesses, or to gratify some famous professor or noble amateur of music at the intercession of Fiorino or Luzzasco, or by the authority of their superiors; but never extemporaneously nor in haste, nor do they play all compositions, but only, as I said about the great concert of the Duke, those works judged to be prepared.

9 THE RISE OF WOMEN AS VIRTUOSO SINGERS

In the preceding reading, Bottrigari mentions the "three most noble ladies" who performed for the Duchess of Ferrara's "private music." His reference is, in fact, to the famous concerto delle donne, *which in the 1580s created a vogue for the high voice and established women as professional singers in the secular realm, under the patronage of Duke Alfonso II d'Este and Duchess Margherita Gonzaga at Ferrara. Although there were female amateurs who sang and played among the ladies-in-waiting at the Ferrara court prior to 1580, in the following decade the group made up of Laura Peverara, Anna Guarini, and Livia d'Arco evolved into a specialized and professional ensemble. They were joined by Tarquinia Molza in 1583. Under the direction of Luzzasco Luzzaschi, this* concerto delle donne *sang at private gatherings for the duke and duchess and their guests, often performing a secret repertory that was the property of the duke alone for some years.*

The Ferrara concerto *attracted wide interest, and soon imitations of the group sprung up at the courts of Mantua, Florence, Rome, and elsewhere. Collectively, the activity of these virtuoso singers had ramifications for the style of the late-sixteenth-century madrigal, with its scoring for two or three difficult parts in the treble clef, and in the seventeenth century for the new genre of opera, with its roles for trained women singers.[1] Con-*

Anthony Newcomb, *The Madrigal at Ferrara, 1579–1597*, 2 vols. Princeton Studies in Music no. 7 (Princeton, N.J.: Princeton University Press, 1979), 1:24–26.

1. Anthony Newcomb, "Sirens, Muse, or Musiciate: Professional Women Musicians in Sixteenth-Century Italy," in *Women Making Music: Studies in the Social History of Women Musicians and Composers,* ed. Jane Bowers and Judith Tick (Berkeley, Calif.: University of California Press, 1982).

temporary accounts attest to both the excellence of the Ferrara
concerto and the delight Duke Alfonso *took in these singers.*

Ambassador Orazio Urbani to the Florentine court:

26 June 1581

Cardinal Madruccio was entertained on the day of his arrival
with the usual music of the ladies, which takes place every day
without fail. The Duke is so inclined to and absorbed in this
thing that he appears to have placed there not only all his delight
but also the sum total of his attention. One can give no greater
pleasure to the Duke than by appreciating and praising his ladies,
who are constantly studying new inventions.

Cavalier Grana to Cardinal Luigi d'Este:

August 1581

His Highness was kind enough to seem glad to see me, and
after dinner in the rooms of the Duchess [of Ferrara] he had
those two ladies sing. At the end they sang a very beautiful new
piece, and at that time His Highness was kind enough to call
me to listen to it closely, for in truth besides being very beautiful
it was decorated with such lovely and *diversi passaggi*[2] that one
could not [hope to] hear better.

Alessandro Lombardini to Luigi d'Este about the visit of the
Duc de Joyeusse:

23 July 1583

In the morning the Duke went to find his Highness [the Duc
de Joyeuse] at his rooms, and they remained there together for
a while. They heard Mass in the small chapel and then went to
eat, with music as usual by trombones, cornets, and other instruments. After dining they retired [to their chambers] with great
ceremony as usual, the one wanting to accompany the other,

2. Literally various passages, or sections of music containing brilliant displays
of virtuosity.

and they stayed there until about 3:00 P.M. Then the Duke took him [the Duc de Joyeuse] to the rooms of the Duchesses, who were together, and, after a few ceremonies and without sitting down, they went into the first room where Luzzaschi was with the harpsichord. La Turcha (Peverara), La Guarina, and the other one, d'Arca, came in as well, and all three sang very nicely, alone, in duets, in trios altogether; they sang Echo dialogues, and many other beautiful and delicious madrigals. His Highness had put in the hands of His Excellency a book with all the things that the ladies were singing, whence they were greatly praised by that Prince and by the other gentlemen.

Finally, composer Alessandro Striggio's highly favorable report on the Ferrara concerto to his patron, Francesco de' Medici, at Florence.

July 29, 1584

Then for two hours the Duke favored me by having me hear his *conserto di donne* [*sic*], which is truly exceptional. These ladies sing excellently both with instruments and from part books, [and] they are sure in contrapuntal improvisation.[3] The Duke continually favored me by showing me in writing all of the works which they improvise upon, with all the runs and passages that they do. I hope that within eight–ten days Your Highness will permit me to return to Mantua, where I've left my wife and children, and there I will be able to compose more easily, in imitation of these songs of Ferrara, some for Your Highness's concerto.

Joanne M. Riley, ''The Influence of Women on Secular Vocal Music in Sixteenth Century Italy'' (Master's thesis, Wesleyan University, 1980), pp. 87–88.

3. The term *contrapuntal improvisation* as used here means the ornamentation of individual vocal lines in a polyphonic piece, such as a madrigal.

BAROQUE

Francesca Caccini's career is a leading example of how work as a professional singer led to composition in opera and other vocal genres for women in the Baroque era. As a daughter of the eminent singer-composer Giulio Caccini, Francesca (1587–1640?) enjoyed a tremendous head start in musical training at her father's school, as well as in growing up at the Medici court at an exciting time, when monody[1] and opera were new developments. Caccini made her debut as a singer in 1600 at barely thirteen years of age in the premiere of the first opera, Euridice, *by Jacopo Peri, with some numbers by her father. In 1607 she officially entered the service of the Florentine court.*

As a composer Caccini was active by the age of eighteen, and she wrote continuously thereafter: secular songs for her court appearances, sacred songs for Lenten concerts, and operas and other dramatic entertainments, for which she joined with other musicians at the court. Caccini's Primo libro *of 1618 represents the most extensive collection of early monodic music by a single composer up to that time. Her only other major extant work, from what appears to have been a sizable output, is the opera* La liberazione di Ruggiero dall'isola d'Alcina (The Liberation of Ruggiero from the Island of Alcina).

Caccini frequently collaborated with Michelangelo Buonarroti the Younger,[2] of whom she thought highly, as the two letters here indicate. In the first she discusses their work on parts of a festa, *a dramatic form similar to opera but less elaborate in production. This* festa—*which included an* invenzione, *or short comic scene—has not been identified.*

Maria Giovanna Masera, "Alcune lettere inedite di Francesca Caccini," *Rassegna Musicale* 5/3 (April 1940): 176–77, 179–80.

1. Accompanied solo song.
2. Grandnephew of the painter and sculptor.

My Most Illustrious and Most Honorable Signore

Your Lordship's hasty departure grieved me as much for the need we have of you as for the reason for which you left. Yet the news Your Lordship sends me makes me hope that your nephew will soon be out of danger, may it so please Our Lord.

I am doubly obliged to Your Lordship on account of the verses you sent me for Signora Giralda, for I can imagine the trouble with which you must have composed them, having cause to think of other things than poetry. They arrived most opportunely because, although we have rehearsed my music in the presence of Her Majesty, Madame, and the princesses, the Grand Duke has not yet heard it. However, we daily expect to be commanded, especially as one night we were assembled and ready until three o'clock in the morning, but because of the arrival of an ambassador, our performance was postponed to another night. This was fortunate because Madame asked why Signora Giralda did not yet sing alone, to which I answered that Your Lordship had not had the time to write your verses because a nephew of yours was in danger of death. I promise Your Lordship that Madame showed such sorrow that she could not have shown more.

Everyone's delight in the *invenzione* when it was said to be yours and in my prologue and envoi, and, in short, in the music as a whole, I can neither write nor express. Suffice it that I assure you it has been some time since I saw Her Majesty and Madame laugh so heartily. The entire room resounded with loud laughter, and Madame in particular spoke so well of Your Lordship that in truth you could not desire more. I reserve all the particulars to word of mouth; I will only tell you that in a cheerful voice Madame said to Her Majesty and to the entire audience that Your Lordship has no equal and that Your Lordship is able to compose in all styles and to suit yourself to all occasions, either serious or gay, easy or difficult. In short, she showed how delighted she was. As for the ladies, they carried themselves well and did themselves great honor.[3]

I do not want to neglect to inform Your Lordship of another particular I had forgotten, that is, that Madame liked the wit of

3. The group of female singers Caccini directed.

Lady Playing the Virginals, **Wenceslaus** Holler, 1635. The virginal, a small portable instrument of the harpsichord family, was once a popular home instrument.

The Sense of Hearing, Abraham Bosse, 1636. In this family concert, the five members are perhaps singing a madrigal, while two of the singers play supporting instrumental parts on the lute and the viola da gamba.

Woman with a Lute, Joannes Vermeer, ca. 1664.

the greedy doctors above all, and she repeated it two or three times. Now that Signora Giralda is singing, the *festa* will be perfect, and it will be ready, it so happens, before the Signor Grand Duke hears it.

I regret that Your Lordship does not think you can be here, but I do not want to fail to advise you to give some thought, if you can, to that little comedy for eleven actors, for we will be precisely that many. Let it be pleasing in its story, humorous, and with varied characters. Although we have not yet fully made up our minds, I have so much in hand that I want to warn you now in order that you not be taken by surprise, but can think about the plot in the meanwhile so that, at need, you will only have to write it out. I pray you, do not speak of this.

Forgive me if I have bothered you too much. May it please God that you return soon with the return of joy and health to your nephew. In closing, I send you my respects. My husband remembers you always, while I pray God for all truly good things for you.

From Florence 18 December 1614
Your Most Illustrious Lordship's
Always most ready to serve you.

                                    Francesca Caccini Signorini

I have not made use of those verses Your Lordship sent me for Signora Medicca because Your Lordship's other verses "Non passar tra quelle prode ("Do not pass through those shores") seemed more appropriate to me. I set them to the tune of "Addio selvaggi monti" ("Farwell wild mountains"), and they fit very well.

In 1617 Caccini made a tour to various Italian cities, giving concerts together with her husband Giovannibattista Signorini, who was also a singer. She wrote to Buonarroti about their success from Genoa:

My Illustrious Signore
I have not forgotten the debt of a letter that I owe Your Lordship, but I have been prevented by infinite tasks that would not let

me be unless sometimes I fled from them. I give you news that we are well, by the grace of God. The favors and courtesies that we have enjoyed everywhere we have passed and that were accorded to us in this city are most extensive and more believable when seen than when explained, so that I will tell Your Lordship part of them by word of mouth, and I will let you see many effects.

Suffice it that I would rather lose my life before the desire to study and the affection I have always had for virtue, because this is worth more than all treasure and all grandeur.

I gave your letter to Signore Chiabrera who has answered it. He is living in the same house of Signore Cardinal Francesco Brignole where we are lodged, truly a house that could be called the sea of all goodness, all amity, and courtesy. Whenever Signore Gabriello drinks, he with great pleasure often drinks toasts to you, and I return them on Your Lordship's behalf; thus we often commemorate you together. By chance in our rooms we have found among many other portraits of famous men the portrait of Michelangelo Buonarroti which has given and often gave us reason for discussing Your Lordship's merits; and Signore Gabriello has felt great pleasure that in Florence there is a descendant of such a great man who carries the imprint of his virtues and his very name, as does Your Lordship.

So, as you hear, we are passing the time virtuously and merrily, discussing and working. At Lucca, *Festa della Dame,* which gave the greatest pleasure, lives in the memory of all. There I sang many canzonettas of Your Lordship's, but I have not attempted this here because the idioms of our language are not understood here as at Lucca.

May Your Lordship hold us in your good grace and give us news of yourself. Next week, having received the three letters from Florence, we will quickly depart for Savona and from there towards Milan for Florence. Meanwhile, with my husband kissing your hands, I pray Our Lord for your every good.

From Genoa 26 May 1617.

Francesca Caccini Signorini

11 ELISABETH-CLAUDE JACQUET DE LA GUERRE: COMPOSER AND HARPSICHORDIST

Elisabeth-Claude Jacquet de la Guerre (1664/65?–1727) was the first major female composer of instrumental music. A harpsichordist from her earliest years, La Guerre made important contributions to the developing chamber music tradition in France, and she also wrote an opera and other theatrical works, cantatas, and much solo music for her own instrument. La Guerre's father was a harpsichord maker, and beginning in her childhood she enjoyed the patronage of King Louis XIV.

In the first of three source documents for La Guerre below, a commentator for the Paris monthly Mecure galant *describes her youthful prowess as of 1677. La Guerre was probably thirteen years old—not ten, as indicated.*

For four years a wonder has appeared here. She sings at sight the most difficult music. She accompanies herself, and accompanies others who wish to sing, at the harpsichord, which she plays in a manner which cannot be imitated. She composes pieces, and plays them in all the keys asked of her. I have told you that for four years she has been appearing with these extraordinary qualities, and she still is only ten years old.

In 1691 La Guerre wrote a ballet, Les jeux à l'honneur de la victoire, *the music of which has been lost. The libretto, however, is extant and bears the following dedication to the king. At*

Edith Borroff, *An Introduction to Elisabeth-Claude Jacquet de la Guerre* Musicological Studies 12 (Brooklyn, N.Y.: Institute of Mediaeval Music, 1966), pp. 6, 12–13, 17–19. Reprinted by permission of the publisher.

*this time French ballet combined dramatic action and singing
with dance.*

When this play was presented to me, I was at once extremely
eager to undertake it. Everything having Your Majesty's glory
as its end is marvelously exciting; and when the desire to please
you is joined to it, what further aim could one have? It is by
such a just incentive that I have always been prompted to work.
From the most tender age (this memory will be eternally precious
to me), presented to your illustrious court, where I have had
the honor to be for several years, I learned, Sire, to consecrate
to you all of my waking hours. You deigned at that time to accept
the first fruits of my gifts, and it has pleased you to receive several
further productions. But these particular marks of my zeal did
not suffice for me, and I welcome the happy opportunity to be
able to make a public (offering). That is what led me to write
this ballet for the theatre. It is not just today (but earlier) that
women have written excellent pieces of poetry, which have had
great success. But until now, none has tried to set a whole opera
to music; and I take this advantage from my enterprise: that the
more extraordinary it is, the more it is worthy of you, Sire, and
the more it justified the liberty that I take in offering you this
work.

*An important tribute to La Guerre is the biographical entry
awarded her after her death by Titon du Tillet in his* Parnasse
français *of 1732, a monumental record of the achievements of
French poets and musicians. The reference in Tillet's third para-
graph regarding La Guerre's playing is probably to the public
concerts she gave in her home, beginning shortly after her husband's death in 1704 and continuing until her retirement in
1717. These concerts were among the earliest of their kind in
Europe.*

Elisabeth-Claude Jacquet de la Guerre. Musician, born in Paris,
died in the same city June 27, 1729, at the age of about 70 years,
buried at Saint Eustache.

Mademoiselle Jacquet from her tenderest youth made known
her talents and her extraordinary disposition for music and for

the art of playing the harpsichord. She was hardly fifteen years old when she appeared at the Court. The King took much pleasure in hearing her play the harpsichord, which caused Madame de Montespan to keep her three or four years with her to amuse herself agreeably, as well as persons of the Court who visited her, in which the young lady succeeded very well.

The marriage that she made with Marin de la Guerre, organist of the church of Saint Séverin, obliged her to follow him and return to Paris. The merit and the reputation of Mme. de la Guerre could only grow in that great City, and all the great Musicians and fine Connoisseurs went eagerly to hear her play the harpsichord: she had above all a talent for improvising and for playing fantasies extemporaneously, and sometimes for an entire half hour she followed an improvisation and a fantasy with songs and harmonies extremely varied and in excellent taste, which charmed the Listeners.

Madame de la Guerre had a very great genius for composition, and excelled in vocal Music the same as in instrumental, as she made known by several works in all kinds of music that one has of her composition, to wit: an opera entitled *Cephale & Procris,* a Tragedy in five Acts with a Prologue, produced in 1694 and printed in folio. II. Three books of Cantatas, of which a number are with instruments, volumes in folio, by [Christophe] Ballard: the words of the *Cantatas* of these first two Books are on subjects drawn from Holy Scripture, of which I believe [Antoine Houdar de] La Motte author of the greatest part. III. A collection of *Pieces for the Harpsichord;* a Collection of *Sonatas,* a *Te Deum* for full Choruses, which she had performed in 1721, in the Chapel of the Louvre, for the Convalescence of His Majesty (Louis XV). Her last works have not yet been printed, and are in the hands of her heirs.

One can say that never had a person of her sex had such talents as she for the composition of music, and for the admirable manner in which she performed it at the Harpsichord and on the Organ. She had had an only son, who at eight years of age surprised those who heard him play the Harpsichord, whether in performance of pieces, or in accompaniment; but death carried him off in his tenth year.

12   THE VENETIAN CONSERVATORIES

*In the seventeenth and eighteenth centuries, music con-
servatories flourished in Venice within the four* ospedali *for
females known as I Mendicanti, La Pietà, L'Incurabili, and Gli
Derelitti. These hospitals, or orphanages, intended to teach desti-
tute Venetian girls a trade, and over time their music schools
achieved such excellence so as to attract paying pupils from
all over Europe. Girls at the conservatories had the unique opportunity for training in voice and many instruments, together with
extensive performing experience, including playing in orchestras.*

*Initially these female musicians drew audiences to their cha-
pels for services, and they also played for private occasions at
noble homes. With the eighteenth century, however, they gave
full concerts, often as state occasions in honor of distinguished
visitors. The subsequent careers of only a few of the most notable
students have been traced to date, namely Maddalena Lombardini-Sirmen and Regina Strinasacchi, violinists who trained in
the mid-eighteenth century. Many leading men, such as Antonio
Vivaldi, Johann Hasse, and Giovanni Pergolesi, were* maestri
di capella *at the conservatories, and their work in composition
surely benefited from having the schools' performing resources
at their disposal.*

*There was no standard length of residence at the conservato-
ries, and some women remained for many years. This latter circumstance coupled with the fact that the women lived a restricted life, requiring permission to come and go,[1] probably
accounts for Charles de Brosses's comment that the women at*

1. Jane Bowers, "The Emergence of Women Composers in Italy, 1566–1700,"
in *Women Making Music: Studies in the Social History of Women Musicians
and Composers,* ed. Jane Bowers and Judith Tick (Berkeley, Calif.: University
of California Press, 1982).

*La Pietà lived "cloistered like nuns." De Brosses was a French
government official who sojourned in Italy in 1739–40. A second
contemporary account is by Charles Burney, the noted English
music historian and chronicler of eighteenth-century musical
life, who visited Venice during his first continental tour in 1771.
Later in the century the conservatories declined, as part of the
general decline of the Venetian Republic.*

Charles de Brosses:

The *ospedali* have the best music here. There are four of them,
all for illegitimate or orphaned girls or those whose parents cannot
support them. These are brought up at the State's expense and
trained exclusively in music. Indeed they sing like angels, play
the violin, flute, organ, oboe, cello, bassoon—in short, no instrument is large enough to frighten them. They are cloistered like
nuns. The performances are entirely their own, and each concert
is composed of about forty young women. I swear that nothing
is more charming than to see a young and pretty nun, dressed
in white, a sprig of pomegranate blossom behind one ear, leading
the orchestra and beating time with all the grace and precision
imaginable. . . .

Of the four orphanages I go most to the *Ospedali della Pietà*.
It ranks first for the perfection of its symphonies. What well-
drilled execution! That is the only place to hear a first attack
from the strings such as, quite undeservedly, the Paris Opéra is
renowned for.

Frid. Aug. 10 [1771]

Dr. Charles Burney:

I had this morning a long visit from Signor [Gaetan] Latilla,
and procured from him several necessary particulars relative to

Gala Concert in the Casino Filharmonico, Francesco Guardi, eighteenth century. An orchestra made up of women musicians from the four Venetian conservatories is depicted at a concert for a visiting dignitary.

the present, as well as the past state of music here. He says the conservatories have been established at Venice about 200 years, as hospitals. That at first the girls were only taught canto fermo [plainsong] and psalmody (like our church girls);[2] but in process of time, they learned to sing in parts, and, at length joined instruments to the voices. He says that the expense on account of the music is very inconsiderable, there being but five or six masters to each of these schools for singing and the several instruments, as the elder girls teach the younger; the *maestro di cappella*, only composes and directs; sometimes, indeed, he writes down closes to suit particular airs, and attends all the rehearsals and public performances.

Frid. Aug. 17 [1771]

This evening, in order to make myself more fully acquainted with the nature of the conservatories, and to finish my musical enquiries here, I obtained permission to be admitted into the music school of the Mendicanti (of which Signor Bartoni is maestro), and was favored with a concert, which was wholly performed on my account, and lasted two hours, by the best vocal and instrumental performers of this hospital: it was really curious to *see*, as well as to *hear* every part of this excellent concert, performed by female violins, hautbois, tenors, bases, harpsichord, French horns, and even double bases. There was a prioress, a person in years, who presided; the first violin was very well played by Antonia Cubli, of Greek extraction; the harpsichord sometimes by Francesca Rossi, *maestra del coro*, and sometimes by others; these young persons frequently exchange instruments.

The singing was really excellent in different styles; Laura Risegari and Giacoma Frari, had very powerful voices, capable of filling a large theater; these sung *bravura* songs, and capital scenes selected from Italian operas; and Francesca Tomj, sister to the Abate of that name, and Antonia Lucuvich, (this second a Sclavonian [Slavic] girl) whose voices were more delicate, confined them-

2. In Burney's England the singing of metrical psalms in church (which was usually the only singing in the service) was often led by the "charity children" of the parish.

selves chiefly to pathetic songs, of taste and expression. The whole was judiciously mixed; no two airs of the same kind followed each other, and there seemed to be great decorum and good discipline observed in every particular; for these admirable performers, who are of different ages, all behaved with great propriety, and seemed to be well educated.

It was here that the two celebrated female performers, the Archiapate,[3] now Signora [Maria] Guglielmi, and Signora Maddalena Lombardini-Sirmen, who have received such great and just applause in England, had their musical instructions.[4] If I could have stayed a few days longer at Venice, I might have been tempted to continue there by such an offer from a friend who had interest sufficient to procure me a sight of the *interior discipline* of these admirable musical seminaries; and I declined this obliging offer with the greater reluctance, as there is not in all Italy any establishment of the same kind.

3. Word not included in dictionaries available to the editor. "Archi" suggests head, or first.

4. Guglielmi was a singer, while Lombardini-Sirmen in addition to her work as violinist, composed.

CLASSIC PERIOD

13   MUSIC AS AN ACCOMPLISHMENT

During the Classic period the number of women involved in domestic music making increased significantly because of the popularity of singing and playing the piano, and also because the middle class was expanding. Music was considered a social "accomplishment" for women, which reflected on the gentility of one's family, filled leisure time and drove away ennui, and in the case of young women, ideally led to a good match. There were other accomplishments too, among them drawing, painting, fancy needlework, and embroidery, but music was the favorite, since "it could be shown off best while actually being accomplished."[1] The theory of accomplishments for women lasted well into the nineteenth century. It did not require that a woman should be talented in a particular pursuit. On the other hand, and this point needs to be stressed, gifted and serious amateur musicians were active too.

In her novels Jane Austen pokes considerable fun at music as a feminine accomplishment. The first excerpt for this reading begins as Elizabeth, the heroine of Pride and Prejudice *(1813), addresses Mr. D'Arcy. The instrument is a piano. Female amateurs at this time also typically played the harp and guitar.*

"Did not you think, Mr. Darcy, that I expressed myself uncommonly well just now, when I was teasing Colonel Forster to give us a ball at Meryton?"

"With great energy—but it is a subject which always makes a lady energetic."

Jane Austen, *Pride and Prejudice* (New York: New American Library, 1961), pp. 22–23.

1. Arthur Loesser, *Men, Women, and Pianos: A Social History* (New York: Simon and Schuster, 1954), p. 268.

"You are severe on us."

"It will be *her* turn soon to be teased," said Miss Lucas. "I am going to open the instrument, Eliza, and you know what follows."

"You are a very strange creature by way of a friend!—always wanting me to play and sing before anybody and everybody! If my vanity had taken a musical turn, you would have been invaluable, but as it is, I would really rather not sit down before those who must be in the habit of hearing the very best performers." On Miss Lucas's persevering, however, she added, "Very well; if it must be so, it must." And gravely glancing at Mr. Darcy, "There is a fine old saying, which everybody here is of course familiar with—'Keep your breath to cool your porridge'—and I shall keep mine to swell my song."

Her performance was pleasing, though by no means capital. After a song or two, and before she could reply to the entreaties of several that she would sing again, she was eagerly succeeded at the instrument by her sister Mary, who having, in consequence of being the only plain one in the family, worked hard for knowledge and accomplishments, was always impatient for display.

Mary had neither genius nor taste; and though vanity had given her application, it had given her likewise a pedantic air and conceited manner, which would have injured a higher degree of excellence than she had reached. Elizabeth, easy and unaffected, had been listened to with much more pleasure, though not playing half so well; and Mary, at the end of a long concerto, was glad to purchase praise and gratitude by Scotch and Irish airs at the request of her younger sisters, who with some of the Lucases and two or three officers joined eagerly in dancing at one end of the room.

In Emma (*1816*), *Jane Fairfax, who must contemplate becoming a governess, is more "accomplished" in music than the heroine Emma. Both young women have played and sung at a party, and the following morning Emma feels remorse.*

Jane Austen, *Emma* (New York: New American Library, 1964), pp. 183–84, 218–19.

The Song, Francesco Bartolozzi, after H. Bunbury, late eighteenth century. The accompanying instrument appears to be a long-necked form of the mandolin.

Lady with a Harp: Elizabeth Ridgely, Thomas Sully, 1818.

The other circumstance of regret related also to Jane Fairfax, and there she had no doubt. She did unfeignedly and unequivocally regret the inferiority of her own playing and singing. She did most heartily grieve over the idleness of her childhood, and sat down and practised vigorously an hour and a half.

She was then interrupted by Harriet's coming in; and if Harriet's praise could have satisfied her, she might soon have been comforted.

"Oh, if I could but play as well as you and Miss Fairfax!"

"Don't class us together, Harriet. My playing is no more like hers than a lamp is like sunshine."

"Oh dear, I think you play the best of the two. I think you play quite as well as she does. I am sure I had much rather hear you. Everybody last night said how well you played."

"Those who knew anything about it must have felt the difference. The truth is, Harriet, that my playing is just good enough to be praised, but Jane Fairfax's is much beyond it."

"Well, I always shall think that you play quite as well as she does, or that if there is any difference, nobody would ever find it out. Mr. Cole said how much taste you had! And Mr. Frank Churchill talked a great deal about your taste, and that he valued taste much more than execution."

"Ah, but Jane Fairfax has them both, Harriet."

"Are you sure? I saw she had execution, but I did not know she had any taste. Nobody talked about it; and I hate Italian singing; there is no understanding a word of it. Besides, if she does play so very well, you know, it is no more than she is obliged to do, because she will have to teach. The Coxes were wondering last night whether she would get into any great family. How did you think the Coxes looked?"

On another occasion Emma pays a call on Mrs. Elton, the minister's new wife, who upon her marriage moved from Maple Grove to Emma's village of Highbury. Mrs. Elton faces the ubiquitous problem of "keeping up one's music after marriage." Emma has just changed the subject of the conversation to music.

"I do not ask whether you are musical, Mrs. Elton. Upon these occasions a lady's character generally precedes her, and Highbury has long known that you are a superior performer."

"Oh no, indeed! I must protest against any such idea. A superior performer! Very far from it, I assure you; consider from how partial a quarter your information came. I am dotingly fond of music—passionately fond; and my friends say I am not entirely devoid of taste; but as to anything else, upon my honour, my performance is *mediocre* to the last degree. You, Miss Woodhouse, I well know, play delightfully. I assure you it has been the greatest satisfaction, comfort, and delight to me to hear what a musical society I am got into. I absolutely cannot do without music; it is a necessary of life to me; and having always been used to a very musical society, both at Maple Grove and in Bath, it would have been a most serious sacrifice. I honestly said as much to Mr. E. when he was speaking of my future home and expressing his fears lest the retirement of it should be disagreeable; and the inferiority of the house too—knowing what I had been accustomed to—of course he was not wholly without apprehension. When he was speaking of it in that way, I honestly said that *the world* I could give up—parties, balls, plays—for I had no fear of retirement. Blessed with so many resources within myself, the world was not necessary to *me*. I could do very well without it. To those who had no resources it was a different thing, but my resources made me quite independent. And as to smaller-sized rooms than I had been used to, I really could not give it a thought. I hoped I was perfectly equal to any sacrifice of that description. Certainly, I had been accustomed to every luxury at Maple Grove; but I did assure him that two carriages were not necessary to my happiness, nor were spacious apartments. 'But,' said I, 'to be quite honest, I do not think I can live without something of a musical society. I condition for nothing else; but without music, life would be a blank to me.'"

"We cannot suppose," said Emma, smiling, "that Mr. Elton would hesitate to assure you of there being a *very* musical society in Highbury; and I hope you will not find he has outstepped the truth more than may be pardoned, in consideration of the motive."

"No, indeed, I have no doubts at all on that head. I am delighted to find myself in such a circle; I hope we shall have many sweet little concerts together. I think, Miss Woodhouse, you and I must establish a musical club and have regular weekly meetings at your house or ours. Will not it be a good plan? If *we* exert ourselves, I think we shall not be long in want of allies. Something of that nature would be particularly desirable for *me* as an inducement to keep me in practice; for married women, you know—there is a sad story against them, in general. They are but too apt to give up music."

"But you, who are so extremely fond of it—there can be no danger, surely?"

"I should hope not; but really, when I look around among my acquaintance, I tremble. Selina has entirely given up music; never touches the instrument, though she played sweetly. And the same may be said of Mrs. Jeffereys—Clara Partridge that was—and of the two Milmans, now Mrs. Bird and Mrs. James Cooper; and of more than I can enumerate. Upon my word, it is enough to put one in a fright. I used to be quite angry with Selina; but really, I begin now to comprehend that a married woman has many things to call her attention. I believe I was half an hour this morning shut up with my housekeeper."

"But everything of that kind," said Emma, "will soon be in so regular a train——"

"Well," said Mrs. Elton, laughing, "we shall see."

Emma, finding her so determined upon neglecting her music, had nothing more to say; and after a moment's pause, Mrs. Elton chose another subject.

14   MARIANNE VON MARTINEZ: COMPOSER AND SINGER

In 1772 Charles Burney made a second musical tour from England to the continent, where, in Vienna, he met composer Marianne von Martinez (1744–1812) and heard her sing and perform her own music at the keyboard. Martinez's parents were longtime friends of the poet-librettist Pietro Metastasio in Vienna, and it was Metastasio who oversaw Martinez's education, arranging for her to study keyboard with Haydn and singing and counterpoint with Nicola Porpora.

Martinez wrote many large-scale works, among them a Mass and Mass movements, oratorios, cantatas, a symphony, and two piano concertos. Burney, however, heard only some of her shorter compositions, which he describes in his travel journal, excerpted here. After Metastasio's death, in 1728, the Martinez family was heir to his estate and thereby gave large and frequent musicales. In the 1790s Marianne von Martinez founded and directed a singing school in her home.

Sunday morning, [September] 6th [1772]

The discourse then became general and miscellaneous, till the arrival of a young lady, who was received by the whole company with great respect. She was well dressed, and had a very elegant appearance: this was Signora Martinez,[1] sister to Signor Martinez, deputy librarian at the imperial library, whose father was an old

Charles Burney, *An Eighteenth-Century Musical Tour in Central Europe and the Netherlands*, vol. 2 of *Dr. Burney's Musical Tours in Europe*, ed. Percy A. Scholes, 2 vols. (London: Oxford University Press, 1959), pp. 106–7, 117. Copyright © 1959 by Oxford University Press. Reprinted by permission of the publisher.
    1. Although Burney spelled the composer's last name as Martinetz, the modern usage is Martinez, and the reading has been amended accordingly.

friend of Metastasio. She was born in the house in which he now lives, and educated under his eye: her parents were Neapolitans, but the name is Spanish, as the family originally was.

After the high encomiums bestowed by the Abate Taruffi on the talents of this young lady, I was very desirous of hearing and conversing with her; and Metastasio was soon so obliging as to propose her sitting down to the harpsichord, which she immediately did, in a graceful manner, without the parade of diffidence, or the trouble of importunity. Her performance indeed surpassed all that I had been made to expect. She sung two airs of her own composition, to words of Metastasio, which she accompanied on the harpsichord, in a very judicious and masterly manner; and, in playing the ritornels,[2] I could discover a very brilliant finger.

The airs were very well written, in a modern style; but neither common, nor unnaturally new. The words were well set, the melody was simple, and great room was left for expression and embellishment; but her voice and manner of singing, both delighted and astonished me! I can readily subscribe to what Metastasio says, that it is a style of singing which no longer subsists elsewhere, as it requires too much pains and patience for modern professors: *è perduta la scuola; non si trova questa maniera di cantar; domanda troppa pena per i professori d'oggi dì.*

I should suppose that Pistocco [*sic*] Bernacchi,[3] and the old school of singing, in the time of cantatas, sustained, divided the voice by minute intervals, and expressed words in this manner, which is not to be described: common language cannot express uncommon effects. To say that her voice was naturally well-toned and sweet, that she had an excellent shake,[4] a perfect intonation, a facility of executing the most rapid and difficult passages, and a touching expression, would be to say no more than I have already said, and with truth, of others; but here *I* want words

---

2. The instrumental conclusion to the songs.
3. Francesco Pistocchi (1659–1726) was the founder of the "Bolognese school" of singing, a brilliant style requiring virtuosity typical of instrumental music of the time. Antonio Bernacchi was a famous pupil of Pistocchi's.
4. A trill.

Mme. Favart, François Hubert Drouais, 1757. A portrait of the celebrated French singer and actress Mme. Marie Justine Benoit Favart (1727–72).

that would still encrease the significance and energy of these expressions. The Italian augmentatives would, perhaps, gratify my wish, if I were writing in that language; but as that is not the case, let me only add, that in the *portamento*,[5] and divisions of tones and semitones into infinitely minute parts, and yet always stopping upon the exact fundamental, Signora Martinez was more perfect than any singer I had ever heard: her cadences too, of this kind, were very learned, and truly pathetic and pleasing.

After these two songs, she played a very difficult lesson, of her own composition, on the harpsichord, with great rapidity and precision. She has composed a *Miserere*, in four parts, with several psalms, in eight parts, and is a most excellent contrapuntist.

The company broke up sooner than I wished, as it was Metastasio's time for going to mass. During this visit, I discovered that Signora Martinez, among her other accomplishments, both reads and speaks English. She invited me to come again, as did the divine poet; so that I now regard myself as *amico della casa*.

Friday, [September] 11th [1772]
From hence I went to Metastasio, where I was immediately admitted, though he was in dishabille, and just going to dress.

Mademoiselle Martinez was at her musical studies, and writing; she directly complied with my request, of sitting down to the harpsichord. Metastasio desired her to shew me some of her best studies; and she produced a psalm for four voices, with instruments. It was a most agreeable *Mescolanza*, as Metastasio called it, of *antico e moderno*; a mixture of the harmony, and contrivance of old times, with the melody and taste of the present. It was an admirable composition, and she played and sung it in a very masterly manner, contriving so well to fill up all the parts, that though it was a full piece, nothing seemed wanting. The words of this psalm were Italian, and of Metastasio's translation.

After this she obliged me with a Latin motet, for a single voice, which was grave and solemn, without languor or heaviness; and

5. Gliding from one tone to the next through all the intermediate pitches.

then played me a very pretty harpsichord sonata of her own, which was spirited, and full of brilliant passages.

I could not finish this visit till I had petitioned Mademoiselle Martinez to oblige me with copies of some of her compositions, which she readily granted, and I had my choice of whatever had pleased me most among the pieces which I had heard.

15   MARIA THERESIA VON PARADIS: PIANIST ON TOUR

The expansion of concert life in the late eighteenth century made public concertizing and touring financially attractive, and the activity of pianist Maria Theresia von Paradis (1759–1834) illustrates how women were early contenders in the market, chiefly as pianists, singers, and violinists. Born in Vienna and blinded by accident at the age of two, Paradis early attracted the patronage of Empress Maria Theresa. She was also fortunate in gaining a broad education, studying piano with the imperial court composer Leopold Kozeluch, singing and dramatic composition with Antonio Salieri, and also composition with Abbé Vogler.

Besides concertizing in Vienna, Paradis made an extended tour in 1784–86 to Paris, London, Berlin, Prague, and many other cities in between. During her stay in Paris she gave fourteen public performances. Eleven of these were in the Concert Spirituel series, and a representative review of one concert is translated below. Presumably she performed works of her own composition for piano, and she also wrote stage works, cantatas, chamber music, and songs. In her later years Paradis—like Martinez before her—founded and headed a music school in Vienna, with the express purpose of improving music education for women.

Mademoiselle Paradis is the one artist whom our nation is not able to praise too highly. This gifted keyboard player is truly astonishing. Blind since the age of two, she has reached an unbelievable level of perfection in the knowledge of her instrument.

"Spectacles. Concert Spirituel," *Mercure de France*, Apr. 24, 1784, pp. 176–77.

. . . The lack of one faculty [surely] affects the sensitivity of the others. When one thinks of the necessity she has, to commit to memory an infinite number of small details that a single glance makes plain, one does not know whether to admire more the perfection of her playing, or the patient efforts that were necessary for her to achieve it. More faultless, more precise, more polished playing is not known. The concertos [Paradis played], which are by M. Hozeluck [*sic*], her teacher, seem well-made, in a pleasing and original style.

16   CORONA SCHRÖTER AND JULIE CANDEILLE: TWO COMPOSERS SPEAK OUT

This final reading from the Classic period presents state-ments by two composers regarding the public and their work, the first by Corona Schröter (1751–1802), who occupied the post of chamber musician at the Weimar court for the major share of her career. Schröter's father, an oboe player, was her first teacher, and subsequently she became one of Johann Adam Hiller's earliest students at the singing school he founded in Leipzig to provide good instruction for both women and men. Schröter came to composition through her work as a singer, and she primarily wrote lieder, two collections of which she published in 1786 and 1794. Her announcement of the 1786 collection in Carl Friedrich Cramer's Magazin der Musik *reflects a perception of negative attitudes by society toward women com-posers.*

I have had to overcome much hesitation before I seriously made the decision to publish a collection of short poems that I have provided with melodies. A certain feeling towards propriety and morality is stamped upon our sex, which does not allow us to appear alone in public, and without an escort: Thus, how can I otherwise present this, my musical work to the public, than with timidity? For the complimentary opinions and the encouragement of a few persons . . . can easily be biased out of pity. The work of any lady, moreover, will indeed arouse similar pity to some extent in the eyes of other experts. . . .

Marcia J. Citron, "Corona Schröter: Singer, Composer, Actress," *Music and Letters* 61/1 (January 1980): 21.

In contrast to Schröter's timidity, the French singer and composer Julie Candeille (1767–1836) spoke out boldly in the Journal de Paris *in 1795 as she denounced the intriguers against her latest stage work* La bayadère (The Indian Dancing Girl), *in which she created the principal role. Earlier, when the success of her* Catherine, ou La belle fermière (Catherine, or The Beautiful Farmer's Wife) *was substantial, with 154 performances, some critics suggested that her father, who was also a composer, and a particular writer with whom she had a liaison, had assisted her. Hence Candeille's indignant and spirited defense in 1795 might reflect this earlier slighting as well. Candeille was also active as a composer of instrumental music, a pianist and harpist, and an actress.*

When persecution pursues me, when injustice and calumny seek my ruin, I must, for my supporters—and myself—repudiate the treacherous insinuations of those who would still wish to rob me of public esteem after having cheated all my efforts to give pleasure.

Never did an insensitive *pride*, never did an arrogant *pretension*, guide me in the service of the arts. Submissiveness and necessity led me to the theater; propensity for and the love of this work emboldened me to write. These two sources united are my sole means of survival. The need to support my family, other more onerous responsibilities, my present needs, and above all the uncertainty of the future—these are my reasons for speaking out. I dare to believe that had they known, my detractors themselves would not have been able to resolve to make me the object of ridicule and aversion, while I become that of forebearance and countenance.

Arthur Pougin, "Une charmeuse: Julie Candeille," *Le menestrel* 49 (Nov. 4, 1883): 388–89.

1820–1920

Women as Concert Artists and in Opera

17 CLARA SCHUMANN: PIANIST

Throughout a career of more than fifty years, Clara Schumann (1819–96) was considered the foremost woman pianist of her time and a peer of Sigismond Thalberg, Anton Rubinstein, and Liszt. Her concert programs and her high musical standards changed the character of the solo piano recital in the nineteenth century. She introduced much new music by her husband Robert, Chopin, and Brahms, and she was also distinguished as being the first pianist to perform many of Beethoven's sonatas in public.

Born in Leipzig, Clara Schumann was carefully trained from the age of five as a pianist and a musician by her father, Friedrick Wieck. Her great progress she attributed to Wieck's program of moderate work matched by physical exercise in the same proportion, attendance of good operas and other performances, and contact with distinguished musicians.[1] She made her debut at the Leipzig Gewandhaus at age nine in 1828, the same year she met Robert Schumann, who was then eighteen. Between 1828 and 1838 Clara launched a highly promising career, and her friendship with Robert deepened into love. Wieck, however, refused to consent to their marriage, in part because he did not want to share Clara with any man. Excerpts from Clara and Robert's correspondence, below, begin in November 1837, when Clara and her father were on tour to Vienna. Her debut in this musical capital was a triumph.

Berthold Litzmann, *Clara Schumann: An Artist's Life Based on Material Found in Diaries and Letters,* trans. Grace E. Hadow, 2 vols. (London: Macmillan, 1913), 1:119–21, 127–32, 313–14, 336–38; 2:148, 156–57, 237–38, 257–58, 260–61, 376. Reprinted by permission of Macmillan, London and Basingstoke.
  1. Letter of Clara to La Mara, Oct. 10, 1882, in Litzmann, 2:365–66.

Clara to Robert:

[Prague] Friday the 24th [1837]. Evening
To-morrow we set out for Vienna by the flying-coach. You
will get this letter on Monday, and now I give you a week in
which you can write much and clearly! Nanny has just been
saying that my eyes have been heavy ever since the evening when
I pored over your letter for 2 hours. See, of what you are guilty!
Do not forget, either, to write to me about your plans, for I am
much interested in them.

—I have been thinking a great deal about my circumstances
during these days, and I must call your attention to something.
You rely on the ring! Good heavens! that is but an external bond.
Had not Ernestine[2] too, a ring from you, and what is of more
importance, your promise? And yet you have torn that bond asun-
der. The ring is of no consequence. . . .

I too, have thought most seriously about the future. One thing
I must say to you; I cannot be yours until circumstances have
entirely altered. I do not want horses or diamonds, I am happy
in possessing you, but I wish to lead a life free from care, and I
see that I shall be unhappy if I cannot always work at my art,
and that I cannot do if we have to worry over our daily bread.
I require much, and I realise that much is needed for a comfortable
life. Therefore Robert, ask yourself if you are in a condition to
offer me a life free from care. Think that simply as I have been
brought up, I have yet never had a care, and am I to bury my
art now? . . .

. . . Yesterday, I played in the theatre for the last time, and
was (contrary to the regulations) recalled 4 times after each piece.
I played my concerto [in A minor, op. 7], and [Adolf] Henselt's
variations; hardly anyone remembers ever having seen it so full
before. I do not, however, want to stay here, Vienna draws me
to herself. I am sad when I come into a strange town where I
am entirely unknown and many thoughts pass backwards and
forwards through my brain. Ah God! I feel as if my heart would

2. Robert was once engaged to Ernestine von Fricken.

burst. If ever I do not write to you within 4 weeks, do not be angry with me, for it will be owing to want of time, and I can only write in the evenings. I shall not have many evenings to myself in Vienna—they will have to be given up to social duties. I can write no more, as it is late. This is a very dull letter—you must put up with it and take it for love, for it is written in pure love

> by Your Clara.

Robert to Clara:

L[eipzig] Nov. 28th

First as to the most important part of your letter, where you say that you can never be mine unless circumstances have completely altered. Your father's spirit stood behind you and dictated that; but you have written it, and you are right to think of your external happiness. We must be quite clear about this. The only thing that troubles me, is that you make the objection for the first time now, which you should have made to me when I first frankly explained my circumstances to you, as otherwise it would certainly never have entered my head to write to your father, if I had thought that you still had so many scruples.

What I wrote before, first to you and afterwards to your father, about my wealth, was true then and still holds good now. It is not over-powering, but such that many a girl, even many a pretty and good one, might give me her hand on it and say, 'It will be hard to make both ends meet, but you shall find me a good housekeeper etc. etc.'—At that time you thought so too, perhaps—Now you think differently—my mind reels.

To business. Unless a gift falls from heaven, I do not see how I can increase my income in a short time as much as, on your account, I could wish. You know the kind of work I do, you know that it is purely intellectual, that it cannot be carried on at any moment like manual labour. . . . I have shown that I can persevere; mention any young fellow of my age who has made for himself so wide a sphere of activity in so short a time. It goes without saying, that I should like to extend it, to earn more, and in this I shall not fail; but I do not believe that this will achieve as much as you wish, or as you perhaps have now; on the other hand I can with a clear conscience rely upon being able to support one wife or even two wives, in about two years' time, without any great anxiety, though certainly not without continuing to work.

Dear Clara, the last page of your letter brought me down to earth, and I should like to embrace all the clod-hoppers. You might have expressed it more romantically though; I find it difficult to say a word in answer. . . . As I said, your father held the pen; the coldness of the lines has something killing in it. . . . And now too, that you think so little of my ring— —since yesterday I have cared no more for yours, and no longer wear it. I dreamt that I was walking by a deep pool, and an impulse seized me and I threw the ring into it— —then I was filled with a passionate longing to throw myself after it. . . .

. . . I will write more to-morrow; my head is on fire, and my eyes are heavy with grief over you. Farewell, however.

Clara to Robert:

Vienna Wednesday Dec. 6th 1837

As great as my joy on receiving your letter, was my sorrow on reading the first page—could you so wound me, draw from me such bitter tears? Is it Robert who so misunderstood me, who read so ugly a meaning into my words—have I deserved this? Yes, I know that many beautiful and perhaps as good girls as I are at your disposal, and better housewives than any artist is supposed to be—yes, I know it, but it is not well that you should mention such a thought to me, to me who live but for you and in you, or that such a thought should come to you, if you love me indeed. . . . You think that I harbour unattainable wishes? I want but two things, your heart and your happiness.

How could I be calm if you were burdened with cares on my account? Could I be guilty of the base desire that you should turn your genius into a drudge so that I might follow my pleasure? No, my thoughts are not so base; perhaps you will learn to know me better, later. My imagination can picture no fairer happiness than to continue living for art, but quite quietly, so that we may both owe many a pleasant hour to it. So we agree in all things, and I fall upon your heart and say: 'Yes Robert, let us live like this!' Do you think that I too, do not love passionately? Oh yes! I too can be passionate, but passion ceases when our hearts are full of care, then you would indeed feel yourself brought down to earth. I see that much is required for a simple life——but do not doubt on this account, that everything will all right. I have steadfast faith, your ring says to me daily: 'Believe, love, and hope.'

Clara to Robert:

[Vienna, December]
Today, the 13th, Fischhof[3] said to me: 'I have a letter from Schumann,' and I shook all over as I do every time I hear your name — The most terrible of all questions is always: 'Who is this Schumann? where does he live? does he play the piano?' — 'He composes.' — 'What are his compositions like?' Then I want to say, like you, 'He is a person with whom you have nothing at all to do, who stands so far above you that you are incapable of understanding him, and who cannot be described in words, etc.' I had to puzzle out several words in your letter to-day, which Fischhof could not read. How glad I was to see the writing, and when I saw your name at the bottom, my heart was at once glad and sad. — I could have wept for pain and joy! — Ah! Robert, believe me, I have many sorrowful hours! No pleasure is complete to me when you are not there! How many polite things I have to say to people, and all the while I am conscious of nothing but the thought of you.

. . . But do not judge Father harshly because of what I wrote about him; he does not now try to persuade me to give you up, because he knows that that hurts my feelings, depresses and disheartens me, and makes it difficult for me to give concerts

3. Josef Fischhof, a Viennese musician and contributor to Robert's *Neue Zeitschrift für Musik*.

and to practise—he thinks his letter has put an end to everything. . . .

But it hurts me when you wish to cast a stone at Father because
he wishes for some small recompense for all the hours which
he has devoted to me. He wishes me to be happy, and thinks
that is to be obtained by riches; can you be angry with him for
it? He loves me above all things, and would not thrust me, his
child, away from him if he saw that my happiness could be
founded on you alone, so, for love of me, forgive him his natural
vanity. Consider that he has treated you like this only for love
of me. You too love me, and you make me happy when you
forgive him; I would not have him misunderstood by you—every
man has his faults; I have and so have you—you will allow me
to say so!

Clara to Robert:

[Vienna, December] The 21st
My second concert took place to-day, and was another triumph.
Of the many items in the programme my concerto had the best
reception. You ask if I always play it by my own wish—certainly
I do, for it has been well received everywhere, and has given
satisfaction to connoisseurs and to the public in general. Whether
or no it satisfies me is another question. Do you think that I
am so weak as not to know well enough what are the faults of
the concerto? I know them, well enough but the audience does
not, and what is more need not, know. Do you think I would
play it, if it took as little everywhere as it did in Leipzig? Certainly
when one has been here one never wants go North again, where
men have hearts of stone (you are, of course, excepted). You
ought to listen to a storm of applause here. I had to repeat the
Bach fugue and the Henselt variations. No pleasanter feeling than
that of having satisfied a whole audience.

So much for me—Now for you. . . . I was much amused at
the place in your letter where you write, 'And so we will come
back to our house, laden with treasure.' Good heavens! what
are you thinking of? Treasures are no longer to be got by instru-

mental art. How much one has to do in order to bring away a
few thaler from a town. When you are sitting with Poppe at 10
o'clock in the evening, or are going home, I, poor thing, am arriving at a party, where I have to play to people for a few pretty
words and a cup of warm water, and get home, dead tired, at
11 or 12 o'clock, drink a draught of water, lie down, and think,
'Is an artist much more than a beggar?' And yet art is a fine
gift! What, indeed, is finer than to clothe one's feelings in music,
what a comfort in time of trouble, what a pleasure, what an exquisite feeling, to give happy hours to so many people by its means!
And what an exalted feeling so to follow art that one gives one's
life to it! — I have done that, and all the rest, to-day, and I lay
myself down, happy and contented. Yes, I am happy but shall
be perfectly so, only when I can fling myself on your heart and
say, 'Now I am yours for ever—I and my art.'

*After a lawsuit against Wieck was settled in their favor, Clara
and Robert Schumann were married on September 12, 1840,
the day before Clara's twenty-first birthday. During their fourteen years together they attempted to combine Robert's work
in composition with Clara's career as a concert pianist. Naturally
there were conflicts, and although Clara did not perform in public and tour as much as she wished, her life with Robert greatly
enriched her artistic powers. In turn, Clara influenced Robert's
compositions and was often the performer to introduce them
to the public. The following letter and entries by Robert in a
diary that the couple kept together were written when the Schumanns had just one child, Marie. With each of her subsequent
seven children, Clara's domestic responsibilities increased.*

*Clara to her friend Emilie List after her return from concertiz-
ing in Copenhagen:*

[Leipzig, May 30th, 1842]
Yes, I really went to Copenhagen alone (that is without Robert,
but with a lady from Bremen) and separated myself from him,
but this shall never happen again if God wills. I will explain

the whole matter to you, so that you may understand our step.
. . . In Hamburg [where the Schumanns had gone for a performance of Robert's Symphony no. 1 in B-flat major, op. 38] they
strongly advised us to visit Copenhagen, and we also received
various invitations from thence, so that we made up our minds
to accept, and at once began to prepare for my concert.

But as the time drew on, Robert saw more and more clearly
the impossibility of leaving his paper[4] in strange hands for perhaps
two months (the three weeks, for which he had arranged, were
ended) and so we decided to give up the journey. I thought the
matter over, however. I am a woman, I shall not be neglecting
anything, I earn nothing at home, why should I not by means
of my talent, gain my mite for Robert? Could anyone think ill
of me for so doing, or of my husband for going home to his
child and his business? I laid my plan before Robert, and it is
true that at first he shrank from it, but in the end he agreed,
when I represented the matter to him as reasonably as possible.
It was certainly a great step for a wife who loves her husband
as I do, but I did it for love of him, and for that no sacrifice is
too great or too hard for me. In addition to this I now found a
nice girl who with the greatest joy offered to come with me; a
girl belonging to one of the most highly respected families in
Bremen, and with whom my husband knew that I should be
safe. We left Hamburg on the same day, Robert for Leipzig, and
I, by way of Kiel, for Copenhagen—I shall never forget the day
of our parting!

Robert in the diary during Clara's trip to Copenhagen:

[Leipzig, March 14th]
The separation has once more made me very conscious of my
peculiar and difficult position. Am I to neglect my own talent,
in order to serve you as a companion on your journeys? Have
you allowed your talent to lie useless, or ought you to do so,
because I am chained to the paper and to the piano? Now, when

4. The *Neue Zeitschrift für Musik.*

you are young and in full possession of your powers? We found the solution. You took a companion with you, and I came back to the child and to my work. But what will the world say? Thus I torture myself with thinking. Yes, it is most necessary that we should find some means by which we can both utilise and develop our talents side by side.

Robert in the diary:

[Leipzig, October]

She played well and finely, as she always does. I am often sorry that I so frequently hinder Clara in her study, because she will not disturb me when I am composing. For I know well that any artist who appears in public, however great he may be, can never give up certain mechanical exercises, but must always keep the elasticity of his fingers, so to speak, in practice. And for this, my dear artist often has no time. So far as the deeper part of musical education is concerned, Clara certainly has not stood still, but, on the contrary, has advanced; now she lives in good music alone, and her playing is therefore the sounder and at once more intellectual and more tender than it was.[5] But she often has not the time to bring technique to the point of absolute certainty, and that is my fault; and yet I cannot help it. Clara realizes that I must develop my talent, that I am now at the best of my powers, and that I must make use of my youth. Well, so must it be when artists marry; one cannot have everything; and after all the chief thing is the happiness which remains over and above, and we are happy indeed in that we possess one another and understand one another, understand and love with all our hearts.

Because of his deteriorating mental health, in 1854 Robert Schumann entered a sanitorium at Endenich near Bonn, where two years later he died. Clara was pregnant at the time Robert became terminally ill, and soon after the birth of their eighth child she set out on the first of the many concert tours that

5. Together they had been studying Bach's fugues, Mozart's overtures, and the Beethoven overtures, symphonies, and piano sonatas.

were to become a regular feature of her life for more than thirty years. She was motivated, certainly, by the necessity of providing for a large family, but she also seems to have felt a need for artistic self-expression that had been largely unfulfilled. Furthermore, total involvement in music performance, much of it Robert's music, gave solace.

Clara's friendship with Brahms and the violinist Joseph Joachim provided some comfort throughout Robert's illness and the aftermath of his death. These friendships, like so many others Clara made, became lifelong. In Brahms, Clara also enjoyed the association with creative genius that she had known with Robert. She followed the acceptance of Robert's music with natural gratification.

Clara Schumann recognized her own importance as a pianist, and in the years following Robert's death she clearly considered herself first an artist and only afterward a parent. While Clara toured, the Schumann children were deposited with family friends and grandparents and in boarding schools. Clara wrote to her children constantly, and she arranged family reunions whenever she could, often for the complete summer. As soon as they were old enough, the eldest Schumann daughters took over the management of the family and of Clara's concert tours and teaching.

Clara to her half-brother, Woldemar Bargiel:

London, May 3rd 1857

I have not very good to news of myself to send you from here—I am often overwhelmed with home-sickness, and do not know how to endure it. So far it has been a very bad season, and if it does not improve in June . . . I shall come back. . . . I have had only 2 engagements this month, if all goes well and I get 2 more I shall have just enough to pay my expenses . . . so you see I have a right to be anxious. And I am not being successful with lessons either. Here things always move very slowly. Tomorrow, I play in public for the first time—and oh! I do not feel in the mood for it.

Clara in her diary:

London, June 7th

What bitter struggles I have endured all through the day, how heavily the thought of to-morrow[6] weighed on my heart! Oh! if only I had my beloved friend here, and could end my tears upon his heart. But the heart which has lost Him, the most glorious husband in the world, can know no end to tears. Spirit of my Robert look down on me, comfort, strengthen your unhappy wife—ah! I can write no more.

[London] June 8th

. . . Today Johannes [Brahms] set the stone over my dear one's grave—my whole soul went with him.

[Zurich] Dec. 19th

To please Wagner[7] I played Robert's *Études Symphoniques* [op. 13]. . . .

[Zurich] Dec. 21st

From a pecuniary point of view the tour has been very successful, that is I am now in a position to pay all the debts which I incurred by moving house. But now I have to earn enough to support us till next winter.

[Munich] Dec. 22nd

Arrived in Munich in the evening, still filled with impressions of Switzerland and the Alps, which I have breathed in as one inhales the perfume of flowers.

Clara to Joachim:

Munich Dec. 27th

. . . The day before yesterday I played Robert's concerto [in A minor, op. 54] in the *Odeon* here, and was much applauded.

6. Robert's birthday.
7. Richard Wagner, who was at that time in Zurich.

Clara Schumann and Joseph Joachim, Adolph Friedrich Menzel, 1854.

Afterwards, the orchestra gave me a beautiful laurel-wreath, which I would so gladly have passed on to him, even if it were but laying it on his grave. I have had no lack of wreathes altogether, but I have never received one without thinking how many of its leaves belong to you and Johannes. If I could deck you with them as my heart and conscience dictate, nothing would be left for me. No one else knows how much I have to thank you for; and indeed no words can express it, but I feel it warmly and eternally.

Clara in her diary:

[London] May [1865]

I find a marked change, since five years ago, in the attitude towards Robert. To my great surprise I now find a large number of Schumann devotees—one of the most zealous is [George] Grove, whom, apart from that, I like more and more, and with whom I feel quite at home.

[London] May 3rd

I played Beethoven's E-flat major concerto [concerto no. 5, op. 73] at the Musical Society. I succeeded in playing it wonderfully well, and the applause was enormous. . . . We see the Joachims[8] every day, which always gives me a sense of being at home.

[London, May] 15th

A red-letter evening in my mind, for such a reception must really warm anybody's heart. The manager of the Popular Concerts [S. Arthur] (Chappell) had arranged a Schumann evening, at which only Robert's works were to be performed. Joachim played the A minor quartet [op. 41, no. 1], and I played the C-sharp minor Études [*Symphonic Etudes*, op. 13] and some little things. The reception given to me was warmer than any I have ever known, and I was really moved by it. It was long before I could seat myself at the piano. Ah! if Robert could have lived to see

8. Joachim's wife, Amalie, was a singer.

it, he would never have thought that he (for the greater part of the applause was for *Him*) could have received such recognition in England.

Clara to Brahms:

London, March 19th 1868
186 Piccadilly

I have been long in finding time to answer your letter, and how much joy and sorrow I have known in the mean time! It has been a period of great anxiety, as you will already have heard in Berlin. I must not begin to tell you about it, or I should never stop. I have good hopes that Felix[9] may quite recover if he spends this summer with us, but I cannot think what is to become of Ludwig. It is true that he has just got another post in Leipzig but how long will it last? How different they are! One makes me anxious by his idleness, and because he will not work, and the other by over-working. It was fortunate that I insisted that Felix must see a proper doctor, as I had been struck by his looks in the autumn, and consequently the matter was at once taken seriously. — Julie has been in Frankfort for the last 3 weeks, and seems much better than she was last summer. Thus things ever go up and down, and the poor mother's heart is never at peace. It was doubly hard that these anxieties should come upon me here, but the struggle increases one's power of resistance, as I have once more found in my own experience. But I have begun by writing about us and I wanted to talk to you about yourself. . . . And so you are really going to settle down in Vienna? I do not think it is such a bad thing. I too, should like to live there, if I could find what I wanted. . . . You seem to imagine that I have made enough money and that I am now travelling for my own amusement.[10] But one does not exert oneself to such an extent for pleasure. Besides, the present moment, when my powers

9. Felix, Ludwig, and Julie in this letter are three of Clara's eight children.
10. In his letter of February 2, 1868, Brahms advised Clara to give up concertizing. See *Letters of Clara Schumann and Johannes Brahms, 1853–96*, ed. Berthold Litzmann, 2 vols. (London: Macmillan, 1913), 2:218–19.

are at their greatest and when I am most successful, is hardly
the time at which, as you advise, to withdraw into private life.
During the past year I have been received everywhere with such
warmth . . . and, with few exceptions, I have played so well,
that I cannot quite see why I should stop just at this moment.
. . . But I will think the matter over. I cannot weigh it properly
until I know what reasons have moved you to say all that to
me, and why you did it at a time when it might have made an
impression on me which would have paralysed all my powers
. . . it was inconsiderate of you—to say the least of it.

Clara in her diary:

[April]
I was to have gone to the performance of Johannes' *Requiem*
[the German Requiem, op. 45] at Bremen, but I was too depressed
to make up my mind to it. However, Rosalie [Leser] and Marie
[her daughter] urged me so strongly that on April 9th I really
did go to Bremen. I travelled to Wunstorf with [Ernst] Rudorff,
and there I met Joachim and his wife who were also on their
way to Bremen. We arrived just in time for the rehearsal—Johannes was already standing at the conductor's desk. The *Requiem*
quite overpowered me. . . . Johannes showed himself an excellent
conductor. The work had been wonderfully studied by [Karl]
Reinthaler. In the evening, after the rehearsal, we all met together—a regular congress of artists.

[Bremen, April] Friday, Good Friday, the 10th
Performance of the *Requiem*, and in addition to this Frau Joachim sang an aria from the *Messiah*, as I never heard her sing
before, exquisitely accompanied by her husband on the violin.
The *Requiem* has taken hold of me as no sacred music ever
did before. . . . As I saw Johannes standing there, baton in hand,
I could not help thinking of my dear Robert's prophecy, "Let
him but once grasp the magic wand and work with orchestra
and chorus," which is fulfilled to-day. The baton was really a
magic wand and its spell was upon all present, even upon his

bitterest enemies. It was a joy such as I have not felt for a long time. After the performance there was a supper in the *Rathskeller*, at which everyone was jubilant—it was like a musical festival. A crowd of friends were together, among them [Julius] Stockhausen . . . [Max] Bruch, the Dietrichs [Albert and Clara], [Julius] Grimm, Rieter [J. Melchior Rieter-Biedermann] . . . but curiously enough, except for some ladies who had been singing in the chorus, there was no-one from Hamburg . . . except Johannes' father.

Reinthaler made a speech about Johannes which so moved me that (unfortunately!!!) I burst into tears. I thought of Robert, and what joy it would have been to him if he could have lived to see it. . . . Johannes pressed me to stay in Bremen for another day. . . . I wish I had not given way to him.

Clara to Brahms:

Baden-Baden, Oct. 15th

. . . You wished for no answer, but you are still labouring under a mistake. . . . Your letter[11] is not the wall that stands between us. . . . But indeed there is no question of any wall to be torn down, all that is needed is a little friendliness and a little more self-control . . . these would more than suffice to make our meetings far happier than ever. . . . It lies in your hands alone, dear Johannes, whether the clouds shall roll away or whether a wall is really to rise between us, which would fill me with the deepest sorrow. As to your letter, I had long ago dismissed it from my mind— It is you who remind me of it. . . . Your conception of a concert tour seems to me remarkable! You look upon it merely as a means of earning money: I do not. I feel myself called upon to reproduce beautiful works, Robert's above all, so long as I have the strength, and even if it were not absolutely necessary I should still go on tour, though not in the exhausting fashion in which I am often compelled to at present. The practice of my art is a great part of me myself, it

11. The same letter of February 2, 1868.

is the air in which I breathe. On the other hand, I would rather starve than play in public with only half my powers.

Brahms to Clara:

Hamburg, Oct.

I wanted a very quiet hour, dearest Clara, in which to put into words my heart-felt thanks for your letter. As I have not been able to find one, they shall at least come flying at my usual letter tempo. There is so much that is true in your letter—if not all—I must confess that with remorse and regret; but with pleasure and satisfaction I realise how kind it is—only an angel like you could have written so kindly. A thousand thanks; shall I believe, or dare I only hope, that your goodness will never again have cause to turn into forbearance?

Life is a wild polyphony, but a good woman like you, can often bring about some exquisite resolution of its discords.

Have you found the variations for two pianos,[12] and could we not play them in Vienna? I have to go there and November will suit me perfectly.

At the age of fifty-nine Clara Schumann undertook a full-time position at the Hoch Conservatory in Frankfurt, where she taught from 1878–92. Her contract allowed her time for touring. Clara in her diary:

Frankfurt, Oct. 29th [1884]

Every day, at present, I dictate Robert's letters to me;[13] they give me great pleasure but at the same time make me very sad. What imagination, what intellect, what delicate perception combined with manly strength, and what love!! The very weight of riches and happiness is almost oppressive, and it is a good thing that my work takes me quite out of myself, otherwise, my health

12. Robert Schumann's Andante and Variations in B-flat major, op. 46.
13. Clara edited the collection *Jugendbriefe von Robert Schumann*, which was published in Leipzig in 1885, and in English translation in 1888.

would certainly suffer. These letters awaken my longing more
than words can say, and my heart's wounds bleed afresh. What
have I possessed and lost! And yet how long have I gone on
living and working. Where does one . . . find the strength? I
found it in my children and in art—they have sustained me by
their love and art too has never played me false.

Concert life and the proliferation of art music are slow to develop in a new country, but by the middle of the nineteenth century these traditions were becoming well established in the United States. Increasingly, Americans intent on careers as concert and opera artists journeyed to Europe to complete their preparation and to gain performing experience. Pianist Amy Fay (1844–1928) was an early participant in, as well as an unwitting promoter of, this migration. After studying at the New England Conservatory and with John Knowles Paine at Harvard College, in 1869 Fay went to Germany, where for the next six years she worked with Carl Tausig, Theodore Kullak, Ludwig Dieppe, and Liszt. Fay's letters to her family at home, in which she enthusiastically described her studies and the great artists she heard in concert, were subsequently collected and published by her sister Melusina Fay Pierce in 1880 as Music Study in Germany. *The book was enormously popular—with twenty-one printings in the United States in the nineteenth century alone—and is generally credited with having influenced thousands of Americans to study abroad, despite the admonishment from the editor that American piano teaching had "developed immensely" since Fay left for Germany in 1869.*

In the following excerpts Fay discusses her introduction to life in a Berlin pension, her studies at Tausig's conservatory, Clara Schumann's playing, and her work with Liszt. For all her admiration of Liszt, Fay in turn earned a high place when Liszt was asked to rank his pupils. Following her successful debut in Frankfurt in 1875, Fay returned to the United States and

---

Amy Fay, *Music Study in Germany* (Chicago: A. C. McClurg, 1880), pp. 13–16, 20–22, 210–14, 222–25.

pursued a notable career as a performer, teacher, and champion
for the advancement of women in music. (See also Readings
28 and 37.)

Berlin, November 3, 1869

Behold me at last at No. 26 Bernburger Strasse! where I arrived
exactly two weeks from the day I left New York. Frau W. and
her daughter, Fräulein A. W., greeted me with the greatest warmth
and cordiality, and made me feel at home immediately. The German idea of a "large" room I find is rather peculiar, for this
one is not more than ten or eleven feet square, and has one corner
of it snipped off, so that the room is an irregular shape. When
I first entered it I thought I could not stay in it, it seemed so
small, but when I came to examine it, so ingeniously is every
inch of space made the most of, that I have come to the conclusion
that it will be very comfortable. It is not, however, the apartment
where "the last new novel will lie upon the table, and where
my daintily slippered feet will rest upon the velvet cushion."
No! rather is it the stern abode of the Muses.

To begin then: the room is spotlessly clean and neat. The walls
are papered with a nice new paper, grey ground with blue figures—
a cheap paper, but soft and pretty. In one corner stands my little
bureau with three deep drawers. Over it is a large looking-glass
nicely framed. In the other corner on the same side is a big sofa
which at night becomes a little bed. Next to the foot of the
sofa, against the wall, stands a tiny square table, with a marble
top, and a shelf underneath, on which are a basin and a minute
soap-dish and tumbler. In the opposite corner towers a huge grey
porcelain stove, which comes up to within a few feet of the ceiling.
Next is one stiff cane-bottomed chair on four stiff legs. Then
comes the lop-sided corner of the room, where an upright piano
is to stand. Next there is a little space where hangs the three-
shelved book-case, which will contain my *vast* library. Then
comes a broad French window with a deep window-seat. By this
window is my sea-chair—by far the most luxurious one in the
house! Then comes my bureau again, and so on *Da Capo*. In
the middle is a pretty round table, with an inlaid centre-piece,

and on it is a waiter with a large glass bottle full of water, and a glass, and this, with one more stiff chair, completes the furniture of the room. My curtains are white, with a blue border, and two transparencies hang in the window. My towel-rack is fastened to the wall, and has an embroidered centre-piece. On my bureau is a beautiful inkstand, the cover being a carved eagle with spread wings, perched over a nest with three eggs in it. It is quite large, and looks extremely pretty under the looking-glass.

After I had taken off my things, Frau W. and her daughter ushered me into their parlour, which had the same look of neatness and simplicity and of extreme economy. There are no carpets on any of the floors, but they have large, though cheap, rugs. You never saw such a primitive little household as it is—that of this German lawyer's widow. We think our house at home small, but I feel as if we lived in palatial magnificence after seeing how they live here, *i.e.*, about as our dress-makers used to do in the country, and yet it is sufficiently nice and comfortable. There are two very pretty little rooms opposite mine, which are yet to be let together. If some friend of mine could only take them I should be perfectly happy.

At night my bed is made upon the sofa. (They all sleep on these sofas.) The cover consists of a feather bed and a blanket. That sounds rather formidable, but the feather bed is a light, warm covering, and looks about two inches thick. It is much more comfortable than our bed coverings in America. I tuck myself into my nest at night, and in the morning after breakfast, when I return to my room—*agramento-presto-change!*—my bed is converted into a sofa, my basin is laid on the shelf, the soap-dish and my combs and brushes are scuttled away into the drawer; the windows are open, a fresh fire crackles in my stove, and my charming little bed-room is straightway converted into an equally charming sitting-room. How does the picture please you?

This morning Frau and Fräulein W. went with me to engage a piano, and they took me also to the conservatory. Tausig is off for six weeks, giving concerts. As I went up the stairs I heard most beautiful playing. [Louis] Ehlert, Tausig's partner, who has charge of the conservatory, and teaches his pupils in his absence, examined me. After that long voyage I did not dare attempt anything difficult, so I just played one of Bach's Gavottes. He said some encouraging words, and for the present has taken me into his class. I am to begin to-morrow from one o'clock to two. It is now ten P.M., and tell C. we have had five meals to-day, so Madame P.'s statement is about correct. The cooking is on the same scale as the rest of the establishment—a little at a time, but so far very good. We know nothing at all about rolls in America. Anything so delicious as the rolls here I never ate in the way of bread. In the morning we had a cup of coffee and rolls. At eleven we lunched on a cup of bouillon and a roll. At two o'clock we had dinner, which consisted of soup and then chickens, potatoes, carrots and bread, with beer. At five we had tea, cake and toast, and at nine we had a supper of cold meat, boiled eggs, tea and bread and butter. Fräulein W. speaks English quite nicely, and is my medium of communication with her mother. I begin German lessons with her to-morrow. They both send you their compliments, and so you must return yours. They seem as kind as possible, and I think I am very fortunate in my boarding place.

Be sure to direct your letters "Care Frau Geheimräthin W." (Mrs. Councillor W.), as the German ladies are very particular about their *titles!*

Berlin, November 21

Tausig has not yet returned from his concert tour, and will not arrive before the 21st of December. I find Ehlert a splendid teacher, but very severe, and I am mortally afraid of him. Not that he is cross, but he exacts so much, and such a hopeless feeling of despair takes possession of me. His first lesson on touch taught me more than all my other lessons put together—though, to be sure, that is not saying much, as they were "few and far between." At present I am weltering in a sea of troubles. The girls in my class are three in number, and they all play so extraordinarily well that sometimes I think I can never catch up with them. I am the worst of all the scholars in Tausig's classes that I have heard, except one, and that is a young man. I know that Ehlert thinks I have talent, but, after all, talent must go to the wall before such *practice* as these people have had, for most of them have studied a long time, and have been at the piano four and five hours a day.

It is very interesting in the conservatory, for there are pupils there from all countries except France. Some of them seem to me splendid musicians. On Sunday morning (I am sorry to say) once in a month or six weeks, they have what they call a "Musical Reading." It is held in a piano-forte ware-room, and there all the scholars in the higher classes play, so I had to go. Many of the girls played magnificently, and I was amazed at the technique that they had, and at the artistic manner in which even very young girls rendered the most difficult music, and all without notes. It gave me a severe nervous headache just to hear them. But it was delightful to see them go at it. None of them had the least fear, and they laughed and chattered between the pieces, and when their turn came they marched up to the piano, sat down as bold as lions, and banged away so splendidly!

You have no idea how hard they make [J. B.] Cramer's Studies here. Ehlert makes me play them tremendously *forte,* and as fast as I can go. My hand gets so tired that it is ready to break, and then I say that I cannot go on. "But you *must* go on," he will say. It is the same with the scales. It seems to me that I play them so loud that I make the welkin ring, and he will say, "But you play always *piano.*" And with all this rapidity he does not allow a note to be missed, and if you happen to strike a wrong one he looks so shocked that you feel ready to sink into the floor. Strange to say, I enjoy the lessons in *Zusammenspiel* (duet-playing) very much, although it is all reading at sight. Four of us sit down at two pianos and read duets at sight. Lesmann is a pleasant man, and he always talks so fast that he amuses me very much. He always counts and beats time most vigorously, and bawls in your ear, *"Eins—zwei! Eins—zwei!"* or sometimes, *"Eins!"* only, on the first beat of every bar. When, occasionally, we all get out, he looks at us through his glasses, and then such a volley of words as he hurls at us is wonderful to hear. I never can help laughing, though I take good care not to let him see me.

Berlin, December 12, 1869

I heard Clara Schumann on Sunday, and on Tuesday evening, also. She is a most wonderful artist. In the first concert she played a quartette by Schumann, and you can imagine how lovely it was under the treatment of Clara Schumann for the piano, [Joseph] Joachim for the first violin, [Heinrich] De Ahna for the second, and [Wilhelm] Müller for the 'cello. It was perfect, and I was in raptures. Madame Schumann's selection for the two concerts was a very wide one, and gave a full exhibition of her powers in every kind of music. The Impromptu by Schubert, op. 90, was exquisite. It was full of passion and very difficult. The second of the Songs without Words, by Mendelssohn, was the most fairy-like performance. It is one of those things that must be tossed off with the greatest grace and smoothness, and it requires the most beautiful and delicate technique. She played it to perfection. The terrific Scherzo by Chopin she did splendidly, but she kept the great octave passages in the bass a little too subordinate, I thought, and did not give it quite boldly enough for my taste, though it was extremely artistic. Clara Schumann's playing is very objective. She seems to throw herself into the music, instead of letting the music take possession of her. She gives you the most exquisite pleasure with every note she touches, and has a wonderful conception and variety in playing, but she seldom whirls you off your feet.

At the second concert she was even better than at the first, if that is possible. She seemed full of fire, and when she played Bach, she ought to have been crowned with diamonds! Such *noble* playing I never heard. In fact you are all the time impressed with the nobility and breadth of her style, and the comprehensiveness of her treatment, and oh, if you *could* hear her *scales!* In short, there is nothing more to be desired in her playing, and she has every quality of a great artist. Many people say that Tausig is far better, but I cannot believe it. He may have more technique and more power, but nothing else I am sure. Everybody raves over his playing, and I am getting quite impatient for his return, which is expected next week. I send you Madame Schumann's photograph, which is exactly like her. She is a large, very German-

looking woman, with dark hair and superb neck and arms. At
the last concert she was dressed in black velvet, low body and
short sleeves, and when she struck powerful chords, those large
white arms came down with a certain splendor.

As for Joachim, he is perfectly magnificent, and has amazing
power. When he played his solo in that Chaconne of Bach's,[1]
you could scarcely believe it was only one violin. He has, like
Madame Schumann, the greatest variety of tone, only on the
violin the shades can be made far more delicate than on the piano.

I thought the second movement of Schumann's Quartette perhaps as extraordinary as any part of Clara Schumann's performance. It was very rapid, very *staccato*, and *pianissimo* all the
way through. Not a note escaped her fingers, and she played
with so much magnetism that one could scarcely breathe until
it was finished. You know nothing can be more difficult than
to play staccato so very softly where there is great execution also.
Both of the sonatas for violin and piano which were played by
Madame Schumann and Joachim, and especially the one in A
minor, by Beethoven [op. 23], were divine. Both parts were
equally well sustained, and they played with so much fire—as
if one inspired the other. It was worth a trip across the Atlantic
just to hear those two performances.

The Sing-Akademie, where all the best concerts are given, is
not a very large hall, but it is beautifully proportioned, and the
acoustic is perfect. The frescoes are very delicate, and on the
left are boxes all along, which add much to the beauty of the
hall, with their scarlet and gold flutings. Clara Schumann is a
great favorite here, and there was such a rush for seats that, though
we went early for our tickets, all the good parquet seats were
gone, and we had to get places on the *estrade,* or place where
the chorus sits—when there is one. But I found it delightful
for a piano concert, for you can be as close to the performer as
you like, and at the same time see the faces of the audience. I
saw ever so many people that I knew, and we kept bowing away
at each other.

1. Partita no. 2, BWV 104.

Just think how convenient it is here with regard to public amusements, for ladies can go anywhere alone! You take a droschkie and they drive you anywhere for five groschen, which is about fifteen cents. When you get into the concert hall you go into the *garde-robe* and take off your things, and hand them over to the care of the woman who stands there, and then you walk in and sit down comfortably as you would in a parlour, and are not roasted in your hat and cloak while at the concert, and chilled when you go out, as we are in America. Their programmes, too, are not so unconscionably long as ours, and, in short, their whole method of concert-giving is more rational than with us. I always enjoy the garde-robe, for if you have acquaintances you are sure to meet them, and you have no idea how exciting it is in a foreign city to see anybody you know.

Weimar, May 21, 1873.

Liszt is so *besieged* by people and so tormented with applications, that I fear I should only have been sent away if I had come without the Baroness von S.'s letter of introduction,[2] for he admires her extremely, and I judge that she has much influence with him. He says "people fly in his face by dozens," and seem to think he is "only there to give lessons." He gives *no* paid lessons whatever, as he is much too grand for that, but if one has talent enough, or pleases him, he lets one come to him and play to him. I go to him every other day, but I don't play more than twice a week, as I cannot prepare so much, but I listen to the others. Up to this point there have been only four in the class besides myself, and I am the only new one. From four to six P.M. is the time when he receives his scholars. The first time I went I did not play to him, but listened to the rest. [Anton] Urspruch and [Johann Georg] Leitert, the two young men whom I met the other night, have studied with Liszt a long time, and both play superbly. Fräulein Schultz and Miss Gaul (of Baltimore), are also most gifted creatures.

As I entered Liszt's salon, Urspruch was performing Schumann's

2. Baroness Olga von Meyerdorff.

Symphonic Studies [*Symphonic Etudes*, op. 13]—an immense composition, and one that it took at least half an hour to get through. He played so splendidly that my heart sank down into the very depths. I thought I should never get on *there!* Liszt came forward and greeted me in a very friendly manner as I entered. He was in very good humour that day, and made some little witticisms. Urspruch asked him what title he should give to a piece he was composing. *"Per aspera ad astra,"*[3] said Liszt. This was such a good hit that I began to laugh, and he seemed to enjoy my appreciation of his little sarcasm. I did not play that time, as my piano had only just come, and I was not prepared to do so, but I went home and practiced tremendously for several days on Chopin's B minor sonata [op. 58]. It is a great composition, and one of his last works. When I thought I could play it, I went to Liszt, though with a trembling heart. I cannot tell you what it has cost me every time I have ascended his stairs. I can scarcely summon up courage to go there, and generally stand on the steps awhile before I can make up my mind to open the door and go in!

This day it was particularly trying, as it was really my first serious performance before him, and he speaks so very indistinctly that I feared I shouldn't understand his corrections, and that he would get out of patience with me, for he cannot bear to explain. I think he hates the trouble of speaking German, for he mutters his words and does not half finish his sentences. Yesterday when I was there he spoke to me in French all the time, and to the others in German,—one of his funny whims, I suppose.

Well, on this day the artists Leitert and Urspruch, and the young composer Metzdorf, who is always hanging about Liszt, were in the room when I came. They had probably been playing. At first Liszt took no notice of me beyond a greeting, till Metzdorf said to him, "Herr Doctor, Miss Fay has brought a sonata." "Ah, well, let us hear it," said Liszt. Just then he left the room for a minute, and I told the three gentlemen that they ought to go away and let me play to Liszt alone, for I felt nervous about

3. "Through difficulties to the stars."

playing before them. They all laughed at me and said they would
not budge an inch. When Liszt came back they said to him, "Only
think, Herr Doctor, Miss Fay proposes to send us all home." I
said I could not play before such great artists. "Oh, that is healthy
for you," said Liszt, with a smile, and added, "you have a very
choice audience, now." I don't know whether he appreciated how
nervous I was, but instead of walking up and down the room as
he often does, he sat down by me like any other teacher, and
heard me play the first movement. It was frightfully hard, but I
had studied it so much that I managed to get through with it
pretty successfully. Nothing could exceed Liszt's amiability, or
the trouble he gave himself, and instead of frightening me, he
inspired me. Never was there such a delightful teacher! and he
is the first sympathetic one I've had. You feel so *free* with him,
and he develops the very spirit of music in you. He doesn't keep
nagging at you all the time, but he leaves you your own conception. Now and then he will make a criticism, or play a passage,
and with a few words give you enough to think of all the rest
of your life. There is a delicate *point* to everything he says, as
subtle as he is himself. He doesn't tell you anything about the
technique. That you must work out for yourself. When I had
finished the first movement of the sonata, Liszt, as he always
does, said "Bravo!" Taking my seat, he made some little criticisms,
and then told me to go on and play the rest of it.

Now, I only half knew the other movements, for the first one
was so extremely difficult that it cost me all the labour I could
give to prepare that. But playing to Liszt reminds me of trying
to feed the elephant in the Zoological Garden with lumps of
sugar. He disposes of whole movements as if they were nothing,
and stretches out gravely for more! One of my fingers fortunately
began to bleed, for I had practiced the skin off, and that gave
me a good excuse for stopping. Whether he was pleased at this
proof of industry, I know not; but after looking at my finger
and saying, "Oh!" very compassionately, he sat down and played
the whole three last movements himself. That was a great deal,
and showed off all his powers. It was the first time I had heard
him, and I don't know which was the most extraordinary,—the

Scherzo, with its wonderful lightness and swiftness, the Adagio with its depth and pathos, or the last movement, where the whole keyboard seemed to "*donnern und blitzen* (thunder and lighten)." There is such a vividness about everything he plays that it does not seem as if it were mere music you were listening to, but it is as if he had called up a real, living *form*, and you saw it breathing before your face and eyes. It gives *me* almost a ghostly feeling to hear him, and it seems as if the air were peopled with spirits. Oh, he is a perfect wizard! It is as interesting to see him as it is to hear him, for his face changes with every modulation of the piece, and he looks exactly as he is playing. He has one element that is most captivating, and that is, a sort of delicate and fitful mirth that keeps peering out at you here and there! It is most peculiar, and when he plays that way, the most bewitching little expression comes over his face. It seems as if a little spirit of joy were playing hide and go seek with you.

Weimar, June 6, 1873

One day this week, when we were with Liszt, he was in such high spirits that it was as if he had suddenly become twenty years younger. A student from the Stuttgart Conservatory played a Liszt Concerto. His name is V., and he is dreadfully nervous. Liszt kept up a little running fire of satire all the time he was playing, but in a good-natured way. I shouldn't have minded it if it had been I. In fact, I think it would have inspired me; but poor V. hardly knew whether he was on his head or on his feet. It was too funny. Everything that Liszt says is so striking. For instance, in one place where V. was playing the melody rather feebly, Liszt suddenly took his seat at the piano and said, "When *I* play, I always play for the people in the gallery (by the gallery he meant the cock-loft, where the rabble always sit, and where the places cost next to nothing), so that those persons who pay only five groschens for their seat also hear something." Then he began, and I wish you could have heard him! The sound didn't seem to be very *loud*, but it was penetrating and far-reaching. When he had finished, he raised one hand in the air, and you seemed to see all the people in the gallery drinking in the sound. That is the way Liszt teaches you. He presents an *idea* to you, and it takes fast hold of your mind and sticks there. Music is such a real, visible thing to him, that he always has a symbol, instantly, in the material world to express his idea. One day, when I was playing, I made too much movement with my hand in a rotatory sort of a passage where it was difficult to avoid it. "Keep your hand still, Fräulein," said Liszt, *"don't make omelette."* I couldn't help laughing, it hit me on the head so nicely. He is far too sparing of his playing, unfortunately, and, like Tausig, only sits down and plays a few bars at a time, generally. It is dreadful when he stops, just as you are at the height of your enjoyment, but he is so thoroughly *blasé* that he doesn't care to show off, and doesn't like to have any one pay him a compliment. Even at the court it annoyed him so that the Grand Duchess told people to take no notice when he rose from the piano.

On the same day that Liszt was in such high good-humour, a strange lady and her husband were there who had made a long journey to Weimar, in the hope of hearing him play. She waited patiently for a long time through the lesson, and at last Liszt took compassion on her, and sat down with his favourite remark that "the young ladies played a great deal better than he did, but he would try his best to imitate them," and then played something of his own so wonderfully, that when he had finished we all stood there like posts, feeling that there was *nothing* to be said. But he, as if he feared we might burst out into eulogy, got up instantly and went over to a friend of his who was standing there, and who lives on an estate near Weimar, and said, in the most commonplace tone imaginable, "By the way, how about those eggs? Are you going to send me some?" It seems to be not only a profound bore to him, but really a sort of sensitiveness on his part. How he can bear to hear *us* play, I cannot imagine. It must grate on his ear terribly, I think, because everything *must* sound expressionless to him in comparison with his own marvellous conception. I assure you, no matter how beautifully we play any piece, the minute Liszt plays it, you would scarcely recognize it! His touch and his peculiar use of the pedal are two secrets of his playing, and then he seems to dive down in the most hidden thoughts of the composer, and fetch them up to the surface, so that they gleam out at you one by one, like stars!

The more I see and hear Liszt, the more I am lost in amazement! I can neither eat nor sleep on those days that I go to him. All my musical studies till now have been a mere going to school, a preparation for him. I often think of what Tausig said once: "Oh, compared with Liszt, we other artists are all blockheads." I did not believe it at the time, but I've seen the truth of it, and in studying Liszt's playing, I can see where Tausig got many of his own wonderful peculiarities. I think he was the most like Liszt of all the army that have had the privilege of his instruction.

Lillian Nordica (1857–1914) was born into a family of singers in Farmington, Maine, as Lillian Norton. Her mother, Amanda Allen Norton, discovered her talent only after the death of an older sister, who had shown great promise for a professional career. Nordica studied at the New England Conservatory for four years with John O'Neill, graduating in 1876. Subsequently she toured as a soloist with Patrick Gilmore's Band in the United States for a year and a half, and in the spring of 1878 she traveled with the band to Europe, her mother accompanying her.

Throughout the nineteenth century and well into the twentieth, American singers aspiring to major operatic careers found European experience imperative in order to perfect their command of languages and to obtain engagements with opera companies, since so few opportunities for performing existed in the United States. In Nordica's case, it was on the strength of Gilmore's handsome final payment in Paris that she and her mother struck out on a path that kept them abroad for five years. Ultimately they met with great success, but their first years were accomplished on a shoestring. Their lodging and food was minimal, and Lillian gave lessons to pay for her own. Even so, an emergency loan from family members in Boston was necessary to see them through one difficult period. The adaptability and resourcefulness of these provincial New England women seem as remarkable as their courage.

Amanda Allen Norton kept the family in Boston informed about Lillian's progress through her frequent letters, the earliest

Lillian Nordica, *Lillian Nordica's Training for the Opera as Told in the Letters of Amanda Allen Norton and Lillian Nordica,* from *Hints to Singers* by Lillian Nordica, ed. William Armstrong, published 1923, pp. 9–11, 12–15, 17, 23–29, 36–38, 57. Reprinted by permission of the publisher, E. P. Dutton, New York.

of which are excerpted here. In the 1890s Nordica became one of the first native American singers to join the Metropolitan Opera, where between 1893 and 1907 she was a leading Wagnerian soprano. Her stage name, Nordica, was fashioned by her teacher in Milan, Antonio Sangiovanni, so as to sound euphonious to Italian audiences.

Brussels, July 1, 1878

We have been away from home eight weeks. Lillian has sung in sixty-five concerts, and we have traveled 3,000 miles since landing in Liverpool, which, taken altogether, makes a great two months work. . . . Lillian has sung with great success so far. I am anxious for next Thursday, July 4, as that will close her engagement and will cap the climax. Having sung in all the great cities of England and Scotland, also in Dublin and in Holland, if she does well in Paris at the Trocadero [i.e., at the 1878 Exposition] then she will feel ready to settle down and study—and prepare to fill other engagements. She has already received letters from managers in London. Still, we cannot yet say what course we shall take until after July.

Paris, July 16

Now that you may know exactly what we are doing, I shall keep strictly to the subject. We have succeeded in getting the greatest teacher of dramatic action, [François] Delsarte. It is an almost impossible thing to secure his instruction on account of scores of applicants from every quarter. Lilly is also taking lessons in French, two hours every day. . . . She learns very rapidly. It remains to be seen what she can do in dramatic art. At any rate, she has the best teacher known. He says that her voice is remarkable, and that her method is perfect.

Paris, August 25

Lilly wants very much to go to Italy, as it is the advice from all sides to get a perfect knowledge of the language, also that indefinite something which one hears and sees in all the best artists. I do not feel competent to advise, but shall let her act

Lillian Nordica as Elsa in *Lohengrin*. She sang this role at the
first Bayreuth performance of *Lohengrin* in 1894, after coaching
with Cosima Wagner.

according to her own instincts. All I shall do is to *stand by*, which is no small part. Sometimes I am afraid she will do too much.

But money melts, at the rate of forty or fifty dollars a week. Her future is *great*, but she cannot jump into next year. She must creep and plod.

You would be surprised to hear the progress she has made in one month in *Lucia*, *Traviata*, and *Faust*. But she must have time to learn all these things.

Now, as she does not propose to marry *anyone* for helping her, the question is, can she raise three, five, seven hundred or a thousand dollars to get the requisite teaching? [Emilio] Belari and [Alberto, Sr.] Randegger [as coaches], for instance, will give her lessons rather than that such a voice should stop, but Delsarte is poor and must be paid, and the French teacher is a poor woman who depends upon her pay; the ladies who keep the *pensions* have to collect their pay once a week to live.

Hats, gloves, and suitable dresses have to be replaced often, for Lilly is hard on her clothing; these are legitimate expenses and amount to no less than thirty, forty, and sometimes fifty dollars a week. As I keep account of every week's expenses, I know exactly how the money *melts*, as Lily says.

Paris, September 10

It is no child's play to learn an opera. If you think so, listen to five or six hours of digging at *Aida* every day, besides two hours [of] French verbs. . . . Lilly has done an immense amount of work in the last four months, taking into account the seventy concerts. Since the twelfth of August she has had forty lessons with Belari in Italian repertory, and the same number or more from Delsarte in dramatic action, besides her French lesson every day.

I take care of everything connected with her dress and wait upon her by inches, because I know that she is doing all she can consistently. She sings most charmingly, and could, if at home, no doubt have all [the engagements] that she could do. But the question now is, study!!! . . . Lilly commences at nine o'clock every morning a preparatory lesson in acting; at ten a pianist from Belari comes to the house to assist her in learning the notes and Italian operas; at half past eleven she practices until twelve, then breakfast; then French for two hours; at three music study; at four acting with Delsarte. So her whole time is occupied. She generally lies on the sofa while studying or reciting French and in that way gets rested. . . . The truth of the matter is, Lilly can be *great*, but she must have time to study without injury to her health, just the same as others have done. Belari, although he wants the credit of having her make her debut in Madrid, says she must not hurry too fast. She will go with me to the country for a week very soon. She has not taken a moment's rest this year. So we will leave everything behind for a few days, and go to a country house, eat fruit, and drink milk.

Milan, December 12

Sangiovanni says Lilly has nothing to do but to learn her operas, and that her voice, manner, figure, face, and perfect simplicity insure her—with good health—of the greatest fame attached to lyric and dramatic opera. He is surprised that she sings both the *Lucia* and the *Aida*, music so different in character. He also says that she can render the greatest operas of the age if she keeps on, but that she must have sufficient time at it, as it is impossible to accomplish the right work by cramming [just] as it would be to make a man of a boy at twelve years. Hundreds have gone through this man's hands, and he knows whereof he speaks.

His assurance to her is that next autumn she will make her debut. Sometimes though when we think, we feel as if we should flee. The distance between us and home! The work ahead!! The critical world!!! The expense!!!! The danger of losing health!!!!! And then the annoyance of forgoing living and everything else. It would rob me of my sleep if I had not the will of a giant. But I find myself saying, "We have gone too far to give it up."

Milan, December 26

The Christmas of another year is past, and it was a day above all others the most fraught with memories.

Mr. R_____ sent Lilly his disquisition on opera singers. After thoroughly reading it twice I concluded that he must have seen and known a great deal more of the stage than we ever *have* or ever *shall*. Lilly has sung in many of the largest theaters and halls in America, Great Britain, Holland, Belgium, and finally in the French metropolis at the Trocadero, and much of that time travelled with sixty-five gentlemen of all nationalities [i.e., the musicians in Gilmore's band]. . . . And not one word or look was ever heard or seen in the least possible manner approaching disrespect. Not a man of Gilmore's band would do more than raise his hat in complete deference to us as we met them in hotels, theaters, or the street. As for Mr. Gilmore, he has the bearing and the soul of a Christian gentleman.

No matter what the calling, you can find plenty of disaster, ruin, and corruption. Every woman can stand on her own self-made reputation, whether in church, state, or on the stage.

Milan, January 26, 1879

Lilly still likes her maestro [Sangiovanni] very much and is going ahead as fast as is allowable. Her voice is called very heavy and dramatic, but she is cautioned not to sing too much. . . . They want to present *Il Trovatore* at La Scala and have tried twenty-seven voices, but no one has been engaged yet. I am telling you these things to show how scarce dramatic singers are, and that to become first class ones they have to make haste slowly or the voice will exhaust the body. . . . We have settled with the landlord today for all we owe him up to this time, and I have counted over what still remains. We shall have enough for the next month. . . . Do you realize it is nearly a year since we left you? We were just saying that it made our heads swim to think that we were so long and far away from home. It is a great thing for two women to come alone to the Old World and buffet its customs, its climates, and its foods. However, we have been good for it, so far, and with continued health shall be.

Be of good courage at home; each side of the ocean has its obstacles to surmount, and if you will pull with a long and strong pull, we shall do the same, and all will be well. We do the best we know how, sure that in the end (which by the way never comes), the summit we are climbing now will, when reached, reveal new ones perhaps higher.

Nordica's progress was such that Sangiovanni secured debuts for her earlier than his original plan of autumn 1879.

Milan, February 11

Lilly has signed to sing in opera, through the recommendation of Sangiovanni. . . . Of course, the first requisite to success is a *voice,* but the *next* is to fall into the right hands.

The appearances will be what is here called a *prova*[:] in reality a test to settle exactly the ability of the person whom impresarios may hereafter recommend at a stipulated price to managers, coming for material to this great musical business center. . . . Almost all singers have to pay for a debut; in Lilly's case the wardrobe is found, except that she prefers to use her own gloves and boots.[1]

She received a pleasant letter today from Mr. C_____ in which he wishes that she would come home and take the position of soprano in Dr. Webb's church, and sing in concerts and oratorio. He says they would give her a good salary. He also said that she could have sung in the *Messiah* better than the one who did etc., etc. He is not sanguine of her singing in opera, although he says he has no doubt of her success. But she will attempt on the eighth of March! And if her forte is not opera, she feels sure of oratorio, etc. We shall wait and work and hope for the best.

Postponed from March 8 to 10, Nordica's debut in Milan as Donna Elvira in Don Giovanni *was a decided success. In April mother and daughter went to Brescia, where the young American soprano triumphed in* La traviata.

Brescia, April 27

My dear family in America, last night was the first appearance of your absent Lilly in *Traviata,* and I have only to repeat what

1. Nordica did not have to pay for the privilege of a *prova* in Milan, presumably in recognition of her outstanding talent.

the crowded theater demonstrated, people standing in mass giving sound of applause and *brava* that would have done your heart good.

I am repaid for a year's anxiety when I see the musical public of the second city in Lombardy calling imperatively *bis!* [encore] *bis!! bis!!!* 'til she was nine times before the curtain with a smile and a gracious acknowledgement for all from the proscenium boxes to the gallery.

Only think of men and women sobbing as though they were actually witnessing the death of a beautiful girl, who struggles to live, yet must die. The most convincing point of all was, that tears ran down her cheeks as she bade adieu to all the joys of life. After this, when she returned before the curtain, loaded with flowers of exquisite colors, it seemed as though the public would go mad.

The owner of the opera house and impresario came immediately to her dressing room, and gave every possible graceful acknowledgement of her artistic rendering of their beloved *Traviata*. This morning at ten o'clock a string band came under her windows at the hotel and commenced playing the overture to *Traviata*. After finishing it, there were calls for *Nordica! Bellissima Violetta!* When she went to the window a hundred persons were waiting, and they just rent the air with *La Americana Nordica!, La gentilissima Violetta!* Sangiovanni and many others from Milan have come to hear tonight's performance. I know you must think me egotistical, but I am so far from home, and on such a responsible errand, that it would not be strange if I became quite absorbed in the results of the year's work. . . . Lilly says to write to Mr. O'Neill that she has never swerved from his method and teaching, and she also wishes, no matter what may go into the papers, that he may be given his credit.

Nordica went on to further triumphs in Genoa, Novarra, at the Imperial Theater in St. Petersburg, and finally in 1882 at the Paris Opéra. In an undated letter, possibly written during Nordica's seasons in St. Petersburg, Amanda Allen Norton joyfully addressed some family members at home:

Now Billy, Annie, and Edwin, I see the first rays of daylight in rosy tints, just peeping above the eastern horizon. Look this way and keep your patience. . . . The first half of the battle is fought, *and the victory is ours*.

20 MARGARET BLAKE-ALVERSON: CONTRALTO

In contrast to the three artists represented earlier in this section, contralto Margaret Blake-Alverson (1836–1923) was a minor, regional figure, but she nevertheless made an important contribution to the early development of musical life in the American West, in California. Blake-Alverson's father was a Protestant clergyman from Cincinnati, who in 1849 responded to a call to minister to the large influx of men attracted to California by the Gold Rush. He traveled overland with his eldest son, and upon their arrival in Stockton father and son mined gold enough to pay for the passage of the remaining seven children and their mother by boat and mule through the Isthmus of Panama. This second party made the long trip in 1851, and soon after reaching Stockton the six girls—all of whom were musical—organized a choir for their father's First Presbyterian Church as "an incentive for the men to forsake one day [a week] thinking of gold." In the selection below from her autobiography, Blake-Alverson describes an equally notable event, the introduction of the first piano in Stockton at Christmas 1852.

In 1858 Margaret Blake-Alverson traveled once again through the Isthmus of Panama with her husband and seven-month-old child to Boston, where she spent four years studying voice and singing in the chorus of the Handel and Haydn Society, in a church choir in Dedham, Massachusetts, and with other groups. After her return to California, Blake-Alverson worked as a church soloist and a voice teacher in Santa Cruz, San Francisco, and Oakland.

Margaret Blake-Alverson, *Sixty Years of California Song* (Oakland, Calif.: Author, 1913), pp. 29–32.

In her autobiography Blake-Alverson relates how her family decided to run a boardinghouse in Stockton and continues:

We were assigned our parts, and for two years we worked until we were able to secure our own house, which stands today in Stockton as one of the earlier homes and our homestead. While in this house [i.e., the boardinghouse] there were times when we still longed for home and the old surroundings. Sister Mary wanted her instrument which she supposed she would never have again. Our friends, knowing this, quietly consulted father in regard to securing a piano as a birthday offering. But as Christmas Day was the date of her birth, it was too late for the year 1851. We had already entered upon the year 1852, and it would take almost a year to get a piano here, as Mr. Atwill had not imported any instruments as yet. Our friends were good business men and they immediately set about to learn if a piano could not be obtained. All this was unknown to any of us but father. William Trembly and James Harrold, while in San Francisco, inquired at the different musical stores as to arrangements to obtain a piano. Kohler & Chase did not import at that time. They dealt in notions, fancy goods and toys. They were not wholly in the music business until later in the sixties. Mr. Atwill was at the time on Washington street. He did not import largely, and when Messrs. Trembley and Harrold came to him he gladly entered into the plan to get a fine Chickering here by December 25th of 1852. The cost was to be $1,200, delivered in good order. The piano order was given, and how it came to California, whether by steamer or around the Horn, I am not able to say. . . .

. . . Christmas came clear and bright, but mud was everywhere. Rubber boots were indispensable this Christmas. Dinner was served about 1:30 o'clock and everybody seemed to be in the happiest mood. It was sister Mary's birthday and we were especially attentive to her.

The dinner was over and the dessert was almost finished when a rap on the front door sounded loud and rough. Father asked Mary to go to the door as she was nearest. She obeyed and, when she had answered the knock, a teamster handed her a letter and asked if Miss Mary Kroh lived here. She replied in the affirmative, and taking the letter she glanced out of the door and saw a heavy truck with an immense box or case on it. She said, "You must be mistaken." He said, "Are you not Miss Kroh? This is for her." By this time we were getting excited, and with one accord the guests arose to see the result. Father became uneasy at her long silence and came out in time to see her reel against the railing of the stairs. She had read the note and realized that her great desire had at last become a reality and her birthday had brought her the long-wished-for piano. This is what she read in the note:

"A merry Christmas and a happy birthday for Miss Mary Matilda Kroh, from her father and many friends who have appreciated her noble sacrifice of the musical environment of her Eastern home. This instrument is given as a partial compensation for her cheerful and noble performance of her duty to her parents and as full appreciation. James Harrold, C. V. Payton, Charles Greenly, David Trembly, William Cobb, Charles Deering, Gilbert Claiborne, William H. Knight, Samuel Grove, A. M. Thompson, William Gray, Thomas Mosely, William A. Trembly, Henry Kroh, James Holmes, Henry Noel, Austin Sperry, George H. Blake."

When the secret was out, all was excitement. Sister made her exit upstairs and the men took off their coats and helped with a will. Soon the beautiful instrument was out of the box and placed in the parlor. What a rejoicing there was! Father gave orders that Mary must play the first air, and we awaited her coming, but she had not been able to control herself to meet the friends and see the most magnificent gift she ever received. Sister Sarah was dispatched to bring her down stairs. She found her in the attitude of prayer. After much persuasion she came down and father met her and led her to the instrument. She stood for a moment unable to proceed. Seating herself upon the stool, she began to play the Doxology, but her head sank upon the piano. Then the tears gushed forth, the spell was broken and after a short time she was able to proceed. It was now about the hour of seven, darkness had crept on and the curtains were closed and the lights lit. We all became more composed, music was brought out, songs were sung and it was like a new world to us, such unexpected happiness in a far-off city of the Golden West. Father had occasion to answer a call at the front door and before closing he accidentally looked out, and to his surprise the sidewalks and porch were filled with old and young men. Along the side of the house stood scores of men in the street as far as the eye could see, and some were sobbing. On entering the room he said, "We have an immense congregation outside. Get out your familiar tunes—'Home, sweet home,' etc." He then drew aside the curtains and raised the windows, "Now, my children and friends, give these homesick sons and fathers a few songs more before we assemble for the evening worship." We sang until the hour of nine and closed with the Doxology. Once more father went on the porch and thanked the people for their appreciation of the music and dismissed them with the benediction. We closed the windows and curtains and remained with our friends a short time, when they departed fully assured that they had brought happiness to many souls by their magnificent gift to one who was worthy to receive it, my sainted sister, Mary Matilda Kroh.

This is the story of the first piano in Stockton, given to sister, December 25, 1852. This night was not the only night when men assembled on our porch to hear the music. Later on a number of men accosted father and told him that the music on the first night we received the piano had so vividly brought back home surroundings and memories of father and mother, that it was the turning point in the path from which they had strayed and caused them to see the error of their ways and to come back [into the fold of the church]. Such is the influence of song upon the young and the old.

21   SISSIERETTA JONES: SOPRANO

In the post–Civil War period, black musicians began to achieve national recognition as concert artists in the United States. Among them soprano Sissieretta Jones (1868–1933) was the most publicized, after Blind Tom (Thomas Greene Bethune). Born Mathilde S. Joyner in Portsmouth, Virginia, Jones moved with her family at an early age to Providence, Rhode Island, where she studied voice at the Providence Academy of Music. Later she attended the New England Conservatory.

The group of press items in this reading traces Jones's career from a lowly assisting artist as Mrs. Mathilde Jones or Mrs. M. S. Jones in 1888–89 to the full-fledged prima donna in 1892 known as Mme. Sissieretta Jones, the "Black Patti." The reference is, of course, to the white soprano Adelina Patti, and it implies that the contemporary press felt Jones needed identification with a major, white star. The novelty of black performers among white audiences usually faded after two or three years, and accordingly in 1896 Sissieretta Jones left the concert stage to head her own vaudeville company, Black Patti's Troubadours. She pursued this second career successfully for fifteen years. Black artists frequently had problems with white managers, such as Jones's with Major Pond.

4 August 1888. *New York Age*
A rehearsal was held at Wallack's Theatre Wednesday afternoon by a company of colored singers who sailed Thursday morning on the steamer Athos for Jamaica. They will also make a tour through the West Indies, the Windward Islands and the Spanish

Josephine Wright and Eileen Southern, "Sissieretta Jones, 1868–1933," *Black Perspective in Music* 4/2 (July 1976): 192–97, 201. Used by permission of *Black Perspective in Music*.

Main. Mrs. Matilda Jones, a young lady of 20 years, and Mr. W. H. Pierce of Providence will be the stars of the affair. Mrs. Jones is called the "Black Patti" by such men as Abbey, Schoeffel and Grau [managers of the Metropolitan Opera], who should be competent to judge in such matters. Mr. Pierce is said to be one of the finest tenors in the country. The organization [called the Tennessee Concert Company] is under the management of James R. Smith, while C. H. Matthews will remain to look after the bank account. It is one of the most promising enterprises that have ever been planned for colored artists.

20 April 1889, *The Freeman*

Last week, at Dockstader's Theatre, Broadway, New York, a company known as the Georgia Minstrels appeared all week to good business. The troupe consisted of Mme. M. S. Jones, DeWolf Sisters, Messrs. Lew Brown, W. Owens King, Will H. Pierce, Dick Jones, Wesley Norris, Billy Wilson, Horace Western [i.e., Weston], Lew Allen and the Excelsior Quartette.

It may be surprising to note the names of some of the artists who appeared in the Georgia Minstrels in New York last week. An actor's lot is not a happy one; up today and down tomorrow.

17 October 1891, *New York Age*

BERGEN STAR CONCERTS

On Thursday evening, October 17th, a Bergen Star Concert was given at the Bridge Street Church, Brooklyn. . . . Mrs. Flora Batson Bergen and Mrs. Matilda S. Jones were the stars of the evening. . . . Mrs. Jones was greeted with great applause. She has a pleasing voice, completely under control. This is her first appearance in Brooklyn. On Monday evening, Mrs. Bergen and Mrs. Jones appeared at Bethel Church, this city [i.e., Manhattan], before a large and enthusiastic audience and repeated their Brooklyn triumph. . . . Madame Jones's rendition of the Meyerbeer Cavatina[1] made good her claim as an artist of high order. . . .

1. "Robert, toi que j'aime," from *Robert le Diable*.

Sissieretta Jones.

25 February 1892, *Washington Post*

MADAME SISSIERETTA AT THE WHITE HOUSE

Mme. M. Sissieretta Jones, who possesses a voice of extraordinary compass, that has given her the title of the "Colored Patti" and medalist of the age, appeared before President Harrison, his family and guests at the Executive Mansion at 10 o'clock. The selections presented were "Cavatina" by Meyerbeer; "Suwanee River;" Waltz by Pattison, and "Home, Sweet Home." Professor Charles Dunger accompanied her on the piano.

27 April 1892, *New York Herald*

THE "BLACK PATTI" AND A CAKE WALK

> *Five Thousand Persons Witness a Novel Entertainment at Madison Square Garden*

APPLAUSE FOR MME. JONES

> *She Sang the Suawanee River and Selections from Grand Operas and Wasn't a Bit Nervous*

There was a study in black and white at the Madison Square Garden last night. About three-fourths of the scene, though, was in white. The big garden had been prepared for a rather unique entertainment in which the "Black Patti," heralded as "the greatest singer of her race," a lot of oddities, musical and otherwise, all colored, and Levy's American Band took part.

About five thousand persons were in the Garden at nine o'clock. The boxes were well filled, as were the arena seats, by people whom one would not often see at a cakewalk. Many of the ladies wore dazzling toilets, and evening dress was general among the men. . . .

The Black Patti

When Mme. Sissieretta Jones, the "Black Patti," walked up the steps to the platform in the center of the great amphitheatre, her breast was covered with medals and she was smiling broadly. She is of Dianesque proportions, very black, but with pleasing features. She was perfectly self possessed. She began the cavatina from Meyerbeer's opera, "Robert le Diable." After the first few notes the audience saw that the songstress had a remarkably strong voice, which she used with discretion.

Her effort was loudly applauded, as was her first encore, the familiar "Way Down Upon the Suawanee River," which she sang in excellent taste. Recalled again, she sang "The Cows Are in the Clover" very effectively, her upper notes being especially sweet. She received an ovation.

I saw in the audience during the evening Mr. Charles F. Chatterton, Mr. Abbey's right hand man, whose special duty it is to look after the real Adelina Patti and talk French to her. Mr. Chatterton said to me:—

"This colored woman is certainly a very good natural singer, and while I should hardly feel like comparing her voice with Mme. Patti's, I find her negro dialect much better, as shown in her rendering of the "Suawanee River."

Born in Virginia

I talked with the "Black Patti" in her dressing room after she had sung. She said she had not been at all nervous and found the acoustic properties of the Garden superb. She speaks of herself as a Providence girl although born in Virginia. She studied music in Boston. The last time she sang in New York was when Mr. Fred Douglass lectured at Cooper Union. She is living at the Hotel Venus, in West Seventeenth Street. She talks well, though [she is] inclined to be a bit diffident.

After a brief intermission at ten o'clock there was "buck" dancing, a "buzzard lope dance," more jubilee and more of Levy's Band. Then came the inevitable skirt dance, with colored performers, after which the "Black Patti" sang again, her selections being a farfalla, "Valse Chantee" and the song "Sempre Libera" from Verdi's *Traviata*.

Then came the cake walk, in which there were about fifty

very earnest and irresistibly comical contestants. They were still walking after midnight and no one had taken the cake.

The same program will be given at the Garden tonight and to-morrow night.

27 June 1893, *New York Times*

LECTURED THE BLACK PATTI

Judge McAdam Says She is Ungrateful to Major Pond— Must Sing for Him Alone

Sissieretta Jones, the "Black Patti," got a severe lecture yesterday from Judge McAdam of the Superior Court on the evils of ingratitude. Incidentally, she was enjoined from singing under any other management than that of Major James B. Pond.

On June 8, 1892, the Major made a contract with the "Black Patti" for a year. He was to pay her $150 per week, furnish all accommodations for her, and pay all traveling expenses. Some time ago the Major and his colored star disagreed, and they have been contending in the courts for several months over a clause in the contract which gave the manager the privilege of re-engaging the singer for an additional two years under the same terms provided for the first year's work.

The "Black Patti" wanted to engage in business for herself, and Major Pond applied to Judge McAdam for an injunction. In granting the motion, the court said yesterday of Sissieretta:

"She feels now as if she could get along without her benefactor, and she has thrown down the ladder on which she ascended to the position she now enjoys. Every sense of gratitude requires her to be loyal to the Manager who furnished her with the opportunity for greatness, and every principle of equity requires her to perform her engagements according to the spirit and intent of the contract. Talent is of litle value without opportunity, and history records on its brightest pages the names of many who would have died in obscurity but for opportunity."

21 October 1893, *Cleveland Gazette*

WORLD'S FAIR MUSIC

On September 25 it was advertised through the World's Fair grounds that the "Black Patti" would sing in the Woman's Building in the afternoon. One hour before the time of her appearance the large building was literally packed, so eager were both American and foreigner to hear the famous singer. Nor were their expectations disappointed, if we may judge from the ovation which followed her song, "Ocean, Thou Mighty Monster." Public opinion, in accord with the best musical criticism, proclaims her the greatest coming singer. She draws her selections from every source, but her favorite seems to be "Fleur des Alps,"[2] although she sings with good effect "Robert le Diable," both songs being well adapted to bring out the quality and phenomenal range of her voice. When compared with Selika,[3] the tones of her upper register are thinner, but this defect is entirely compensated for by the fuller and deeper tones of the lower. Madame Jones's voice is always musical; there is present, too, that spirit, that musical taste and insight, that is found only in the born artist. One hears such mellow, sweet, rich tones that while she sings, he sits enraptured and as the last tone dies away involuntarily bursts out into applause. She has pleased us often by responding to encores with "Swanee River." May she ever honor that most soulful American folk song.

14 May 1898, *The Colored American* (Washington, D.C.)

BLACK PATTI'S TROUBADOURS

Black Patti (Mme. Sissieretta Jones), who for several years past has won the highest lyric honors on the concert stage, and who is endowed with a marvelous voice, sweet in quality and of extensive range, has abandoned the concert stage in favor of comedy, vaudeville and opera. This great singer is the star of "The Black

2. J.-B. T. Weckerlin.
3. Maria Selika (1849– ?), another black soprano, had appeared earlier in the summer at the exposition.

Patti's Troubadours," an organization comprising fifty celebrated artists and which is said to be the most imposing aggregation of colored performers ever organized. The stage entertainment offered by this company is attractive, sensational and novel. It embraces comedy, burlesque, ballet, vaudeville and opera presented with appropriate scenery, elegant and costly costumes and all the necessary stage surroundings requisite for a perfect and artistic performance.

"At Jolly Coney Island" is the title of a merry and laugh-provoking skit which serves as a curtain raiser and vehicle to give free rein to the company's comedy and singing forces. This travesty is followed by a great vaudeville olio and selections from the various standard grand and comic operas. In the operatic olio Black Patti has great opportunities to display her wonderful voice. She sustains the principal roles of *The Grand Duchess, Carmen, Bohemian Girl, Trovatore, Lucia, Maritana, Tar and Tartar,* and *The Daughter of the Regiment.*[4] The rendition which she and the entire company give of this repertorical opera selections is said to be incomparably grand. Not only is the solo singing of the highest order, but the choruses are rendered with a spirit and musical finish which never fail to excite genuine enthusiasm. The work of Black Patti and the company has received the highest marks of public approval, and the forthcoming performances here will doubtless be highly appreciated. The Troubadours will be at the Grand Opera House for one week, beginning Monday evening, May 16.

4. Offenbach, *The Grand Duchess of Geroldstein;* Balfe, *Bohemian Girl;* W. V. Wallace, *Maritana.* The composer of *Tar and Tartar* could not be determined.

Four Composers

22 FANNY MENDELSSOHN HENSEL

Fanny Mendelssohn Hensel (1805–47) was a major talent destined for composition, but societal and familial restrictions curbed her full development. With her younger brother Felix (1809–47) and two still younger siblings, Rebecca and Paul, she enjoyed a privileged childhood and a broad education with the best of private tutors in Berlin. Fanny's musical gifts were quite as prodigious as Felix's, and into adolescence they pursued piano and composition together. But whereas a career in music was carefully planned by his parents for Felix, Fanny was conditioned to think of her future as being that of a homemaker. Some of Fanny's early songs appeared under Felix's name, since the family did not think it appropriate for Fanny to publish.[1] Selected correspondence by various members of the Mendelssohn family and entries from Fanny's diary provide insight into her situation.

Abraham Mendelssohn to his daughter Fanny:

Paris, July 16, 1820

Your last songs are at Viry,[2] where I shall fetch them tomorrow, and then I must find some one who will sing them decently to me. M. Leo has played me Felix's last fugue, very imperfectly. He pronounces it very good and in the true style, but difficult. I liked it well; it is a great thing. I should not have expected

---

Sebastian Hensel, *The Mendelssohn Family (1792–1847)*, trans. Carl Klingemann, 2 vols. (New York: Harper Brothers, 1881), 1:82–84; 2:31, 101, 103, 108–9, 334.

1. "Heimweh," "Italien," and "Suleika und Hatem," in Felix's op. 8, and "Sehnsucht," "Verlust," and "Die Nonne," in his op. 9 were written by Fanny.

2. A village outside Paris. Abraham was in Paris on business.

him to set to work in such good earnest so soon, for such a
fugue requires reflection and perseverance. What you wrote to
me about your musical occupations with reference to and in comparison with Felix was both rightly thought and expressed. Music
will perhaps become his profession, whilst for *you* it can and
must only be an ornament, never the root of your being and
doing. We may therefore pardon him some ambition and desire
to be acknowledged in a pursuit which appears very important
to him, because he feels a vocation for it, whilst it does you
credit that you have always shown yourself good and sensible
in these matters; and your very joy at the praise he earns proves
that you might, in his place, have merited equal approval. Remain
true to these sentiments and to this line of conduct; they are
feminine, and only what is truly feminine is an ornament to
your sex.

Tuesday [July 18]

They went over your Romances yesterday at Viry, and you
will be glad to hear that Fanny Sebastiani sang 'Les soins de mon
troupeau' very nicely and correctly, and likes them much. I confess that I prefer that song to all the others—so far as I can judge
of them, for they were only very imperfectly performed. It is
bright, and has an easy, natural flow, which most of the others
have not; some of them are too ambitious for the words. But
that one song I like so much that since yesterday I have often
sung it to myself, whilst I remember nothing of the others; and
I think facility one of the most important qualities of a song.
At the same time it is far from trivial, and the passage 'si j'ai
trouvé pour eux une fontaine claire' is even very felicitous; only
it appears to me to give too decided an end to the lines immediately
following the words 's'ils sont heureux.' I strongly advise you
to keep as much as possible to this lightness and naturalness in
your future compositions.

Mother wrote to me the other day that you had complained
of a want of pieces for the exercise of the third and fourth finger,
and that Felix had thereupon directly composed one for you.
Madame [Marie] Bigot thinks that if those fingers do not get

Fanny Mendelssohn Hensel.

on like the others, the true reason is not a want of exercises, but of exercise, of real, earnest practice. She says that you ought to spend a part of your practising time every day in observing quite mechanically the movement of those fingers, without regard to music or expression, and that [J. B.] Cramer has composed a number of pieces calculated to strengthen them; these have to be played again and again, slowly and with constant attention to a firm motion of the two weak ones. She says that in this way and by indefatigable patience she has succeeded in making all her fingers equally strong, and that this is the only way. I hope you will consider this advice.

[November 14, 1828, Fanny's twenty-third birthday]
Every year makes us both 365 days older. Who knows how often I may yet congratulate you on your birthday, and speak a serious word to you? or how long you may be able and willing to hear it?

I will, then, tell you to-day, dear Fanny, that in all essential points, all that is most important, I am so much satisfied with you that I have no wish left. You are good in heart and mind. 'Good' is a small word, but has a big meaning, and I would not apply it to everybody.

However, you must still improve! You must become more steady and collected, and prepare more earnestly and eagerly for your real calling, the *only* calling of a young woman—I mean the state of a housewife. True economy is true liberality. He who throws away money must become either a miser or an impostor. Women have a difficult task; the constant occupation with apparent trifles, the interception of each drop of rain, that it may not evaporate, but be conducted into the right channel, and spread wealth and blessing; the unremitting attention to every detail, the appreciation of every moment and its improvement for some benefit or other—all these and more (you will think of many more) are the weighty duties of a woman.

Indeed you want neither mind nor sense to fulfil them faithfully, and yet there is ample scope left for constant endeavour to strengthen your will, to collect your thoughts, and arrive at a right choice and appreciation of your occupations. Do this as long as you can freely, and before you are compelled. Whilst Providence still allows you to live with your parents, try to do many things better than they do. Give a solid foundation to the building, and there will be no want of ornaments.

But I won't preach, and am not old enough to prate. Accept once more my fatherly wishes, and take my well-meant advice to heart.

Your Father

When Fanny married Wilhelm Hensel, a painter, in 1829, at the age of twenty-four, Felix had already launched a brilliant career as a composer and conductor. Fanny followed her brother's triumphs closely, and surely somewhat vicariously, while devoting her own life to music "at home." Her activity centered on the Sunday musicales she organized at the Mendelssohn family estate in Berlin. These were distinguished at the time for introducing music of the highest caliber. Fanny participated in the programs as a pianist and the conductor of a choral group that she rehearsed each week, and often she included a composition of her own, as she continued to compose, chiefly for voice and piano. Nonetheless, the isolation she experienced at some times must have been overwhelming.

Fanny to her friend Carl Klingemann in London:

Berlin, 15 July 1836

I enclose two pianoforte-pieces, which I have written since I came home from Düsseldorf. I leave it to you to say whether they are worth presenting to my unknown young friend, but I must add that it is a pleasure to me to find a public for my little pieces in London, for here I have none at all. Once a year, perhaps, some one will copy a piece of mine, or ask me to play something special—certainly not oftener; and now that Rebecca has left off singing, my songs lie unheeded and unknown. If nobody ever offers an opinion, or takes the slightest interest in one's productions, one loses in time not only all pleasure in them,

but all power of judging their value. Felix, who is alone a sufficient
public for me, is so seldom here than he cannot help me much,
and thus I am thrown back on myself. But my own delight in
music and Hensel's sympathy keep me awake still, and I cannot
help considering it a sign of talent that I do not give it up, though
I can get nobody to take an interest in my efforts. But enough
of this uninteresting topic.

*Early in 1837 a single song of Fanny's appeared in a collection,
and Felix, who had argued against its publication, thanked Fanny
for going against his wishes. He was, however, opposed to her
undertaking any further publication, and for the time being
Fanny acquiesced. In 1838 Fanny performed in public for the
first time, playing Felix's piano concerto no. 1 in G minor, op.
25. She was thirty-three years old.*

Felix to his mother Leah:*

Frankfurt, June 2, 1837
You write to me about Fanny's new compositions, and say that
I ought to persuade her to publish them. Your praise is, however,
quite unnecessary to make me heartily rejoice in them, or think
them charming and admirable; for I know by whom they are
written. I hope, too, I need not say that, if she does resolve to
publish anything, I will do all in my power to obtain every facility
for her, and to relieve her, so far as I can, from all trouble which
can possibly be spared her. But to *persuade* her to publish anything I cannot, because this is contrary to my views and to my
convictions. We have often formerly discussed the subject, and
I still remain exactly of the same opinion. I consider the publication of a work as a serious matter (at least it ought to be so),
for I maintain that no one should publish unless they are resolved
to appear as an author for the rest of their life. For this purpose,
however, a *succession* of works is indispensable, one after another. Nothing but annoyance is to be looked for from publishing,

---

* *Letters of Felix Mendelssohn*, ed. Paul Mendelssohn-Bartholdy and Carl Mendelssohn, trans. Lady Wallace (Philadelphia: Frederick Leypoldt, 1894), pp. 113–
14.

where one or two works alone are in question; or it becomes what is called a "manuscript for private circulation," which I also dislike; and from my knowledge of Fanny I should say she has neither inclination nor vocation for authorship. She is too much all that a woman ought to be for this. She regulates her house, and neither thinks of the public nor of the musical world, nor even of music at all, until her first duties are fulfilled. Publishing would only disturb her in these, and I cannot say that I approve of it. I will not, therefore, persuade her to this step: forgive me for saying so. If she resolves to publish, either from her own impulse or to please Hensel, I am, as I said before, quite ready to assist her so far as I can; but to encourage her in what I do not consider right, is what I cannot do.

The highlight of Fanny's career was her trip to Italy in 1839–40 with her husband and their young son Sebastian. After visiting Milan, Venice, and Florence, the Hensels settled in Rome for the winter and spring months.

Fanny in her diary:

Rome, Thursday, 23 April 1840

In the evening some people dropped in, and I played much to dissipate the dullness profusely distributed by some English ladies. After they had left I began again *de plus belle*, and played until midnight. [Georges] Bousquet and [Charles] Dugasseau make my task rather difficult, for they never forget a single thing I have played, even though it be months ago. A more improving audience would be hard to find. I also compose a great deal now, for nothing inspires me like praise, whilst censure discourages and depresses me. Gounod[3] is such an enthusiast in music as I have seldom seen. He likes my little Venetian piece very much, as well as the one in B minor that I have composed here; also Felix's duet and Capriccio in A minor [op. 33, no. 1], but above all Bach's concerto, which I have had to play to him at least ten times.

3. Gounod won the Prix de Rome in 1839 and was in residence at the French Academy. Bousquet was also a musician, Dugasseau a painter.

Sunday, the 26th

I went in the early morning with Wilhelm to the garden of the [French] Academy, and it was so beautiful. On Saturday evening we had a long debate, which lasted so far into the night, as to whether we had not better prolong our stay here through next winter; but in the morning good sense and sound arguments prevailed. While walking in the Villa gardens we decided to reward ourselves by staying at least till the end of May, like the famous drunkard, who, after having safely passed three gin-shops, treated his resolution in the fourth. It will cost us both a hard struggle to leave Rome. I could not have believed that it would have made such a deep impression on me. I must not conceal from myself that the atmosphere of admiration and homage in which I have lived may have something to do with it, for even when quite young I never was made so much of as I have been here, and that this is very pleasant nobody can deny. Everything combines to attach me to Rome, and how good it would be for my Wilhelm and his work! But it will not do, so we have made up our minds.

Fanny to her sister Rebecca:

Rome [undated]

I have been composing a good deal lately, and have called my piano pieces after the names of my favorite haunts, partly because they really came into my mind at these spots, partly because our pleasant excursions were in my mind while I was writing them. They will form a delightful souvenir, a kind of second diary. But do not imagine that I give these names when playing them in society; they are for home use entirely.

Fanny to the family at large in Germany:

[May]

Yesterday evening our performance—Bach's triple concerto—came off capitally before a brilliant assembly at Landsberg's,[4] and

4. Landsberg was a former violinist, whom Fanny had known earlier in Berlin.

was received with much applause. I believe I told you that I
was practicing it with Charlotte Thygeson and a clever lady amateur here. Yesterday I could scarcely suppress my delight at finding
myself playing this grand piece in Rome, and thus gaining friends
and admirers for our old master. I am entitled to claim part of
the credit for myself, for it is not everybody who could have
made them understand and feel it. My thoughts when playing
[Johann Nepomuk] Hummel's quintet beforehand were very different, for I don't think I have ever played it since I was studying
with [Carl Friedrich] Zelter. For the concerto Landsberg placed
in a row three superb grand pianos by the same manufacturer,
which he had just gotten back from the *Inglesi*. They occupied
the whole side of the room, and looked very imposing. The room
was very full and very hot, but the evening was most enjoyable.

*In 1846 the bids of two rival publishers in Berlin spurred
Fanny to publish a small number of what she considered to
be her best works: two books of solo songs, a variety of piano
compositions, and a book of part songs, the latter no doubt
written for her choral group. This recognition encouraged her
to write a work of larger scale, her piano trio in D minor, op.
11, which was first performed at a musicale in April 1847. Fanny
Mendelssohn Hensel's last diary entries reflect her happiness
and suggest that she would have gone on to further achievements. She was stricken suddenly during a choral rehearsal on
May 14 and died later that night. Felix was shattered by the
news of Fanny's death, and he survived her by less than six
months.*

Fanny in her diary:

[Berlin, 1847]

Yesterday the first breath of spring was in the air. It has been
a long winter, with much frost and snow, universal dearth and
distress, indeed a winter full of suffering. What have we done
to deserve being among the few happy ones of the world? My

inmost heart is at any rate full of thankfulness, and when in
the morning after breakfasting with Wilhelm we each go to our
own work, with a pleasant day to look back upon and another
to look forward to, I am quite overcome with my own happiness.

23   CLARA SCHUMANN

In her December 21 letter of 1837 to Robert in Reading 17, Clara Schumann refers disparagingly to her youthful piano concerto in A minor, op. 7, and although she continued to compose well into her adult years, she always had ambivalent feelings about her creative work. Her training for composition was excellent, and she was encouraged to compose by both her father and her husband. Her music—chiefly piano works and songs— was published, performed, and reviewed favorably during her lifetime.[1] Yet, the constant example of Robert's work caused her to disparage her own. She knew her strengths as a performer, and as excerpts from her correspondence and diaries here indicate, she fell back on the convention that women lacked in creative powers. With the exception of one work, Clara ceased to compose after Robert's death, presumably because of her hectic performing schedule.

Clara to Robert, 1839:

23 April [Paris]

You ask me if I am not composing anything; I have written one quite tiny piece, but I do not know what I shall call it. I have a particular adversion to showing you anything that I have composed; I am always ashamed.

Berthold Litzmann, *Clara Schumann: An Artist's Life Based on Material Found in Diaries and Letters,* trans. Grace E. Hadow, 2 vols. (London: Macmillan, 1913), 1:241–44, 259, 318–19, 410. Reprinted by permission of Macmillan, London and Basingstoke.

1. Nancy B. Reich, "Clara Schumann," in *Women Making Music: Studies in the Social History of Women Musicians and Composers,* ed. Jane Bowers and Judith Tick (Berkeley, Calif.: University of California Press, 1982).

May

I have received the *Idyll* [from the Three Romances for piano, op. 11], and thank you for it my dear; but I am sure you will forgive me if I tell you that there are some things in it which I do not like. . . . The end, which I liked best, you have completely altered; and yet it impressed everyone to whom I played it. . . . You are not angry with me, are you?

15 July

It is a sin to have composed nothing for such a long time. Father is very annoyed, and I too am unhappy about it, but I am altogether more dissatisfied with myself than I can say.

Clara in her diary, November 1839:

[Leipzig]

I once thought that I possessed creative talent, but I have given up this idea; a woman must not desire to compose—not one has been able to do it, and why should I expect to? It would be arrogance, though indeed, my father led me into it in earlier days.

Robert in the joint diary, February 1843:

[Leipzig]

Clara has written a number of smaller pieces, which show a musicianship and a tenderness of invention such as she has never before attained. But children, and a husband who is always living in the realms of imagination, do not go well with composition. She cannot work at it regularly, and I am often disturbed to think how many tender ideas are lost because she cannot work them out.

Clara in her diary, regarding her piano trio in G minor, op. 17:

2 October 1846 [Dresden]

There is nothing greater than the joy of composing something oneself, and then listening to it. There are some pretty passages

in the trio, and I think it is fairly successful as far as form goes.
. . . Of course, it is only a woman's work, which is always lacking
in force, and here and there in invention.

                                                    18 November
   This evening I played Robert's piano quartet and my trio, which
seems to me more harmless each time I play it.

                                                September 1847
   I received the printed copies of my trio today; but I did not
care for it particularly, after Robert's D minor [no. 1, op. 63],
it sounded effeminate and sentimental.

Unlike Fanny Mendelssohn Hensel and Clara Schumann, who were born into musical families, Ethel Smyth (1858–1944) had to wage a veritable battle to gain her parents' approval and financial support for her education in music and in turn her aspirations as a composer. Smyth grew up at Frimhurst in Frimley, a village southwest of London and near her father's artillery command at Aldershot. Her mother sang and played the piano, but it was only at the age of twelve that Smyth was introduced to art music by a governess who had studied at the Leipzig Conservatory. Shortly thereafter Smyth began playing the early Beethoven piano sonatas and making plans to study in Leipzig herself, Leipzig being the goal of many English music students at the time because of the popularity of Felix Mendelssohn, the conservatory's founder, in England.

At age seventeen Smyth undertook what proved to be a short term of study with a local musician, Alexander Ewing, in harmony, composition, and repertory. Her father did not approve of Ewing and soon terminated the lessons. The following narrative begins when Smyth was eighteen.

Occasionally, though very rarely, I went to a concert in London, being met at Waterloo and convoyed to St. James's Hall by some approved friend, or perhaps by Aunt Susan's maid, and on one occasion was actually presented to Frau [Clara] Schumann and her daughters. This great event was engineered by a friend of mine, Mrs. George Schwabe, of whom more will be related presently, whose mother-in-law—another personality who will reap-

Ethel Smyth, *Impressions That Remained* (New York: Alfred Knopf, 1946), pp. 108–12, 188–91, 211–12. Reprinted by permission of the publisher. Copyright 1919 Longmans, Green & Co., Ltd.

pear in these pages—was an old friend of Frau Schumann's. The extraordinary thing is that in the wealth of impressions I was to gain in after life of that wonderful woman, all recollections of our first meeting have faded, but I gather from a remark in one of Mr. Ewing's letters that she gave my musical aspirations her blessing. She could do no less!

Soon after I struck what may rank as a half-milestone in my journey; for the first time I heard Brahms. The occasion was a Saturday Popular Concert at which the *Liebeslieder Walzer* [op. 52] were sung by four persons, three of whom (the Germans) knew the composer personally and afterwards became factors in my life. They were Fräuleins [Thekla] Friedländer and [Louise] Redeker, Mr. Shakespere, and George Henschel. That day I saw the whole Brahms; other bigger and, to use the language of pedants, more important works of his were to kindle fresh fires later on, but his genius possessed me then and there in a flash. I went home with a definite resolution in my heart. . . .

That night there was a discussion at dinner as to which drawing-room I had better be presented at. Suddenly I announced it was useless to present me at all, since I intended to go to Leipzig, even if I had to run away from home, and starve when I got there. . . .

I almost despair of anyone believing today, so quickly has the world moved since then, what such a step stood for in my father's mind. We knew no artists, and to him the word simply meant people who are out to break the Ten Commandments. It is no exaggeration to say that the life I proposed to lead seemed to him equivalent to going on the streets; hence the strange phrase he hurled at me, harking back in his fury to the language of Webster's or Congreve's outraged fathers: "I would sooner see you under the sod."

After a period of vain efforts to overcome his resistance, which became so terrific that it was no longer possible to broach the subject at all, I quite deliberately adopted the methods used years afterwards in political warfare by other women, who, having plumbed the depths of masculine prejudice, came to see this was the only road to victory. I not only unfurled the red flag, but

Ethel Smyth at the Piano and Singing, John Singer Sargent, 1901.

determined to make life at home so intolerable that they would
have to let me go for their own sakes. (I say "they," but here
again I felt that, whatever my mother might say in public, she
was secretly with me.) In those days no decent girls travelled
alone, third class and omnibuses were things unheard of in our
world, and I had no money; but I would slip away across the
fields to Farnborough Station, travel third to London, and proceed
by omnibus to any concert I fancied. The money difficulty was
met by borrowing five shillings from tradesmen we dealt with on
the Green, or the postman, "to be put down to the General." In
order to be close to [Joseph] Joachim and his companions I would
stand for hours in the queue at St. James's Hall, and ah! the
revelation of hearing Schubert's A Minor Quartet [D. 804]! . . .
All my life his music has been perhaps nearer to my heart than
any other—that crystal stream welling and welling for ever. . . .

From my place I used to watch George Eliot and her husband
sitting together in the stalls like two elderly love-birds, and was
irritated by Lewes's habit of beating time on her arm with his
pince-nez. There is a well-known syncopated passage in Beethoven's Quartet [in A Minor], Op. 132, and I noted with scornful
amusement how the eyeglass, after a moment of hesitation, would
begin marking the wrong beat, again hover uncertainly, and presently resume the right one with triumphant emphasis as if nothing
had happened. All this George Eliot took as calmly as if she were
the Sphinx, and Lewes an Arab brushing flies off her massive
flanks.

The greatest excitement was one day when with beating heart
I forced my way past Mr. [S. Arthur] Chappell's Cerberus into
the artists' room—a place more sacredly awful to me than the
Holy of Holies can ever have been to a young Levite—and made
the acquaintance of Fräuleins Friedländer and Redeker, expressed
to them my admiration of their singing, and fell madly in love
with Redeker, whose rendering of that divine love-song: *Wie bist
du, meine Königin* had all but torn the heart out of my body.[1]

1. Brahms, op. 32, no. 9.

They were goodnaturedly touched by such enthusiasm and begged me to come and see them some morning, which I did, climbing up stairs upon stairs to the room they shared. It was at eleven A.M., they were in *déshabillé,* the beds unmade, and they were sipping port out of an egg-cup. This unaccustomed sight gave me rather a shock, and for a moment I thought of my father, but supposed it was just part of the artist life; and indeed a few months later such a spectacle would have made no more impression on me than did Mr. Lewes's eyeglass on George Eliot.

My financial arrangements with the tradesmen came out of course, as they were meant to, and to my father's ragings I stubbornly replied: "You won't let me go to Leipzig so of course I have to go to London to hear music." From this moment he became convinced that, freed from control, I should squander money right and left, and one of the stock phrases was: "We shall have to sell your mother's diamonds"—a calamity that ranked in our minds with expedients such as debasing the coinage. But in this phrase I thought I saw a weakening of will; he was actually considering possible consequences of surrender! . . .

I had a few friends who backed me up more or less openly and were consequently looked on with disfavour at home. To this rule Barbara Hamley, now Lady Ernle, proved an exception, contriving in a miraculous manner to be my friend and yet keep on excellent terms with the parents, who delighted in her. She effected this miracle by a blend of tact, reasonableness, and sense of humour that must have oiled many locks in her course through life; moreover, but for her sympathy with the Frimhurst rebel, she was a perfectly normal, model young lady, who kept house with great success for her adored and adoring uncle Sir Edward Hamley, then Commandant of the Staff College (one of whose sympathetic traits was a great admiration for my mother). Thus she was in a favourable situation for operations, and her championship of me included a useful element—full comprehension of my father's point of view.

Not so that of Mrs. George Schwabe, daughter of Lord Justice James, a clever, hard-riding, whist-playing, particularly cherished friend of mine, who as radical, and one justly suspected of unorthodox views on religion, naturally considered this opposition to my German plans ridiculous and out of date. So too did Mrs. Napier, wife of her first cousin General William Napier (the historian's son), who was then in command—or rather Mrs. Napier was in command—at Sandhurst. This delightful champion of mine had rebel blood in her own veins, her father, fierce eagle-eyed Sir Charles Napier, whom his daughter was as like as two peas, having eloped with her mother, a Greek. It goes without saying that these two friends of mine were constant subjects of strife, and if my mother, jealous by nature, was especially so in these cases, who can wonder? It was all very well for Mrs. Napier to say right and left: "Of course dear little Ethel must go to Leipzig"— to say it even to my parents themselves, which she did, for she came of a fearless stock. *She* was not my mother, *she* had not to endure daily scenes with my father—scenes which became more frequent and furious as time went on. For towards the end I struck altogether, refused to go to church, refused to sing at our dinner-parties, refused to go out riding, refused to speak to anyone, and one day my father's boot all but penetrated a panel of my locked bedroom door! . . .

There was nothing for it but to capitulate! Fräulein Friedländer was able, by some miracle, to produce adequate testimony to the respectability of her aunt, Frau Professor Heimbach, who lived at Leipzig and would certainly be willing to take me under her wing till her very own mother had a room at my disposal; the terms suggested confirmed Mary Schwabe's reports as to the cheapness of life in Germany; my father named the maximum of allowance he could make me; it was pronounced to be sufficient, with care; and finally, on July 26, 1877, under the charge of Harry Davidson, who knew Germany well, I was packed off, on trial and in deep disgrace, but too madly happy to mind about that, to the haven of my seven years' longing.

Commenting on the headiness of her early correspondence from Germany, Smyth many years later noted: "It must be remembered that those at home were waiting to hear whether

*my claim to having a vocation was illusory or not; so no wonder
I nearly went off my head with joy at the encouragement I
met with, and eagerly reported it.''* **2** *Three early letters from
Smyth to her mother are included below. The first two describe
her experiences during a brief holiday she took after arriving
in Leipzig with Thekla Friedländer and other musicians in Friedländer's circle. The third was written near the end of Smyth's
year at the Leipzig Conservatory.*

*She found the conservatory "trading on its Mendelssohnian
reputation,"* **3** *and she therefore left to continue her studies in
composition privately with Heinrich von Herzogenberg for a
number of years. The glorious aspect of Leipzig, for Smyth, was
the concert and operatic life, through which she absorbed much
music that was new to her.*

Friedrichsroda: August 12, 1877

. . . Henschel is only 27, but he is gradually making a name
for himself, and musicians take on an average 40 years to do
this. One day when I was out of the room Thekla told him I
composed, and on my return he asked me (as he afterwards con-
fessed as a matter of politeness and with no expectations) to see
something I had done. I produced a song—we have no piano,
but of course he reads it through like a book. Mother! he said
such things of my talent! Things I never even dreamed of. He
said it was simply wonderful, and could not believe I had had
no tuition. Of course he found faults, and afterwards told a friend
of his whom I know that they were faults arising from talent.
In the afternoon we went to the von Mildes.[4] He is the first
man in the Berlin Opera, now old, but a great musician with a
voice like a god, and his wife is also very musical. Of course
Henschel was there and several other musicians, and I was asked
to sing some things of mine. Mother! I wish you had been there.
They were astonished, they all came round and said it was "merk-
würdig, wundervoll," and all the afternoon, when Henschel was

2. *Impressions That Remained*, p. 183.
3. Ibid., p. 145.
4. Hans Feodor and Rose Agthé von Mildes, both singers.

strumming, as *he* only can strum, between the songs, he kept on coming back to the modulation at "Schweig' still, mein Herz" in "Rohtraut"[5] which pleased him hugely. Afterwards, when we were all supping, our host proposed the health of the artists and coupled with it the name of "one who has but lately come among us and whom we hope to keep," and once again I was fêted, and oh I wish you had been there! The bliss of knowing that when I went on so about cultivating my talent I was not wrong! For though I felt it myself, I sometimes doubted whether it was only for a woman, and an Englishwoman living in a not musical circle, that I was anything particular in music—whether such talent as I have deserved to have everything else put aside for it. And now I know it does deserve it! The greatest musical genius I know has seen my work and so to speak has given it his blessing, and it is well with me . . . !

Don't think, mother darling, that this makes me lose my head, that I fancy I have only to put pen to paper and become famous. It is just this: men who have lived among musicians all their lives, who have been hand in glove with Schumann and Mendelssohn, and are so with Brahms and [Anton] Rubinstein, say they seldom saw such talent, in a woman *never*, and I can but tell *you* all this. I know though that years and years, perhaps, of hard work are before me, years in which little or nothing I do shall be printed—this I have resolved on—and in which I shall be nobody, and at the end of which is *perhaps* a laurel crown awaiting me in the shape of a name! But the end is worth the uphill struggle, and if application and hard steady work can do anything I ought to get it.

I go up every day into the mountain and compose. Then to the von Mildes I go a good deal, and am very welcome I think— so it seems! Then we go up to the meadows and play croquet, and then up to where Henschel lives and sing, sing, sing! Oh, those three! Thekla is not in good voice, but Meine Koenigin,

5. "Schön Rohtraut" is no. 5 in Smyth's *Lieder und Balladen*, op. 3, published in Leipzig ca. 1886. See Kathleen Dale, "Ethel Smyth's Music: A Critical Study," in Christopher St. John, *Ethel Smyth: A Biography* (London: Longmans, 1974), p. 304.

alias Fraeulein Redeker, is in first-rate voice, and the music we have simply defies description. She is at this moment wandering about in a pink dressing-gown singing *Scenas* out of an opera of Rubinstein's, and it is rather distracting.

Do you know she sings from 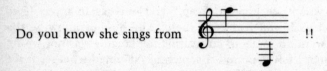 !!

It [Redeker's] is a glorious voice and *won't* be kept in. She is literally bubbling over with singing. Yesterday all four of them sang for a charity in the church, but I never do care for sacred music except, oh! I must except, the bass duet, "The Lord is a Man of War," which is certainly a grand thing. Henschel sang it with [Charles] Santley at the Handel Festival.[6] . . .

Please send on my accounts to Papa! My German gets on A1, I always speak it, even to the Scotch girls. . . .

Friedrichsroda: August 19

. . . Fancy, staying in the house with Henschel is your old Wild-bad friend, Herr von Roumanim; he raves about Mary! He is a pleasant man and bade me remember him most kindly and respect-fully to my Frau Mutter and Fraeulein Schwester! Also I was to tell you that now he wears his hair long, not like a tooth-brush, as when you knew him.

I have had several talks with Henschel about my music and am most awfully happy about it. He thinks more of my talent than ever I did! and has written about me to Brahms with whom he was almost brought up, and to Simrock, the publisher. It is so glorious to be told by competent persons that one's future lies in one's own hands, that the material for realising hopes I hardly ever—I think never—breathed at home even, is there; and I have but to work hard and steadily and then *not be too soon pleased with myself.* Every day I become more and more con-

6. From *Israel in Egypt.*

vinced of the truth of my old axiom, that why no women have become composers is because they have married, and then, very properly, made their husbands and children the first consideration. So even if I were to fall desperately in love with BRAHMS and he were to propose to me, I should say no! So fear not that I shall marry in Germany! I told Henschel my opinion, and he said perhaps I was right, but as he himself has, I am told, an "unglückliche Liebe"[7] on hand, I don't think he is a judge! He *is* so good to me, corrects my songs for me (I have composed lots more), sets me basses on which to construct chorales and all sorts of things; and yet I know if I were Henschel it would be a great pleasure to me to get hold of a new pupil to give a friendly shove-on to during a three weeks' do-nothing stay in a little primitive town. . . . I am, as always, very, very happy and oh so well. . . .

April, 1878

. . . Just imagine what a goose I am. I went to Breitkopf and Härtel—the music publishers *par excellence* in the world. The nephew, who conducts the business, Dr. Hase, I know very well and he is quite one of the most charming men I ever met. But you know how unpleasant it is to do business with a personal friend! Well, he began by telling me that songs had as a rule a bad sale—but that no composeress had ever succeeded, barring Frau Schumann and Fräulein Mendelssohn, whose songs had been published together with those of their husband and brother respectively. He told me that a certain Frau Lang had written some really very good songs, but they had no sale.[8] I played him mine, many of which he had already heard me perform in various Leipzig houses, and he expressed himself very willing to take the risk and print them. But would you believe it, having listened to all he said about women composers, and considering how difficult

7. Unfortunate attachment.
8. Josephine Lang (1815–80) wrote 140 lieder, a good number of which were published during her lifetime. These may or may *not* have sold well, as was reported to Smyth. In 1882, however, Breitkopf and Härtel published a retrospective *Liederbuch* for Lang in two volumes, containing 40 songs.

it is to bargain with an acquaintance, I asked no fee![9] Did you ever hear of such a donkey! I should have asked £2 10s., which would have dissolved one of the dressmaker's bills! So if, Mother darling, after all I have to come down on you for that bill (which I still hope not to do!) please consider it the price of my modesty! . . .

25   LUISE ADOLPHA LE BEAU

The German composer Luise Adolpha le Beau (1850–1927) was regarded by the major critics of her time as the first woman to compose large-scale vocal and orchestral works successfully, beginning in the 1880s,[1] and although this evaluation is historically inaccurate, it attests to her stature among her contemporaries. Even still, Le Beau constantly battled skepticism about her capabilities. Together with her parents, who contributed to her support throughout their lifetimes and encouraged her work in every way, Le Beau lived in a succession of German cities, in search of a congenial home base where she could obtain performances of her works and concertize as a pianist. Typically, however, she was regarded as an outsider. Le Beau wrote sixty-six works, of which thirty-five were published, and she was active also as a music critic and an educator, in which latter role she championed equal opportunities for female students in all aspects of music.

As she approached age sixty, Le Beau began her autobiography, in fulfillment of her father's wish that she should speak out about the obstacles confronting a woman in composition. The episode excerpted for this reading concerns the writing and publication of her fantasy opera Hadumoth,[2] and then Le Beau's subsequent efforts to secure the opera's performance. Her experience illustrates the difficulties composers of her time faced in obtain-

Luise Adolpha Le Beau, *Lebenserinnerungen einer Komponistin* (Baden Baden: Emil Sommermayer, 1910), pp. 155, 161–62, 186–89, 191–92, 211, 213–15. This selection was chosen and translated by Judith E. Olson.

1. Judith E. Olson, "Luise Adolpha Le Beau: Composer, Pianist, and Critic in Late Nineteenth-Century Germany," in *Women Making Music: Studies in the Social History of Women Musicians and Composers,* ed. Jane Bowers and Judith Tick (Berkeley, Calif.: University of California Press, 1982).

2. A copy of the full score is at the Bayerische Staatsbibliothek in Munich.

ing backers. Her autobiography in general attests to the fact that, as a female composer, Le Beau encountered still further difficulties.

Wiesbaden, 1887

For many years I had venerated V[ictor] von Scheffel's *Ekkehard*[3] and had often thought of modelling the Hadumoth episode into a plot for a choral work. I discussed this plan with my parents, and they likewise considered the material quite suitable. The scenario . . . was quickly sketched. I designated precisely which characters applied [and] where arias, recitatives, and ensemble passages or choruses should be sung and asked Frl. Luise Hitz of Munich to set in verse the action laid out in the scenario.

Wiesbaden, 1888–89

In the fall of 1888 I began composing *Hadumoth*, which was based on the episode of the two shepherd children. After the orchestral introduction, which I composed last, Audifax begins with a recitative and aria. He wants to search for a treasure and asks the dwarfs for help (treasure motive). They taunt him and send him away. Hadumoth and Audifax then confer at length how they can win the treasure and through it their freedom. They decide in a duet to go to the Lady of the Forest in order to pray for their freedom at the Festival of the Solstice (flame motive). The two sing (freedom motive) with the following chorus. Dismissed by the Lady of the Forest, the children wander through the night and hope that the treasure will fall from the sky (shooting-star motive). The double chorus follows, in which the monks and Swabians sing the "Media Vita" in the Phrygian mode; the Huns, however, sing their battle-song in the "Magyar" mode. I chose this because I could thus also bring out the contrast of the two parts harmonically. Herewith ends the second scene. Now Hadwig orders the dead to be buried. A funeral chorus follows. Hadumoth, who has not found her Audifax among the

3. Written in 1857, this historical novel proved to be extremely popular in Germany.

dead, goes to the Duchess and entreats her for a gold-piece with
which she can ransom Audifax, who is imprisoned by the Huns.
She obtains it; Ekkehard blesses her, and the parting chorus
sounds, "Farewell, maid, brave and strong" with Hadumoth's solo.
In the fourth scene, she wanders (wander motive) and falls asleep
in the forest. Forest spirits protect her. A fisher awakens Hadumoth, asks where she wishes to go, and leads her at her request
to the Huns' encampment. A drinking song of the Huns, written
in the "Magyar" mode, closes this scene. The fifth begins with
an orchestral passage, which portrays the ride of the two children
as they flee from the Huns' encampment. In his principal aria,
Audifax then recounts the burning of the Huns' encampment
(flame motive), their ride (riding motive), the death of the Lady
of the Forest, and concludes, "O Hadumoth, you mean more to
me than all the treasures of this world!" (love motive). After a
short prayer of thanksgiving (duet) they ride on (orchestral passage), arriving in their homeland in the middle of a festival. A
short fugato, "Hey, who comes riding there!", interrupts the He-
gau Dance and Chorus. They are encircled, congratulated, ab-
solved by Lady Hadwig (freedom motive) and join in a solo-quartet
with Hadwig and Ekkehard, which culminates in the words: "Yes,
in love and trust the treasure is found." A closing chorus with
double fugue extolls the young couple. The orchestral introduction utilizes from the motives the three which relate to the moral
of the whole: the treasure, belief, and love motives. The piano
reduction with all the notes concerning the instrumentation was
already finished in Wiesbaden.

Berlin [ca. 1891]

The *Hadumoth* score was finished. Because such a work could
become known only if the composer himself supplied (or lent)
the parts for the first performance, that then had to be considered.
My father read an advertisement regarding a lithographic machine
and went with me to the factory, in order to become acquainted
with this instrument. We found it usable, and I let one of the
workers demonstrate it to me. Naturally some practice was necessary, and much patience, in order to obtain a clean impression,

but I didn't give up, and my loyal parents helped me as much
as possible. . . . We printed mornings from seven to ten; then I
immediately wrote out again the freshly-lined stone for the following day. Despite much trouble and many interruptions, we enjoyed this mechanical work very much, since we performed it
together, enlivening it with various jokes. . . . We printed for a
full year!—

Berlin [ca. 1891–92]

After the [full] scores and piano reductions were bound, the
much more difficult task of bringing the work to the public began!
I played and sang it for the director of the Philharmonic Chorus,
Herr S[iegfried] Ochs. He favored it and praised various aspects.
He liked the solstice chorus very much. Also the duet with the
falling-star motive. I had written a short trill for the violin and
then a woodwind-chord to depict the falling stars. Herr Ochs
asked me if I would like to use a drum stroke here. If it had
been rockets, then one could certainly use drums, but for the
quiet, poetic falling stars I found this totally misplaced. . . . He
indicated that he wished to perform *Hadumoth*. He also recommended that I go to [Friedrich] Gernsheim, in case he could
perform [it] sooner in his society. This made me distrust Herr
Ochs. . . . The negotiations with Herr Ochs dragged on: he always
acted the same; as if he wanted to perform *Hadumoth*, but kept
putting it off, spoke of intrigues against him, called Berlin a
"world-village," where there was no interest in new music, and
appeared as if he were asking me for money (which I certainly
could not have given him) to cover a deficit. . . . A performance
of my *Hadumoth* never came. . . .

 . . . After I had played *Hadumoth* for [him], Herr Gernsheim
said, "Here there is truly no longer a difference between masculine
and feminine composition." However, his program was also already complete, and he was unwilling to risk another novelty,
although the work had pleased him, since [Georg] Vierling's *Con-
stantin* realized a deficit of three thousand marks. Consequently,
it was thus impossible to have a work performed publically in
Berlin without great sacrifice. If at that time I had had twenty

or thirty thousand marks at my disposal, my compositions would have become better known, for Berlin set the tone for the remaining cities—as musically limited as the public is there!

Recommended by Le Beau's publisher, Paul Simon of Kahnt Nachfolger, Hadumoth *was favorably reviewed by the well-known music critic and writer, Alfred Kalischer.*[4]

Berlin [ca. 1892]

Using Kalischer's review as a reference, I then turned to directors of societies outside [of Berlin] to prepare the way for a performance of *Hadumoth.* In Hamburg I personally brought it to Herr [Otto] Beständig, who told me he would perform it as soon as they performed it in Berlin! Herr [Adolf] Mehrkens looked through the work and praised it highly. Then I sent it from Berlin to the director of the New Singing Society in Stuttgart, Herr E. H. Seyffardt. . . . Herr Seyffardt wrote to me very cordially and with full appreciation for *Hadumoth*—however, he didn't have any more room in his programs in the immediate future. Later in Stuttgart when I spoke with him in person, [he indicated] that he was forced, as it were, by a local publisher to perform another choral work, *Ekkehard,* which was little to his liking. I discovered on this occasion that the composer was willing to pay the honorarium for the soloists. . . . I turned to Friz Steinbach. He replied that he could not perform the work there [i.e., at Meiningen] "in spite of many outstanding musical qualities." It is likely that the Huns' choruses were responsible for that; for these certainly make a performance more difficult, because most societies are short of male voices, and male singing societies do not like to sing along in mixed choirs. The Philharmonic Society in Karlsruhe was directed at that time by Cornelius Rübner. It also would not attempt *Hadumoth* despite the employment of my friends there! They told me later that a composer from Karlsruhe had payed the Philharmonic Society seventeen hundred marks to perform his mass!

---

4. *Neue Zeitschrift für Musik* 59/39 (Sept. 28, 1892): 437–39.

Le Beau also offered Hadumoth *to organizations in Leipzig, Strasbourg, and Frankfurt, none of which accepted it. Finally, on moving to Baden Baden in 1893, she showed the work to the critic and writer Richard Pohl.*

Baden Baden, 1893

Richard Pohl, on the contrary, understood *Hadumoth* much better. Toward the end of the year I played it for him from beginning to end as he read along. He enjoyed the "workmanship, form, invention" as much as my playing, which he deemed "virtuoso" and "much better than a Kapellmeister!" Herr Pohl recommended the work with great praise at a meeting of the Spa Council. I found this out from the Lord Mayor G., to whom I had also been warmly recommended by Her Royal Highness, the Grand Duchess [of Baden]. Indeed, I am especially indebted to that [i.e., her recommendation], in that the Spa Council decided upon a performance of the work. I promised to accompany the rehearsals, since the Kapellmeister did not play the piano.

Baden Baden, Fall 1894

Herr Kapellmeister [Paul] Hein had returned from his vacation at the end of October, and now rehearsed as often as I wanted; we were, however, lacking in men. Each of them wanted to be invited especially to participate. Finally I turned in addition to the elementary school teachers and invited high school students to sing along. The male singing society Hohenbaden took over the performance of the Huns' choruses. . . .

The portrayer of the main role, who had been engaged at my recommendation and had memorized her entire part, became frightened and withdrew three weeks before the concert! This was all the more fatal for me, since I could have obtained good singers, who were now already engaged, and each would still have to learn the part from the beginning! I therefore wrote to the singing-teacher, Prof. Julius Stockhausen in Frankfurt am Main, and asked him to recommend one of his best students. He fulfilled my request and studied the part with Frl. [Johanna] Meyerwisch, who then also sang here.

Before the first full rehearsal, I assembled all of the soloists at my home to familiarize them with the entire work. Notwithstanding, the first collaboration of the orchestra with the choir, which had just gone over the parts, and the newly-gathered solo forces came off somewhat "colorfully," and it was very good that two full rehearsals had been scheduled from the beginning. The second took place on the following Sunday morning. All made the greatest conceivable effort, for Her Royal Highness, the Grand Duchess, had the grace to listen from an adjoining chamber although the Court was in mourning. Friends from Karlsruhe and Württemberg were also present. Richard Pohl gave me highest recognition, saying, "If I were the Grand Duchess of Baden, I would give you the Grand Medal for Art and Science! But you don't need it: You have merit!"

The performance took place on November 19.[5] My parents were both in the hall. I sat with the Spa Council. The *Badeblatt* dedicated a poem to me. Already in the afternoon I received a large palm. The participation of the townspeople was truly moving! Baker, merchant, bookbinder, postman, etc., were sitting in the grand hall long before the beginning of the concert. The participants spared no pains. Frl. [Johanna] Meyerwisch sang the main role with greatest determination. Frau [Iduna] Walter-Chionanus [sang] Hadwig splendidly. Oberländer, [Theodor] Görger, and Herr [Ferdinand] Zerr (the Fisher) acted very well. Exuberant applause ensued after every scene, indeed, even individual numbers. At the end, I was called forward and wanted to present the singers as well, but they were also applauding. Then laurel wreaths, baskets of flowers, and bouquets were brought to the podium. Everyone congratulated [me] and enjoyed themselves. Several friends helped me carry the wreaths and flowers home. My parents had seen nothing of the ovations; they went home before me as agreed upon earlier, and were no little astonished when we all arrived so laden! After a few days, when the excitement was over, they expressed our joy appropriately by giving

5. Evidently this was a concert version.

me a ring to remember the first performance of *Hadumoth*. Subsequently I received more poems by mail. The reviews were all glowing. The Lord Mayor said: "It was a triumph." Local newspapers, as well as those from outside the area (from Stuttgart to Cologne), took notice.

Later performances took place in Constance in 1895 and in Pforzheim in 1900.

A Composer's Wife

26 COSIMA WAGNER

Although some women have chafed at the role of supportive wife to a creative husband, others have found it immensely rewarding. Of these, few can be said to have performed the supportive role more fully than Cosima Wagner (1837–1930) as the wife of Richard. Cosima was the second of three children born to Countess Marie D'Agoult and Liszt, who after their separation in 1844 cruelly used the children as pawns between them. Growing up virtually as an orphan, Cosima developed great strength of character. She was a fine pianist in her youth, and while her mother felt she should pursue a professional career, Liszt was opposed.

In 1857 Cosima married Hans von Bülow, an early follower of Wagner's and subsequently the conductor of the premieres of Tristan *and* Die Meistersinger *in Munich in 1865 and 1868. For Cosima the marriage proved unfulfilling. With Wagner, however, she found great purpose for her life in serving his genius and sharing his work in progress. Cosima and Wagner exchanged vows in 1863, but for numerous and complicated reasons—chief among them Wagner's dependence on the good will of his patron Ludwig II of Bavaria—Cosima kept up the pretense of her marriage to von Bülow over the next five years.*

The diary entry below is the first in a volume Cosima began for her children shortly after she joined Wagner permanently at Triebschen on the outskirts of Lucerne, late in 1868. She had left her two eldest daughters by von Bülow, Daniela and Blondine, behind with their father in Munich, while bringing

Cosima Wagner's Diaries, vol. 1: *1869–1877*, ed. Martin Gregor-Dillon and Dietrich Mack, trans. Geoffrey Skelton (New York: Harcourt, Brace, Jovanovich, 1978), pp. 27–29. © 1978, 1977 by Geoffrey Skelton and Harcourt Brace Jovanovich, Inc. Used by permission of the publisher.

*her two daughters by Wagner, Isolde and Eva, with her. She
was pregnant with Wagner's and her third child, Siegfried. Cosima soon reunited her children, and in 1870, after she was
divorced by von Bülow, Cosima and Richard Wagner were married. Her diaries, which she continued until the composer's death
in 1883, show that she never ceased to agonize over her treatment of von Bülow, even though she believed her union with
Wagner was inevitable. After 1883 Cosima perpetuated the Bayreuth festivals of Wagner's operas and oversaw the performance
rights of his music throughout the world.*

Friday, January 1 [1869]

On Christmas Day, my 31st birthday, this notebook was to
have started; I could not get it in Lucerne. And so the first day
of the year will also contain the beginning of my reports to you,
my children. You shall know every hour of my life, so that one
day you will come to see me as I am; for, if I die young, others
will be able to tell you very little about me, and if I live long, I
shall probably only wish to remain silent. In this way you will
help me do my duty—yes, children, my duty. What I mean by
that you will find out later. Your mother intends to tell you
everything about her present life, and she believes she can do
so.

The year 1868 marks the outward turning-point of my life:
in this year it was granted to me to put into action what for
the past five years had filled my thoughts. It is an occupation I
have not sought after or brought about myself: Fate laid it on
me. In order that you may understand, I must confess to you
that up to the hour in which I recognized my true inner calling,
my life had been a dreary, unbeautiful dream, of which I have
no desire to tell you anything, for I do not understand it myself
and reject it with the whole of my now purified soul. The outward
appearance was and remained calm, but inside all was bleak and
dreary, when there came into my life that being who swiftly
led me to realize that up to now I had never lived. My love
became for me a rebirth, a deliverance, a fading away of all that
was trivial and bad in me, and I swore to seal it through death,

through pious renunciation or complete devotion. What love has done for me I shall never be able to repay. When the stars decreed that events, about which you will find out elsewhere, should banish into isolation my only friend,[1] the guardian spirit and savior of my soul, the revealer of all that is noble and true, that he should be left solitary, abandoned, joyless, and unfriended, I cried out to him: I shall come to you and seek my greatest and highest happiness in sharing the burdens of life with you. It was then that I left you, my two precious eldest children. I did it and would do it again at any moment, and yet I miss you both and think of you day and night. For I love you all, each with an equal love; in your hearts I seek the refuge for my earthly memory when my time is past, and I would sacrifice everything to you—everything but the life of this one person. Our separation will be temporary, and you are still so small that you will not feel it as your mother does. This is my hope.

Early in the morning the Friend came to greet me and wish me a happy New Year. I am always so overcome by his kindness toward me, in my ever deeper awareness of his greatness, that in his presence I always feel I must dissolve into tears. Afterward I dressed Loldchen and Evchen[2] prettily (white satin frocks and garlands of roses) and we went to give him our good wishes. Then we had breakfast, after which he went to work as usual (making a fair copy of the second act of *Siegfried* and completing his essay on the Jews).[3] I took Evchen and Loldchen into the garden. Before lunch (at one o'clock) my beloved read me what he had written. At table he told me more of the range of his essay, and we discussed his position, that is to say, the position of art as laid down by the Jews, which made me see Mendelssohn for the first time as a tragic figure. After the meal he went for his usual walk, after receiving a telegram from the King[4] and

1. Because of the opposition of enemies at the court, Wagner was forced to leave Munich in December 1865. In April 1866 he settled at Triebschen, where Cosima visited him frequently.

2. Cosima's nicknames for Isolde and Eva. Later in the text Isolde is also referred to as Loldi.

3. *Judaism in Music.*

4. Ludwig II of Bavaria.

another from you. The latter affected him as it did me; my heart was heavy and full to bursting, because you were not here with me, but a glance at him consoled me and gave me courage—I was looking into a happy future. Then I arranged the Christmas tree, which was lit today for the second time. At about five o'clock Evchen and Loldchen, dressed again as angels, came down and found the Christmas gifts which had been kept back. Richard played for them, they danced, and I thought of you, my absent ones, so far away, and once again I watched the merry scene through a veil of tears, yet here, too, these tears were without bitterness. Then Richard started up a jumping jack, to Loldi's great joy. While the little ones were enjoying their supper, he played me the "Spring Song" from *Die Walküre*. When you one day hear these sounds, my children, you will understand me. I cannot hear them without being transported right away. — We had tea upstairs in my room; I asked my beloved to dictate something to me today (biography) for superstitious reasons (they say that whatever one does on the first day of the year one continues). Although it was an exertion for him, he wanted in his indescribable goodness toward me to do it, and so there emerged two pages about Schopenhauer which for me are beyond all price. At eleven we parted, after once more reviewing the day together and finding it harmonious and good. When he had gone, I sat down at my writing desk to talk to you. The Friend has given me the golden pen with which he wrote *Tristan* and *Siegfried*, and this I consecrate to these communications of mine to you. Thus I signify to you how sacredly I regard this work of a mother's confidences and anxieties; the pen which has traced the sublimest things ever created by a noble spirit shall now be dedicated solely to the depths of a woman's heart. So God bless you, my children, you who are far away, you who are close by, and you lying still unknown within my womb. May your mother's love be a friendly light to you in your path through life! Do not mistake your mother, though you yourselves will never be able to do what she has done, since what Fate has here decreed is something that will not recur. All whom I love are now at rest, and so I, too, will go to my bed. For you and for him my last and friendliest thoughts!

Women as Amateur Performers, Music Teachers, and Music Patrons

27   THE FEMALE AMATEUR: FROM ACCOMPLISHMENT TO ACHIEVEMENT

With the last third of the nineteenth century the general gains made by women in education, as well as the success of numerous female concert artists, occasioned a new seriousness about the amateur performer. Consequently the long-held concept of music as a social accomplishment for women was replaced by the ideal of music as a serious achievement for the musically gifted student only. This trend was especially notable in the United States beginning in the 1880s, when Etude *magazine, a powerful influence in middle- and upper-class homes, published numerous articles, letters to the editor, and fictionalized accounts that decried dilettantism in favor of rigorous study.* Etude *addressed itself specifically to pianists, but by extension its message applied as well to amateur vocalists and the increasing numbers of women who were taking up other instruments in the last decades of the century. By the turn of the century the noted critic James Huneker applauded the demise of the "piano girl."*

ETUDE: "AN OPEN LETTER AND THE REPLY"

Dear Sir:

While I do not like to dictate to you concerning my daughter's musical instruction, feeling how entirely competent you are to direct it, yet I beg to remind you of a fact which I expressed, if you will remember, in our first interview, viz.: that I do not care to make of my daughter a professional player, but only wish

"An Open Letter and the Reply," Etude 4/11 (November 1886): 259.

to have her accomplished for the high society in which it is my desire and intention she shall move.

From my observation of your manner of instruction, I am led to believe that, owing to your personal elevated ideals of your art, you have, perhaps, set an ideal too high for the attainment of one possessing humbler intents and aspirations.

To be explicit, I think that too much time is expended by my daughter on technical exercises. To use an illustration, suppose I send my daughter to study painting, and for a year or more she is drilled in the practice of drawing or sketching, and for another half year in the art of mixing colors, use of brushes, etc., and at last, after painting her first picture, she is told that the effort is very commendable, but yet it is a mere daub and must be done over yet a hundred times before it can be in any respect presentable before connoisseurs. What must I think? Why I must either question my daughter's intelligence or reflect in some measure on her instruction.

I feel, again, that my daughter is losing interest in her musical work because she seems to suffer from comparison with others of her age, who, with equal advantages, play much finer and win more applause from their associates.

I trust, sir, you will kindly consider this matter, and give, hereafter, more pieces to instruct and less exercises to annoy my daughter, and, at the same time, will consider that I am prompted by no motive of fault finding or criticism of your excellent methods, but am actuated in this appeal to your generosity purely by the interests and necessities of my child.

> Most respectfully,
> Madam von _____

Esteemed Madam:

In reply to your note of yesterday, I beg to offer a few words of explanation.

I am at once pleased and pained at the contents of your letter: pleased with the frankness you display in expressing to me personally your exact feelings and wishes in this matter; but pained to perceive that your conception of a musical education has been formed somewhat superficially, from common observation, and not from a deep study of the subject. I had by no means forgotten your first conversation with me concerning your daughter's musical studies, and indeed, no one could have proceeded more carefully than I in the execution of your wishes then expressed.

You certainly accredit me with sufficient experience to know exactly what degree of musical culture constitutes true accomplishment.

What is termed accomplishment in our best society is really but a clever attempt at masking ignorance. It requires but little knowledge of music, or of language, or of anything else intellectual to "pass" in society. For this reason, dear Madam, you can readily see how perniciously it works upon children's minds to hold up such an ideal of accomplishment as the goal of their youthful efforts. . . .

You speak of exercises as unimportant, and express your preference for pieces. I grant the expression is very natural. We all desire the realization of a thing more than its deferment. But reason tells us, and experience teaches us, that there is no royal road to achievement. All the great men of the world have united in declaring effort to be synonymous with genius itself.

To master such a difficult art as music takes a long time, and a severe course of training.

The training requisite to perform one piece must be as thorough and nearly as long continued as to perform a dozen. You can readily understand that if your daughter had been trained to the point that she could translate with fluency any passage from Virgil, she would have no difficulty in doing the same in a selection from Horace. It should not be her aim to learn from her teacher to recite a number of Latin verses for the amusement of her friends and to receive the false encomium of "learned," when she knows she is not learned.

Therefore, I would commend such a course of training in music as will make her a thorough musician, competent to interpret to her satisfaction and the delight of her friends, the works of the masters in a manner that is above the criticism of connoisseurs. To this end I have made her studies. If she will arrive at excellence she cannot evade any part of the discipline I have assigned to her, not has she ever evinced to me any unwillingness to comply with such demands.

Moreover, your daughter has an exceptional talent, which, if properly developed, will, in time, redound to our credit and satisfaction. . . .

Trusting, my dear Madam, that you will ponder on the weight of these suggestions, and will consider also how deeply I am interested in the true progress and education of your talented child,

> I remain, with great respect,
> Your obedient,
> D. De F. Bryant

JAMES HUNEKER:
"THE ETERNAL FEMININE"

What this present generation of children has to be especially thankful for is its immunity from useless piano practice. Unless there is discovered a sharply defined aptitude, a girl is kept away from the stool and pedals. Instead of the crooked back—in Germany known as the piano back—and relentless technical studies, our young woman golfs, cycles, rows, runs, fences, dances, and pianolas! While she once wearied her heart playing [Louis Moreau] Gottschalk, she now plays tennis, and she freely admits that tennis is greater than [Sigismond] Thalberg. Recall the names of all the great women's colleges, recall their wonderful curriculums, and note with unprejudiced eyes their scope and the comparatively humble position occupied by music. In a word, I wish to point out that piano-playing as an accomplishment is passing. Girls play the piano as a matter of course when they have nimble fingers and care for it. Life has become too crowded, too variously beautiful, for a woman without marked musical gifts to waste it at the piano.

Begun as a pastime, a mere social adjunct of the overfed, music, the heavenly maid, was pressed into unwilling service at the piano,

James Huneker, "The Eternal Feminine," *Overtones* (New York: Scribner's, 1904), pp. 291–93.

and at times escorted timid youths to the proposing point, or
eked out the deadly lethargy of evenings in respectable homes.
Girls had to pull the teeth of this artistic monster, the pianoforte,
else be accounted frumps without artistic or social ambitions.
Unlike that elephant which refused to play a Bach fugue on the
piano, because, as the showman tearfully explained, the animal
shudderingly recognized the ivory of the tusks of its mother,
the girl of the middle century went about her task muddled in
wits, but with matrimony as her ultimate goal. To-day she has
forsaken the "lilies and languors" of Chopin, and the "roses and
raptures" of Schumann, and if she must have music, she goes
to a piano recital and hears a great artist interpret her favorite
composer, thus unconsciously imitating the Eastern potentate who
boasted that he had his dancing done for him. The new girl is
too busy to play the piano unless she has the gift; then she plays
it with consuming earnestness. We listen to her, for we know
that this is an age of specialization, an age when woman is coming
into her own, be it nursing, electoral suffrage, or the writing of
plays; so poets no longer make sonnets to our Ladies of Ivories,
nor are budding girls chained to the keyboard. Never has the
piano been so carefully studied as it is to-day, and, paradoxical
as it may sound, never has the tendency of music been diverted
to currents so contrary to the genius of the instrument. All this
is better for woman—and for the development of her art along
broader, nobler lines.

As women increasingly sought to enter the professions in the last decades of the nineteenth century, the step from serious amateur performer to music teacher was a natural one for many. Indeed, in the United States in 1880 women constituted 43 percent of the musicians and music teachers (the two categories are combined in the census), while by 1910 the figure had climbed to 66 percent. It must be remembered, however, that these healthy percentages also reflect the fact that most avenues of employment were not available to women. Hence by 1900 musc and music teaching ranked fifth in the most frequently pursued vocations by women, following elementary school teaching, medicine, social and religious work, and law.[1] Distinguished educators such as Clara Baur, Julia Ettie Crane, and Emma A. Thomas founded their own music schools and conservatories, and some women worked within the public school system. But the majority of women were private teachers, usually of piano or voice.

After her return to America from Germany in 1875, pianist Amy Fay (Reading 18) combined concertizing with private teaching, chiefly in Chicago and New York. Despite her reputation, Fay still experienced some of the problems that typically handicapped the woman teacher of her time—problems that she analyzed in her Etude *magazine article of 1902, reprinted here. One difficulty Fay does not discuss, although it is well documented elsewhere: women teachers generally could not command the same fees for lessons as men.*

Amy Fay, "The Woman Teacher in a Large City," *Etude* 20/1 (January 1902): 1, 14.

  1. Rudolph C. Blitz, "Women in the Professions, 1870–1970," *Monthly Labor Review* 9615 (May 1974): 56.

AMY FAY: "THE WOMAN TEACHER
IN A LARGE CITY"

We all know the old adage: "Before you cook your hare, first catch him." No doubt, if women music teachers could get plenty of pupils, they would be able to teach them; but here is precisely the difficulty. The woman teacher usually begins her career as an ambitious girl in a small town. She has some talent, and perhaps is the organist of one of the churches in the place of her abode. Her friends and acquaintances think her something remarkable, and she gradually gets a good class of pupils, at very small prices, say ten dollars per quarter.

When I began to teach, we used to have to give twenty lessons for ten dollars, and even then I thought myself favored, because formerly the quarter numbered twenty-four lessons. Still, in one way, the country teachers are more fortunate than the city ones, for the pupils have no distractions or amusements, are interested in their music, and do not miss their lessons. Moreover, they take lessons summer and winter, and one time of the year is the same to them as another.

Now, how is it in the city? Here, in New York, prices are very high for the best teachers of music. Five dollars is not considered an extravagant price to pay per lesson, although it frequently is more than people can afford. On the other hand, city pupils begin their terms late in October, and begin to drop off in April. By the first of June everybody who can goes out of town to avoid the heat, and the music teacher is left, high and dry, "alone in her glory." She has the privilege of living on her income through the summer, and of spending all she has accumulated during the winter. She returns to the city after her own vacation jaunt rested, but short of money.

Now is the time, however, when she ought to have plenty of money to advertise, get herself written up, send out circulars, and call upon her friends (this last costs car-fare) in order to impress upon the public mind that she is there and wants pupils. Otherwise she will go along with very slim classes until the middle of the winter, when she will have worked into her rut again.

A woman is at a disadvantage on account of her sex, and the reason of this is that, as a rule, boys and young men do not study music. Young girls find it more interesting to take of a man teacher, and this would be alright if the young men would return the compliment. They would enjoy taking lessons of a woman in music if she were competent to teach them, and for the same reason, that it is more interesting to study with a teacher of the opposite sex. I have had some excellent men pupils, but, unfortunately, they are all too few and far between!

I was returning to the city last year when a woman of my acquaintance got on the car and took a seat next to me. Said she: "Will you please tell me of some good man teacher in New York? My niece is going to take lessons in music this winter, and she declares she won't take of a woman." I meekly named several men teachers and did not once suggest that in my own misguided opinion I could teach the young girl as well as any of them. I knew it would be of no use, for a man she would have!

This preference for men is so well known that it is almost impossible for a woman to get a good position in the private fashionable schools in the city. They want a "professor," and the parents feel better satisfied when their daughters have lessons from a "gentleman teacher." If women teach in schools, it is usually as under-teachers, poorly paid. If they do not teach in schools or conservatories, they must depend upon their own magnetic qualities to attract pupils. It is a precarious means of support, and I often wonder what becomes of the old music teachers. One never sees them. The elderly teachers must be shelved, and how in the world do they save enough to live on?

Women should urge upon parents to have their boys learn music, as well as their girls, and then there would be plenty of pupils to go round. So long as one sex monopolizes the musical culture of the world, just so long will women music teachers find it hard to make a living.

The problem of missed lessons is a hard one for a woman. Parents realize that when they are dealing with men teachers they must pay in advance, and that, if their children do not take their lessons, they must expect to lose them. With a man, "business is business." Women do not dream of expecting anything else from the "lords of creation." With their own sex it is a very different matter, and, I am sorry to say, they cut off corners in the most unblushing manner.

Says a mother to me: "Mary has not been very well, and she has not practiced much this week; so she wants to be excused from her lesson." The probable state of the case is that Mary's mother has been too lazy to attend to her daughter's practicing, and the shrewd idea is in the back of her head that she will economize.

I have it in my power to charge for the lesson, but the fee will be grudgingly paid. For my part, I prefer to be cheated out of my money to having an unpleasant argument with a pupil.

Some will compound with their consciences by sending word beforehand that they cannot take the lesson. They reason then that "you have your time for something else"; and that is so, but it may be something which does not bring in any money.

Some teachers try to equalize matters by saying that they will make up the lost lesson within the quarter, but must charge for it. This will do, if your pupils live in town, but, if they are some distance out, they will not take the trouble to make the extra trip. If you make it, the loss of time and railroad fare will make your profits extremely small.

Fix it as you will, the woman teacher usually comes out at the small end of the horn, and after she has made up the missed lessons, lost those which come on holidays, like Christmas and New Year's, Good Friday and Thanksgiving Day, and finally triumphantly sends in her bill, paterfamilias delays and dallies about paying it until at least four weeks more have elapsed, and then the next quarter is well along.

29 WOMEN AS PATRONS IN THE CLUB MOVEMENT

The women's club movement, which gained striking momentum late in the nineteenth century both in Europe and the United States, was an unprecedented phenomenon that provided middle- and upper-class women with the opportunity for self-development and the betterment of their communities, as well as a means of overcoming isolation at home. Women in the clubs engaged in a broad variety of philanthropic and social reform projects, and many clubs fostered literature and the arts. In the United States, where men by default "left culture to the ladies," club women were the chief promoters of cultural interests throughout the nation. Regarding their work in the music clubs, in particular, women organized festivals and lending libraries, sponsored local talent and managed concert artists on tour, and oversaw music in the public schools. They also conducted courses of self-study for members and gave club concerts, sometimes performing music by women composers.

The music club movement in the United States received an important impetus at the Centennial Congress in 1876, when Fanny Raymond Ritter challenged women to assume the role of collective music patrons in her address to the Association for the Advancement of Women. Ritter's challenge is presented below, together with Fanny Morris Smith's description of the personal rewards to be found in club work from 1900.

Fanny Raymond Ritter, *Woman as Musician: An Art-Historical Study* (New York: E. Schuberth, 1876), pp. 16–17.

Fanny Raymond Ritter

. . . Not all ladies, however, are fortunate enough to boast a Gluck, a Handel, a Beethoven, a Michelangelo, a Tasso, among her everyday friends; not all women possess the wealth and power of a Princess Belgiojoso or a Baroness Rothschild;[1] but every American lady who possesses the indispensable kindness of heart, refinement, generosity and culture, as well as influence—the wives of men of intellectual power, inherited wealth, or great commercial prominence, more especially—can accomplish a great deal in her own small circle.

Ladies can do this in many ways: by reasonably persistent self-culture; by aiding in the formation of libraries of musical literature, of collections of rare musical instruments, and of private societies for the home practice of music; by condemning all that is unworthy of, and extraneous to art; by discountenancing the insinuating charlatanism of impudent adventurers, or vulgar speculators, and by seconding the claims to social and public distinction of genuine artists; by dissuading aspirants of insufficient talent from the profession of art, which, rightly pursued, is a secular ministry, but which, to be really successful as such, demands remarkable qualities in its highpriests; by sustaining the efforts of gifted women artists, compelled by sacred duty or sublime adversity, to make a public display of their talents; [and] by lending their influence to, and bestowing pecuniary aid on, every worthy artistic enterprise. These grateful offices fall most naturally into the hands of the *women* of America, since, from the very nature of life here, the time of men of influence is almost wholly occupied with the claims of business or politics; few among them study music at all in their youth, and how many who do, are able, on leaving college and entering the actual school of life, to prosecute musical practices and studies, and to carry them to any practical result, amid the conflicting claims of some profession, of commerce, or statesmanship?

1. Cristina Barbiano di Belgiojoso ran a famous salon in Paris in the 1830s and 1840s. Betty Rothschild, the wife of Beau James, was active in the same capacity in Paris from the 1820s to the 1860s.

With lady amateurs, then, will chiefly rest the happy task of preparing, by a beneficent use of such abilities as they may possess, the soil which must foster the young germs of future American art, and of hastening the day of its appearance, though this may be long in coming; for history teaches us that the formation of so-called national "schools" of art, acknowledged as such by other nations and the world at large, and not only by friends at home, must be the work of long centuries rather than of years.

One of the finest recommendations of music to our sex, as an art worthy of universal cultivation is, that it not only penetrates to the mind of the hearer, but to the heart also, thus widening and enlivening the faculties, and rendering them better prepared, by sympathy, to receive humane and elevated impressions. For what is all culture, even the highest, save a means to an end? And what is that end, if not the vivifying and humanizing of the heart, even more than the purifying and strengthening of the intellect? . . .

Fanny Morris Smith

This is the month when club women are inaugurating the work for the coming year, when new club members are entering, and old members dropping out of club life. If the year's work is to mean all it should to each club woman, it will be because she looks at it and goes about it in the right way.

What, if we sift it to the last grain, is the origin and reason for women's clubs? Is it ambition, or love of culture, or need of combination, gregariousness? Or is it something deeper still—and of more vital consequence. I am sure, if we think carefully, we should recognize the truth: it is a longing for more life, fuller life, higher life—that brings women together in club work.

As society grows more complex, the constant tendency is to isolate women in the home: women need not work in the fields or administer the affairs of business as they did in earlier times.

Fanny Morris Smith, "The Beginning of the Club Year," *Etude* 18/11 (November 1900): 410–11.

Men have gradually aggregated all the functions of business life, at least in America. Women have been left with none of the cares or responsibilities that reach out into national or even civic life. Women have been obliged to concentrate their thoughts on the administration of a large number of small, vexing, and perplexing details that make up the unparalleled difficulties of American housekeeping. Everything has turned inward—nothing left outward.

Now life grows by extension (not expansion) and health and vigor increase with mental and soul growth. As a means of escape from self-contradiction, out into the larger common life of an intimate circle of kindred minds, the women's club is the greatest blessing of modern development.

It is obvious that this blessing is only possible to those who are fit for it. It is to those who are anxious to give and share that the blessing of woman's organized life comes back, in good measure, pressed down, running over! To those who enter club work to get and snatch and keep there is no blessing at all— only bitterness and unrest and disappointment.

You are tired out with economical housekeeping. You are weary of keeping up an artificial life of cruel etiquette; you are perplexed in the daily and hourly solutions of loving helpfulness, or discipline, or comfort; you are lonely because the opportunity for loving self-denial has been taken from you, and time hangs heavy on your hands. Then go into club life—and make an honest and serious effort to throw your thought and will into the new and extrapersonal channel which it offers. Live an hour with Mozart or Beethoven or Liszt—realize and help others to realize what life meant to them. Spend a day at the club music class and enter into the feelings of the working girls assembled there. Lend a hand in starting the young artist, bred a quarter of a mile from your own door, and share her hopes and fears. Do your part in getting up the book club, and make the best reading list your own. In short, get out of yourself into that kind of helpfulness that organization best promotes, and the year will be the richest of your life.

Women as Orchestral Musicians

**30 THE VIENNA DAMEN ORCHESTER
IN NEW YORK, 1871**

As earlier readings have indicated, women played a great variety of instruments at Italian convents late in the Renaissance and also at the famous Venetian conservatories in the seventeenth and eighteenth centuries. In contrast to these special situations, however, it was only in the latter half of the nineteenth century that the choice of instrument widened among women in general, beyond the so-called "feminine" instruments of the period—the piano, harp, and guitar. First the violin and subsequently the flute and lower strings were successfully pursued by large enough numbers of women so as to be deemed acceptable. And by the end of the century women had taken up all instruments, despite the admonitions in the contemporary press that as players of wind instruments other than flute, and as players of brass, they lacked the strength and furthermore would ruin their looks.

Among these new instrumentalists many sought professional employment, and some, notably violinists, joined the ranks of concert artists. The major share, however, looked to orchestral work, and since the standard all-male orchestras were closed to them—the lone exception being the female harpist—women banded together to form their own institutions, the Damen Orchester and the Lady Orchestra. The trend originated in the German-speaking countries and later spread to England and the United States. For American women an immediate model was provided by the Vienna Damen Orchester, which visited New York in the fall of 1871 for two weeks of performances featuring waltzes. As the following review of the Vienna group's first performance clearly indicates, an all-women's orchestra had a definite curiosity value that attracted audiences.

September 13, 1871, *New York Times*

VIENNA LADY ORCHESTRA

The first performance of the Vienna Lady Orchestra was given at Steinway Hall on Monday evening, to the expressed pleasure of a very large and fashionable audience. The spectacle was certainly a novel one. The platform was changed into a bower, and under the roses were sheltered, instead of the familiar *profanum vulgus* of music makers, a score of blushing maidens attired in purest white, and armed after the orthodox style for their harmonious work. The sight of an instrumentalist of the gentler sex has little rarity about it, but the view of an organized force of female musicians was, until Monday, never offered in this country. On this fact was founded a very large share of the first success of the Vienna Lady Orchestra, and on it will rest their prospective triumphs. We would not, however, underrate the cleverness and culture the company displayed. Its members execute with precision and spirit the rather unpretentious selections where of their program is made up, and some of the solo talent is to be highly commended. The chief opportunity for fault-finding is suggested by the lack of heavy wood and string instruments and by the absence of brass. The dry notes of the piano and the broken chords of the harp are quite insufficient to support a substantial ground for the violins, the violoncellos, the dwarfed double bass, and the flutes. The delivery is on that account devoid of color, and the sound rather thin. Another cause for complaint is furnished by the undue prominence of a big drum, and the untunefulness of a small one, both being in altogether too frequent use. We need not be so cautious in praising the recital of the Vienna Lady Orchestra, as to dealing with the composition, and as we stated above, we can join in the admiration generally shown for the vivacity and unity of the readings. . . .

"Vienna Lady Orchestra," *New York Times*, Sept. 13, 1871, p. 5.

31 CAROLINE B. NICHOLS AND THE BOSTON FADETTE LADY ORCHESTRA

The early American lady orchestras in New York and Boston confined themselves to popular music, playing in beer gardens and theaters, but by 1900 there were several women's groups that performed light and standard classical repertory, the most famous being the Boston Fadette Lady Orchestra,[1] under the direction of Caroline B. Nichols. Trained originally as a violinist, Nichols founded the orchestra in 1888 with the aid of her brother-in-law, George H. Chickering, of the Chickering piano firm, and for the next thirty-two years she was active at its helm in Boston and on tour.

An engagement in Pittsburgh occasioned this interview with Nichols in the Pittsburgh Gazette. *Note that the orchestra was being featured in vaudeville: women's orchestras at this time had to be flexible in order to survive. Nichols took great satisfaction in the fact that over the years of the Boston Fadette's existence she prepared more than 600 young women for self-supporting careers as orchestral players.*

February 23, 1908, *Pittsburgh Gazette Times*

HOW ONE WOMAN CARVED OUT A NEW AVENUE
OF BREAD WINNING FOR HER SEX

One of the most fascinating pages in the history of orchestral music in America is that which traces the career of the Fadettes

---

"How One Woman Carved Out a New Avenue of Bread Winning for Her Sex," *Pittsburgh Gazette Times*, Feb. 23, 1908, section 4, p. 6. Reprinted by permission of the *Pittsburgh Post-Gazette*.

1. The name "Fadette" was taken from George Sand's 1884 novel *La petite Fadette*.

woman's orchestra of Boston from its origin, through its early struggle for recognition and final triumph as the only ranking symphony orchestra composed entirely of women. It is a story that reads like a page from romantic fiction. The presence in this city this week in vaudeville performances at the Grand Opera house of the Fadettes makes a recital of this story particularly apropos.

No chronicle of the career of the Fadettes that did not take into account the source of the gifts with which the members of the organization have been endowed could be complete. So, we find the fifty young women who respond to every pulsation of the baton of Caroline B. Nichols descended from a race of cultured musicians.

Hereditary influence makes for good as well as evil for those to whom it is transmitted, and yet we hear so much less about inherited talents than of the criminal taint. If proof were needed, and it is not maintained that proof is necessary, the Fadettes woman's orchestra of Boston furnishes ample evidence that the gifts of the fathers are inherited by the children, even to the third and fourth generations. There are [fifty] members in the Fadette Orchestra, and not one of them but can trace back gifts to some forbear who achieved at least local fame in the pursuit of music. . . .

While the Fadettes have been in existence twenty years, their professional career extends little over a decade. The personnel of the organization has undergone almost a complete change in that time, Dan Cupid having made tremendous inroads, while death has taken a number of the most valued members. Indeed, not one of the original members save Miss Nichols, the director, remains with the organization today. More than 100 left because of marriage, and eight have died.

Caroline B. Nichols, the snow-haired but youngish-looking director of the Fadettes, is a thorough musician in every interpretation of the term. While the violin is her solo instrument, she plays almost anything that is placed in her hands and besides has a thorough knowledge of the literature and theory of music. She is a great and enthusiastic advocate of music as a field for breadwinning for women and has done more than any other woman to develop this field. . . .

"There are twenty–thirty woman's orchestras of a professional character in the United States today," she said recently, "and while none of them has gained the fame that has come to the Fadettes they are all managed to make a good living for their members. If young women are going to earn their living, why not put them at something that will be refined, elevating in its influences, and artistic in its development? Don't you think the violin is better than the typewriter? Hasn't the girl who makes her living with a fiddle a better opportunity and greater social prestige than her sister who works her way through life playing the keys of a typewriter in a stuffy office? Mind you I do not disparage the typist! But I say all things considered isn't it better to fit a girl to earn her living by music than in a commercial pursuit of any sort? I only use the typewriter as an illustration because there are more girls doing that sort of thing perhaps than in any other single avenue of breadwinning open for women. If a girl is going to devote herself to music, it is better that she take up the violin, or almost any other instrument, in preference to the piano. There are so many piano teachers, they are so poorly paid, and so few are competent that the opportunities are not promising."

"The field for women musicians is growing," Miss Nichols said thoughtfully. "Why when the Fadettes began to appear for professional engagements, people looked askance, and the men musicians smiled and said wait until the public hears them. Well, the public did hear them, and the public liked them so much that we've never had an open week from that day to this that was not of our own making. We can play fifty-two weeks a year if we wish, and we usually do, and we have run as long as twenty weeks in Keith's Theater in Boston—Boston, mark you, where they have the greatest symphony organization in America, perhaps in the world."

"So far as the comforts and conveniences of such an organization as ours," said the conductor, "we have all the comforts of home. We travel first class, live in good hotels, have our little family of congenial companions, and as many of our engagements are for long runs, particularly in the summer and fall, you can readily understand we are not put to any inconveniences. We never play less than a week anywhere."

CAMILLA URSO ON PROFESSIONAL EQUITY FOR WOMEN VIOLINISTS, 1893

Women instrumentalists in the turn of the century period had a strong supporter in concert violinist Camilla Urso (1842–1902), who at the 1893 Woman's Musical Congress in Chicago attested to the affinity of women with her instrument and made the case for women violinists as orchestral players. Born in Nantes, France, Urso at the age of seven became the first female student of violin at the Paris Conservatory. In the early 1850s she immigrated to the United States with her family and appeared as a child prodigy. Later, as a mature artist, she performed widely in the United States, Canada, Europe, and Australia, providing inspiration to countless girls and young women.

The Woman's Musical Congress was held during the World's Columbian Exposition in Chicago and drew the largest number of amateur and professional American women musicians ever assembled. Planned specifically as an event to bring recognition to the recent achievements of women in the music field, the congress sponsored recitals of works by women composers and lectures by leading performers and educators, such as Camilla Urso.

WOMEN AND THE VIOLIN: WOMEN AS PERFORMERS
IN THE ORCHESTRA

So many times have I been asked, Why I learned to play the violin, that to cut matters short I would answer the question by another: Why should I not have learned the violin?

Susan Kagan, "Camilla Urso: A Nineteenth-Century Violinist's View," *Signs* 2/3 (spring 1977): 731–34. © 1977 by the University of Chicago Press. Reprinted by permission of the University of Chicago Press.

For women to play the violin or any string instruments with bow is not of recent date; centuries ago, ladies of high birth and station used to charm away the leisure hours and entertain their friends with their playing. Indeed as exalted a personage as Elizabeth, Queen of England, amused herself with the violin and an instrument of this denomination of the old and imperfect fashion, has been traced to her possession.[1]

The virgin queen's case was not an isolated one; the squadron of Catherine of Medici, as her maids were called, the followers of Marguerite de Navarre, the ladies in Boccaccio's Decameron are represented as playing on the viol, and painters of the 16th and 17th centuries represent St. Cecilia, the patron of musicians, playing on the Treble viol, the precursor of the violin in its present shape. The treble viol required from the performer a position and handling similar to those exacted by the violin.

Giuseppi Tartini in his school at Padua (Italy) had excellent female scholars. Maddalena Lombardini-Sirmen, one of these, attained fame as a performer and composed considerable violin music; most of her works were published at Amsterdam (Holland).[2]

In 1784, Mozart composed his sonata in B-flat major, for violin and piano [K. 454], for his friend Regina Strinasacchi. This lady was a celebrated performer on the violin and Mozart often played with her in concerts.

To record the name of women who have attained celebrity in the art of violin playing is not my object. I only wish to show in the preceding paragraphs that my action in choosing the instrument was not a whim, nor a case of rare occurrence, nor a novel one.

I believe myself however to have been the first girl violinist heard in the United States after I was brought over here from the Paris Conservatoire by an American Impresario to play in concerts. I was then ten years.

1. It is now thought that Queen Elizabeth played the virginals and also possibly the lute. Urso's subsequent references to women musicians associated with Catherine de Medici and Marguerite de Navarre could not be confirmed.

2. As noted in the introduction to Reading 12, Lombardini-Sirmen and Regina Strinasacchi, who is mentioned subsequently by Urso, received their initial training at the Venetian conservatories.

The development of violin playing amongst women in Europe, America, Australasia, is truly prodigious of recent years and a teacher of long date in New York was saying recently that was it not for his female scholars he would have to retire. The old objection against women playing the violin was that it lacked grace in the appearance and movements of the performer, until women coming before the foot-lights demonstrated the absurdity of the notion and to an admiring public proved that a pretty woman, handsomely attired, arms and shoulders bared, violin and bow in hand is more picturesque and possess[es] more attraction than the male performer dressed in the conventional dress suit.

Sundry reasons may be mentioned why the art of violin playing of all others should be cultivated by ladies anxious to acquire musical talents.

First, the lightness and grace of the violin. To look at it, to watch its wonderful contours, its perfection of form is a pleasure always renewed, never tiresome. Ask the violin amateurs; they will look over and over again the same instrument discussing new points to admire, never tired to take it up. Secondly it is easily handled and carried. Thirdly, no other instrument is so truly melodious; a simple ballad played on the violin will charm and give intense pleasure. Like the voice it responds to one's emotion and mood. Fourthly, as a solace, no better, no more responsive friend one finds than this delightful instrument and one gets so attached to it, that any slight accident, a crack, a jar, makes one feel grieved as if a dear companion gets injured. . . .

I have tried to show that as an "art d'agrément," the violin is perfectly within the ability of women and "en rapport" to their tastes and I will approach the subject of its utility to many students who could turn an honest penny by their acquired talent. But few can become virtuosi and many really good players must stay at home, who were they given an opportunity, would be glad to help their family and themselves.

Why leave all this talent go for nothing and not utilize it in the orchestras? Women as a rule play in better tune than men.

They play with greater expression, certainly, than the average orchestral musician. In Dublin, in Melbourne, I have employed lady violinists to reinforce my orchestra. They performed their part very well and with great attention to details. They were quick to understand, prompt at rehearsals, obedient and attentive to the conductor's remarks and not inclined to sneak away under a pretext or another if the rehearsal was a trifle long; they gave good work for the money paid them. If such an incentive as paid employment in this way was given to the many female violinists now doing nothing, what a benefit it would be to many of the theatres!! The scratching to be heard in some of these is enough to excuse our gentlemen escorts to leave their seats between the acts.

I know in advance the objection that will be brought out against my proposition: and what of the household duties of these women? It would be too easy to enumerate the thousands of comediennes that are in public every day; but I shall point that in most orchestras the place of harpist is supplied by women. This admitted, why should not [other] ladies be employed in the same orchestras??

33 SHOULD WOMEN PERFORM IN THE SAME ORCHESTRA WITH MEN?

In 1903 the Musical Union in New York became affiliated with the American Federation of Labor and in so doing was compelled to accept qualified women musicians as members. Interviews with three local musicians about this situation and about the general question of women in orchestral work are presented below, followed by comments from a conductor at the Paris Opéra.

Gustave Kerker, Musical Director at the Casino Theater

It would be like oil and water to put men and women in the same organization. Women musicians alone may be alright, but they don't belong with men. The Musical Union is making a big mistake admitting women to membership. Neither sex will derive any real benefit from such an arrangement, except in the matter of wages. Labor Unions have established rates, and naturally women musicians who belong to the union will be entitled to the same money as the men receive, whereas in the past many have played for less.

Another mistake in joining a labor union is that musicians have lowered themselves from the status of artists to that of laborers. Women harpists are admitted to be more desirable than men, the harp being essentially a woman's instrument. It requires such delicate fingering, you will find everywhere women are in demand

"Opinions of some New York Leaders on Women as Orchestral Players," *Musical Standard* [London] 21 (Apr. 2, 1904): 217–18; "La femme musicienne d'orchestre," *Le guide musical* 50 (July 31–August 7, 1904): 572.

for this work. But here a line should be drawn in the orchestra. Nature never intended the fair sex to become cornetists, trombonists, and players of wind instruments. In the first place they are not strong enough to play them as well as men; they lack the lip and lung power to hold notes which deficiency makes them always play out of tune. One discordant musician might not be noticed in an orchestra, but if you have several women members or a whole band composed of them, the playing verges on the excruciating. Another point against them is that women cannot possibly play brass instruments and look pretty, and why should they spoil their good looks? . . .

Do I think our theaters will eventually employ women musicians? No, most emphatically to that question. In the first place, very few musical directors would want them because women cannot be depended upon for rehearsing and the hard work demanded of musicians. Woman, lovely woman, is always to be admired, except when she is playing in an orchestra. She is certainly not in her own sphere, and any leader will find this out after he has had a few quarrels and instances of feminine disagreements.

Nathan Frank, Concertmaster of the Metropolitan Opera Orchestra

More women will take up music now that they can become professionals of equal standing with men. The fact that positions of good and established salaries are open to their sex will encourage them to become good artists. I predict that the future will see many women filling orchestral positions, especially in theaters, and some, indeed, may advance so far as to become eligible to an opera organization. . . . There is no harder orchestra work to do than operas; it requires tremendous physical strength and endurance, combined with an intuitive power to anticipate, as it were—to follow—the singer. No two opera artists sing alike; one night we have Mme. [Johanna] Gadski in the role of Elsa, and perhaps a night or two later another artist will sing the role in a very different style. Now a thorough musician has to understand just how to accompany each one after scarcely any rehearsing. Musical instinct and physical qualification are not all the requirements, either, to make a successful orchestral player. Tremendous lung power is needed for all the wind instruments, and few women possess this. In some points women would be more desirable than men in orchestral work. They would be easily guided, they would be punctual and reliable and would not be tempted, as so many men are, to send substitutes whenever they got a chance to make a little more money playing somewhere else.

Ada Heinemann, a Player in the Orchestra at the Atlantic Garden Music Hall

We never go there [i.e., to the Musical Union's headquarters]. In fact, we should feel very much out of place among the men, and even though our membership in the union entitles us to vote, we do not take advantage of this privilege. However, we do anticipate some good from it in the near future. The chances are that we will be called upon to take men's places when we can do so, and this means a broadening of our field. If I had a chance to substitute for a man I should do so in a minute. By accepting them [i.e., substitute engagements] women gain a foothold in the orchestral world, and that is what we are ambitious for. Now we are limited to concert work or to organizations composed entirely of women. I am sure a great many of us could hold our own with the majority of men; all we need is the chance to show them what we are capable of and willing to do. There is no reason why an orchestra leader should not engage a woman cornet player or a violinist, if she is good, just as quickly as he would a man. Sex should make not a difference whatsoever, if the woman can play an instrument well.

Paul Taffanel, Conductor at the Opéra and Head of the Orchestra Class at the Paris Conservatory

I have only praise for the women instrumentalists who have been admitted to the orchestra class at the Conservatory. Committed, punctual, all very talented—two play first desk—they fill well the positions they hold. One supposes that they would do as well in a concert orchestra.

As far as the theater! . . . The situation is entirely different, and at the Opéra, for example, there is opposition to the introduction of women into the orchestra. The physical obstacles seem almost insurmountable to me. We demand of our musicians four hours of work daily: from eight o'clock [in the evening] until midnight; we demand regular attendance at rehearsals; in sum, an effort that is almost impossible to obtain from a woman.

I will add that it is hardly a French custom to bring young men and young ladies together in the same work; our musicians enjoy great freedom in behavior among themselves; at intermission they come [and] go as they please. We are not able to restrain their freedom, nor [are we able] to take responsibility for the problems that could result for women from this same independence.

If other theaters want to experiment [in hiring women orchestral players], they certainly will be interesting to watch, and whatever the result, it will be an important indication for women instrumentalists. Until then it seems that women desiring to play in an orchestra have greater opportunities in concert work.

34 GEORGE UPTON: A CLASSIC FORMULATION OF THE THEORY OF WOMEN'S INNATE INFERIORITY

The heightened activity of women as performers, music teachers, and patrons in the club movement in the late nineteenth and early twentieth centuries was paralleled in the field of composition by a significant increase in the number of women seeking to enter the ranks of art-music composition. There had been, throughout the nineteenth century, a large number of women composers in the realm of popular music, amateurs mainly, writing parlor songs and dance music for piano. Their activity was seemingly deemed acceptable, or so lack of comment in the contemporary literature would indicate. By contrast, the influx of women into the loftier realm of art music—Le Beau and Smyth were part of this generation and at its forefront—occasioned a strong opposition that raged for more than thirty years. Alarmed by women's growing presence, critics decried what they saw as a feminization of music, with its inevitable deterioration, and they developed theories that maintained the innate inferiority of women as composers.

George Upton, the Chicago music critic, was an early formulator of one such theory in his influential book Woman in Music, *of 1880, which is excerpted for this reading. Women, Upton allows, could serve as muse for inspiration to male composers, and they could also interpret, especially as singers; but they could not write music—that is, great music. The proof was that women had not written great music in the past.*

Conceding that music is the highest expression of the emotions, and that woman is emotional by nature, is it not one solution

George Upton, *Woman in Music* (Boston: J. R. Osgood, 1880), pp. 21–28.

of the problem that woman does not reproduce them because she herself is emotional by temperament and nature, and cannot project herself outwardly, any more than she can give outward expression to other mysterious and deeply hidden traits of her nature? The emotion is a part of herself, and is as natural to her as breathing. She lives in emotion, and acts from emotion. She feels its influences, its control, and its power; but she does not see these results as man looks at them. He sees them in their full play, and can reproduce them in musical notation as a painter imitates the landscape before him. It is probably as difficult for her to express them as it would be to explain them. To confine her emotions within musical limits would be as difficult as to give expression to her religious faith in notes. Man controls his emotions, and can give an outward expression of them. In woman they are the dominating element, and so long as they are dominant she absorbs music. Great actresses who have never been great dramatists may express emotions because they express their own natures; but to treat emotions as if they were mathematics, to bind and measure and limit them within the rigid laws of harmony and counterpoint, and to express them with arbitrary signs, is a cold-blooded operation, possible only to the sterner and more obdurate nature of man. As I have said, so long as the emotions are dominant, she absorbs music. When the emotions lose their force with age, her musical power weakens. Almost every man who has learned to play an instrument, or to sing, be it ever so poorly, and be his troubles or his cares ever so pressing, continues to play or to sing as long as he has strength. . . .

The large majority of women drop their music long before the hair grows gray, or at the first touch of sorrow. This may be due partly to the effect of forced and unwholesome practice in these days when it is thought that every girl, whether she have musical intelligence and ability or not, must learn to play the piano, and partly to the engrossing demands of household cares; but these causes do not explain what is a general rule: while, in the matter of care, even the pressure of business does not divert man's attention from his music; on the other hand, he turns to it, even in his old age, for rest and solace.

There is another phase of the feminine character which may bear upon the solution of this problem, and that is the inability of woman to endure the discouragements of the composer, and to battle with the prejudice and indifference, and sometimes with the malicious opposition, of the world, that obstruct his progress. The lives of the great composers, with scarcely an exception, were spent in constant struggle, and saddened with discouragements, disappointments, the pinching of poverty, the jealousies of rivals, or the contemptuous indifference of contemporaries. Beethoven struggled all his life with adverse fate. Schubert's music was hardly known in his lifetime, and his best works were not known until after his death. Schumann is hardly yet known. There is scarcely a more pitiable picture than that of the great Handel struggling against the malicious cabals of petty and insignificant rivals for popular favor, who now are scarcely known even by name. Berlioz's music is just beginning to be played in his native country. Wagner has fought the world all his life with indomitable courage and persistence, and has not yet established a permanent place for his music. There is scarcely a composer known to fame, and whose works are destined to endure, who lived long enough to see his music appreciated and accepted by the world for what it was really worth. Such fierce struggles and overwhelming discouragements, such pitiless storms of fate and cruel assaults of poverty, in the pursuit of art, woman is not calculated to endure. If her triumph could be instant, if work after work were not to be assailed, scoffed at, and rejected, there would be more hope for her success in composition; but instant triumphs are not the rewards of great composers. The laurels of success may decorate their graves, placed there by the applauding hands of admiring posterity, but rarely crown their brows.

It is a curious fact, that nearly all the great music of the world has been produced in humble life, and has been developed amid surroundings of poverty and in the stern struggle for existence. The aristocracy has contributed very little to music, and that little can be spared without detriment. Nearly all the masters have been of lowly and obscure origin, and have lived and died

in comparative poverty; for, with rare exceptions, musical composition has been miserably unremunerative until within the last
fifty years. The enduring music has been the child of poverty,
the outcome of sorrow, the apotheosis of suffering. Sebastian Bach
was the son of a hireling musician. Beethoven's father was a dissi-
pated singer. Cherubini came from the lowest and poorest ranks
of life. . . .

But even assuming that woman had the disposition and the
leisure to devote to musical composition, would she *then* succeed?
The bluntest answer to this is, that she has not succeeded when
she has had the opportunity. But there is another way, perhaps,
of arriving at an answer. Woman reaches results mainly by intu-
itions. Her susceptibility to impressions, and her finely-tempered
organization, enable her to feel and perceive, where man has to
reach results by the slow processes of reason. So far as music is
a matter of emotion, she is more immediately sensitive to it than
man: she absorbs it more quickly, if not so thoroughly; she dis-
criminates with more nicety, and often judges with more impar-
tiality; she recognizes what is true and what is false more quickly.
If music were only an object of the perceptions, if it simply addressed itself to the senses, if it were but an art composed of
ravishing melody, of passionate outbursts, of the attributes of
joy, grief, and exaltation, and vague, dreamy sensations without
any determinate ideas, woman possibly would have grasped it
long ago, and flooded the world with harmony as she has with
song; but music is all this and more, for these are only effects.
It is not only an art, but an exact science, and, in its highest
form, mercilessly logical and unrelentingly mathematical. The
imagination does not have a free flight, but is bounded within
the limits of form. The mere possession of the poetical imagination
and the capacity to receive music in its fullest emotional power
will not lead one to the highest achievements in musical art.
With these subjective qualities must be combined the mastery
of the theoretical intricacies, the logical sequences, and the mathematical problems, which are the foundation principles of music.
In this direction woman, except in very rare instances, has never
achieved great results. Her grandest performances have been in

the regions of romance, of imagination, of intuition, of poetical feeling and expression.

For these and many other reasons growing out of the peculiar organization of woman, the sphere in which she moves, the training which she receives, and the duties she has to fulfil, it does not seem that woman will ever originate music in its fullest and grandest harmonic forms. She will always be the recipient and interpreter, but there is little hope she will be the creator.

However this may be, there is a field in which she has accomplished great results; namely, her influence upon the production of music. She has done so much *for* music, that it is not exaggeration to claim, that, without her influence, many of the masterpieces which we now so much admire might not have been written at all; that the great composers have written through her inspiration; and that she has, in numerous notable instances, been their impulse, support, and consolation.

35 HELEN J. CLARKE: REGARDING UNEQUAL EDUCATION IN THE PAST

As the "woman composer question" evolved, women's supporters argued that women had traditionally been hindered by a lack of training, and they demanded equal educational opportunities. They were certainly correct, for it was only late in the century that conservatories generally allowed women to enroll in theory and composition classes. Helen J. Clarke stresses the problems of deficient education and women's lack of practical experience in the following excerpt from her rebuttal to Edith Brower's "Is the Musical Idea Masculine?"[1] Brower had answered this question with an emphatic yes, and like Upton she maintained that women could not handle the abstract— for example, form in music.

We do not hear of women being subjected to any such drill in the gradually developing laws of counterpoint and later of harmony. Even within the last decade, the writer has heard of German teachers who absolutely refused to teach women the science of harmony, because, as they declared, no woman could understand it. If such a feeling is possible in this enlightened century, it is easy to picture what might have been the attitude in the past toward the training of women in the direction of creative work in music. This fact needs peculiar emphasis, because in Germany the two tendencies, on the one hand, of musical development, and, on the other, of suppression of women have been most marked.

Helen J. Clarke, "The Nature of Music and Its Relation to the Question of Women in Music," *Music* [Chicago] 7 (March 1895): 459–61.

1. *Atlantic Monthly* 73 (March 1894): 332–39.

Against the argument that women have had no opportunities, Miss Brower adduced that woman had a lute put into her hands before the pen. That is just the trouble; she has had so much and no more. She has until comparatively recently been taught to execute but not to create.

Another way in which conditions have been peculiarly favorable for the development of the composing faculty in men is that they have always breathed in the midst of musical environments. When a Bach or a Haydn is discovered to have a voice, he immediately becomes a choir boy, and being a boy he knows he may someday become choir master, so he observes the effects which may be produced from the organ, or the effects in chorus singing— all of which he lays up in his mind and digests as artistic food.

Likewise, when a Handel or a Beethoven plays an instrument ere long he plays in an orchestra, and so has constant opportunity of observing the qualities and capabilities of the instruments, the timbre, the intensity of sound and so on. Only by such means can he hope ever to use instruments effectively. And this artistic expression is no more than artistic diet without which the artistic faculty can no more grow and develop than could a human body develop physically without food.

I repeat, that, considering the peculiarly important part played by form in music, and by form I do not mean necessarily classic form, but form in all its modern developments—more of this artistic diet is needed in the development of a creative talent than in any other art. . . .

. . . I do not intend to argue from these facts that women are great composers. The proof of this must lie alone in her production of great musical works. I think, however, as I have tried to show, that the nature of music is such that certain conditions in the past have militated greatly against her highest development in the art, and notwithstanding the fact that the lute was put into her hand before the pen, these causes are not any innate inferiority of mind or heart, of intellect or emotion, but a lack of that transcendant power of expression in form, which in music, especially, can only come, and has only come even to the greatest of musicians, after the most profound and careful study of the laws of composition and of the masterpieces of the art.

Until women have had the same sort of training, above all, the same musical environments, the same opportunity to devote themselves body and soul to the art of composition, it is manifestly unfair to declare them mentally and emotionally incapable of great work.

The difficulties that women must overcome are far greater than those which meet men at the dawn of their musical career. They must come into competition with all the great works which have preceded them, and they must struggle in the face of a prejudice against their possession of genius so deeprooted and widespread that even their faith in themselves wavers, and the desire to attain without which no goal can be made is thus shorn of the strong impulse that should "aim at the stars" and is content if it but "hits the moon."

36   MR. MEADOWS-WHITE: REGARDING THE
"GREAT COMPOSER" ASPECT
OF THE QUESTION

*The "woman composer question" also sparked many in-
vestigations of women's actual history as composers. As a result,
supporters of women could point to a tradition for female composers, and they responded that whereas women did not figure
among history's few greatest composers, many women—together
with countless men—had pursued viable careers in composition,
gaining recognition in their own time.*

*The English composer Alice Mary Smith (1839–84) was a
minor figure who achieved some distinction in the 1880s. A
performance of her cantata* Ode to the Passions *was well received
in London in 1883 and occasioned much comment about the
potential of female composers. At a session of the Musical Association that documented women in composition beginning in
the sixteenth century, the husband of Alice Mary Smith, Mr.
Meadows-White, was asked for his reactions to the "woman
composer question," from his standpoint as a "very clever man
married to a very clever woman." Mr. Meadows-White responded:*

I think the Chairman has given the very best reason why I
should be silent, because if I am married to a very clever woman
my position must be one of inferiority at home, a position I should
find it difficult to escape from when I came abroad. But I confess
that on this particular subject I have not very much to say. My
conviction is this, that excellence in music as in other things is

Stephen S. Stratton, "Woman in Relation to Musical Art," *Proceedings of the
Musical Association* 9 (1882–83):136–39.

reached by the same methods for women as for men. I cannot help thinking that one reason why women have not had such success in composition as men is partly owing to this, that composition has not been made so much a study by them as by men. Another reason may be that the general education of women has not been the same as that of men. . . .

There is no doubt that where there is one woman who from circumstances has been able to cultivate such studies, there have been thousands and millions of men whose education has gone as far as their capacity allowed them, and naturally enough by the law of averages—though I do not say this accounts for it entirely—you would expect to find the number of very eminent women in such studies less than that of eminent men. Five or six great composers have been named—Bach, Mozart, Beethoven, and two or three other great names to whom we all turn at once—but, consider how many generations, how many centuries have passed before these few names which are in the category of great composers have arisen![1] No doubt if you search and read lists you will find a great number of men who have composed, but when you look back over the past these great men stand up four, five, or six at the most. Now to produce those five or six names look at the personas who have put pen to ruled paper, and have produced works more or less of merit in their time.

Mrs. Meadows-White has been kindly alluded to in the paper, but I am perfectly certain of this—and I desire to say so, for I know there are other ladies here equally distinguished in musical composition—I am sure she would be the last person to say that she has advanced very far on the road towards the eminence which Handel or Mozart or any of the great masters attained. She has only moved up to a certain point by the same means as any person, man or woman, who gets forward has done, that is to say, taking pains in the cultivation of those gifts which she has.

There is no doubt that a woman when she is married has other duties which may prevent her from occupying all her time in

1. Generally, little was known about music before 1700 at this time.

musical composition. Still, I may say it does not follow that, because a woman is married, she ceases to have any encouragement to go on in that path in which she has been successful. . . . I may add from experience that there is nothing inconsistent with the little eminence my wife has attained in music with the good management of domestic affairs.

In the opinion of Amy Fay, the greatest obstacle facing women in the past had been their failure to take their own talents and aspirations seriously. Fay's reference to John Ruskin is to his Of Queen's Gardens, *"a lecture investigating the true dignity of woman, and her mode of help to men."*[1] *Ruskin proclaimed that woman's intellect, unlike man's, "was not for invention or creation, but for sweet ordering, arrangement, and decision. . . . Her great function is to praise."*[2] *"Knowledge should be given her as may enable her to understand and even to aid the work of men."*[3]

Women have been too much taken up with helping and encouraging men to place a proper value on their own talent, which they are too prone to underestimate and to think not worth making the most of. Their whole training, from time immemorial, has tended to make them take an intense interest in the work of men and to stimulate them to their best efforts. Ruskin was quite right when he so patronizingly said that "Woman's chief function is praise." She has praised and praised, and kept herself in abeyance.

But now, all this is changed. Women are beginning to realize that they, too, have brains, and even musical ones. They are, at last, studying composition seriously, and will, ere long, feel out a path for themselves, instead of being "mere imitators of men."

Amy Fay, "Women and Music," *Music* [Chicago] 18 (October 1900): 506.

1. *The Complete Works of John Ruskin,* ed. E. J. Cook and Alexander Green (London: George Allen, 1905), 14:112.

2. Ibid., p. 122.

3. Ibid., p. 125.

For the matter of that, men have been imitators of each other at first. We all know that Mozart began to write like Haydn, and Beethoven began to write like Mozart, before each developed his own originality of style, and as for Wagner, he has furnished inspiration and ideas for all the composers who have succeeded him. Why, then, should we expect of women what men could not do (although Minerva was said to have sprung fully armed from the brain of Jove)? If it has required 50,000 years to produce a male Beethoven, surely one little century ought to be vouchsafed to create a female one!

It is a very shallow way of looking at the matter to say that "women have not been handicapped in music, because more girls than boys have been taught to play the piano or the harpsichord."[4] What does such teaching amount to? Really very little. To be a great creator in art, one must be trained to it from one's earliest years by a gifted parent or teacher. Mozart and Beethoven had fathers who fully realized the capacity of their sons, and they made them study early and late, "every day i' the hour," as Shakespeare says. No doubt, an hour of such work as these composers did in their youth, would be worth many days of the kind of musical preparation demanded of girls of this or any other period.

4. As maintained by A.L.S. in "Women and Music," *Musical Courier* 41/5 (Aug. 1, 1900): 33.

*Mabel Daniels's experience in integrating the score-read-
ing class at the Munich Conservatory in 1902—which she describes here in two letters to a friend—illustrates how women
in the past have had to fight generalizations about what women
should and should not do. Daniels graduated from Radcliffe College in 1900 and went to Munich to study composition with
Ludwig Thuile at the recommendation of her Boston teacher,
George W. Chadwick, head of the New England Conservatory
and a former classmate of Thuile's at Munich under Joseph
Rheinberger. In addition to her work in composition, the high-
lights of Daniels's year in Munich were her vocal studies and
attending performances of Wagner's operas. She returned to Boston to pursue a long and distinguished career as a composer.*

4 October [1902]

Such a glorious Allegro vivace day! The sun is shining, the
air is crisp and cool, and the sauciest of breezes is coquetting
with the tree-tops in the Platz. It gets into one's blood, a morning
like this, and the wildest dreams seem possible of fulfillment. I
came home from my lesson humming the theme of the scherzo
of Beethoven's Eighth Symphony [in F major, op. 93]. It seemed
to fit the buoyancy of my mood as nothing else could.

I can see you smile now and hear you say, "It's quite evident
she is happy in her new surroundings." Exactly so, my dear, and
there are so many delightful things to tell you that I don't know
where to begin. However, the Conservatory forms one of the most

---

Mabel Daniels, *An American Girl in Munich* (Boston: Little, Brown, 1905),
pp. 39–44.

vital elements of my new life here, so I'll start by telling you
of my visit there.

Be it known then, that the Royal Conservatory of Munich,
to give it its full title, opened the 18th [of September], and
promptly at nine o'clock I made my way thither. What a rambling
building it is, and how replete with association! So many musicians have studied here at some time or other, although Rheinberger and many of the teachers who have made it famous are now
memories of the past. With a certain indefinable thrill I realized
I was actually within these walls.

Instead of the *"Herein!"* which I expected to hear in response
to my knock on the door of the director's room, [Bernhard] Stavenhagen himself opened the door. I wonder if you heard him
play when he was in America. He's a handsome man, not much
above thirty, with blue eyes, firm chin, straight nose, and curly
blond hair and mustache.

In fact, he has all the delightful characteristics of a German
and none of the unlovely ones. Besides this, he is tall, a rarity
in men of this nation.

"Eine Amerikanerin!" he said pleasantly, pushing a chair forward. "I speak a lee-tle English, but" he went on in German,
"perhaps we will make more progress if I stick to my mother
tongue."

"I speak a very little German," said I, smiling, not feeling the
least afraid of him, and forthwith explained my situation and
what I wished to do at the school. A little man, whose face,
beard, and hair all seemed the same reddish color, was looking
over a pile of letters in the corner of the room. He now glanced
up at me curiously as I began my inquiries about the Partitur
Lesen [score reading] class of which I had read in the catalogue.

You know that five years ago women were not allowed to study
counterpoint at the conservatory. In fact, anything more advanced
than elementary harmony was debarred. The ability of the feminine intellect to comprehend the intricacies of a stretto,[1] or cope
with double counterpoint in the tenth, if not openly denied,
was severely questioned. The counterpoint class is now open to

1. In a fugue, the imitation of the subject in close succession.

women, although as yet comparatively few avail themselves of
the opportunity. Formerly, too, all the teachers in the conservatory
were men, but one finds today two women enrolled as professors
among the forty on the list.

"I should like to enter the Partitur Lesen class," said I inno-
cently, not then having learned all this.

Stavenhagen looked back at the little man. The little man
looked back at Stavenhagen. If I had thrown a bombshell they
could not have appeared more startled. The little man at once
abandoned his letters and stood staring, a few feet in front of
me.

"There have never been any women in the class. I am right,
am I not, Herr Sekretariat?" said Stavenhagen.

"You are right, Herr Direktor," responded the other. He held
his hands behind him and gazed at me as one might at a curious
species of animal. I felt I ought to be tagged, like those poor
creatures in the zoo. "Rare. From North America."

"Is the class full, Herr Sekretariat?" inquired Stavenhagen.

"About thirty men have registered, Herr Direktor," solemnly
answered the secretary.

There was a pause.

"Have you ever played string quartets from score, Fräulein?"
inquired the director.

"Yes, Herr Direktor," said I, with that supreme calmness which
comes at times when one is inwardly much disturbed. Again there
was a pause. Even I began to be impressed with the solemnity
of the occasion.

"Of course," said the director, "because a Fräulein never has
joined the class is no reason why a Fräulein never can."

"Not at all," said the secretary. The gravity of his expression
was worthy of a crisis in the affairs of state.

The two men walked to the other side of the room, and while
they conversed in whispers I stood gazing out of the window at
the equestrian statue in the *Platz*, unable to hide the smile at
the corners of my mouth. Although conscious of my many peculiarities, I had never before considered myself an abnormal being,
and to be so regarded struck me as amusing.

It seemed to take them a long time to come to a decision.

When my impatience had subsided to a state of hopelessness, Stavenhagen came forward.

"Your request is unusual, Fräulein," he began, "but—but— well, you may come on Friday at three o'clock."

With a sign of relief I bowed myself out in approved German fashion, feeling as might the immortal Napoleon after a hardwon victory.

8 November, Munich

I will acknowledge that I felt rather strange on the first meeting of the score reading class, when, on entering the room with a score of Haydn's symphonies under my arm, I encountered the astonished gaze of thirty pairs of masculine eyes. You could have heard a pin drop, the place was so still, as I walked by the different groups and took a seat near the window. Then a low whispering started among the students. Evidently I had created a sensation. A moment later the big door opened and Stavenhagen came in. Everyone rose, or straightened himself up at once. With a little nod which seemed to include us all, the director took his seat by the piano and the lesson began. Each one was called on to play a number of bars written in four different clefs, the old soprano, the tenor, the alto, and the bass—Stavenhagen selecting a new chorale each time. It was not till near the end of the hour that he called my name. Just as I took my seat before the keyboard, feeling intensely nervous and fearing lest my fingers tremble visibly, I heard one of the men smother a laugh. That settled it! I was bound to do or die, and with a calmness quite unnatural I played the bars set before me without a mistake. Nobody laughed when I had finished, and now that the first shock is over, the students treat me with upmost courtesy. Indeed, they seem to have accepted me as inevitable, although occasionally I catch one of them staring at me with an expression which says so plainly as words: "What on earth does a woman want of score reading?"

39 A COROLLARY TO THE QUESTION: SEXUAL AESTHETICS IN MUSIC CRITICISM

As a corollary to the "woman composer question," critics of the late nineteenth century developed a system of sexual aesthetics that analyzed music in terms of feminine and masculine traits. Feminine music, which women were expected to cultivate exclusively, was by definition graceful and delicate, full of melody, and restricted to the smaller forms of songs and piano music. Masculine music, by contrast, was powerful in effect and intellectually rigorous in harmony, counterpoint, and other structural logic. Symphonies, operas, and similarly large-scaled works lay in the realm of masculine music, and as women in increasing numbers came to write in large forms they were decried as venturing beyond their proper sphere.

Two reviews of Amy Marcy Beach's Gaelic Symphony, in E minor, op. 32—the first symphony by an American woman—provide initial examples of the application of sexual aesthetics for this reading. Beach's symphony in the post-Brahmsian tradition was first performed by the Boston Symphony Orchestra on October 30, 1896, and in his response the noted critic Philip Hale is generally enthusiastic. Hale does, however, attribute what he finds as excessively heavy orchestration in parts of the score to Beach's feelings of inferiority as a female composer. A second reviewer of an 1898 performance faults Beach's logic and contrapuntal skill, while noting especially the womanly grace and delicacy of the Siciliana or scherzo movement. Thus the system of sexual aesthetics found both virtues and defects in a composition by a woman to be the inevitable result of her gender.

Philip Hale, "Mrs. Beach's Symphony Produced Last Night in Music Hall," *Boston Sunday Journal*, Nov. 1, 1896, p. 2.

MRS. BEACH'S SYMPHONY PRODUCED LAST NIGHT
IN MUSIC HALL

. . . It is fortunately not necessary to say of the "Gaelic" symphony, "This is creditable work for a woman." Such patronage is uncalled for, and would be offensive. Nor is it necessary to say, "A praiseworthy endeavor." The endeavor is of little importance. The result is more to the purpose.

. . . Let me say frankly that this symphony is the fullest exhibition of Mrs. Beach's indisputable talent. I think it should be ranked as a whole above her Mass [op. 5], which was performed by the Handel and Haydn [Society]. The themes themselves may or may not be of importance; we will talk this over together later; certainly the treatment of them in the first, second and fourth movements often excites honest admiration and gives genuine pleasure. I except the slow movement for it seems to be the most labored and at the same time the weakest.

First of all, this music, as a rule, sounds well. For the jest is true, that there is music which is better than it sounds. Charming ideas of Schumann, for instance, are often shockingly dressed in orchestral robes. But in this symphony of Mrs. Beach's there is the evidence of orchestral instinct rather than the suspicion of loose experimenting. . . . Mrs. Beach wrote in this instance as though she were sure of the effects she had thought out. You do not at once feel that piano music has been fitted this way and that way and anyway to the orchestra.

Occasionally she is noisy rather than sonorous. Here she is eminently feminine. A woman who writes for orchestra thinks, "I must be virile at any cost." What Saint-Saëns said of Augusta Holmes is true of the sex.

Of the four movements, the second stands out in sharpest relief. There is plenty of good stuff in the first; there is an elemental swing as well as a force that almost approaches grandeur in the finale; there are many excellent things in the detail on which I would fain dwell, but the scherzo is to me the most complete, rounded and truly musical of the movements.

Mrs. Beach, who was applauded heartily, acknowledged the tribute of the audience modestly.

BOSTON SYMPHONY CONCERT

The symphony of Mrs. Beach is too long, too strenuously
worked over, and attempts too much. Its composer is a Boston
lady of musical ability, a pianist, and the possessor of a good
memory. Almost every modern composer has left a trace in her
score, which in its efforts to be Gaelic and masculine end in
being monotonous and spasmodic. The second movement is the
most unfeigned, although the first starts out bravely enough and
the last, which contains good material, is spun out. The slow movement is unqualifiedly tiresome, for the composer never knows
where to stop. Mrs. Beach scores with a generous eye for color,
and that color soon becomes cloying. What she says in her work
has been said a thousand times before, and better said, yet there
is no gainsaying her industry, her gift for melody—even "Du
lieben Augustine" is not forgotten—and her lack of logic. Contra-
puntally she is not strong. Of grace and delicacy there are evi-
dences in the Siciliana, and there she is at her best, "But yet a
woman."

*The English composer Ethel Smyth, whose formative years
are the subject in Reading 24, specialized in opera. A review
of the New York performance of her* Der Wald (The Forest) *in
1903 at the Metropolitan Opera demonstrates another theme
in sexual aesthetics: A woman did not compose well—rather,
she composed "like a man."*

A NEW OPERA IN NEW YORK

Not as the music of a woman should Miss Smyth's score be
judged. She thinks in masculine style, broad and virile. She has
fully mastered the modern orchestral mode. Her melodic vein
is pronounced. Its contours are bold and straight. There is no
seeking after phrases with which to please the groundlings. And
there is no timidity in avoiding the obvious harmony and the
hackneyed progression. . . .

"Boston Symphony Concert," *Musical Courier* 36/8 (Feb. 23, 1898): 29–30.
"A New Opera in New York," *Musical Courier* 46/11 (Mar. 18, 1903): 12.

Miss Smyth's instrumentation avoids the leaning towards violin episodes in unison, so noticeable in the orchestral works of other women—[Cecile] Chaminade and [Augusta] Holmes, for instance. The orchestra is used as a unit, and its separate factors are combined with cleverness and several times with exceedingly good counterpoint. . . . Her climaxes are full-blooded, and the fortissimos are real. There is no sparing of brass, and there is no mincing of the means that speak the language of musical passion. In this respect (and it is not the only one) the gifted Englishwoman has successfully emancipated herself from her sex.

Performers were also subject to the yardstick of sexual aesthetics, among them pianist Teresa Carreño, who built and sustained an international career of great renown in the 1890s until her death in 1917. The formidable program Carreño played that occasioned the review excerpted here consisted of Chopin's Sonata in B minor, op. 58, the Schumann sonata no. 2 in G minor, op. 22, Edward MacDowell's Sonata in E minor, op. 59 ("Keltic"), and a group of Liszt pieces.

CARREÑO WELCOMED IN CHICAGO

Madame Carreño comes to us again at the height of her artistic powers. Age seems to have no further hold over her except to steady the exuberant fire of her earlier years into the unflickering glow of heated anthracite. She has passed on beyond the heights of virtuosity to the realm of pure art, and has reached a place where that poise comes which should be called mastery. But this is not quite the word; there is in that word some taint of masculinity, and Madame Carreño is the finest type of the "eternal feminine." There is in her playing the mental grasp, the breadth of conception, which the male would arrogate to himself as his peculiar attribute, and yet her playing, no matter how full and rich in artistic insight, is womanly, with that charm, that tenderness,

Chicago Evening Post, Nov. 5, 1909; quoted in "Carreño Welcomed in Chicago," *Musical Courier* 59/22 (Dec. 1, 1909): 10.

that sensibility, which is her crown. There should be some word coined for those women who reach the heights of art where they are the peers of men, but, praised be the fact, still with that untouched which marks the woman.

1920–1981

A Patron and an Educator

**40   ELIZABETH SPRAGUE COOLIDGE:
PATRON OF CHAMBER MUSIC**

Elizabeth Sprague Coolidge was known as the "Patron Saint" and the "Lady Bountiful of Chamber Music," and her contribution was crucial to the establishment of a chamber music tradition in the United States. During her lifetime, and indeed still, her name has been synonymous with top-caliber performances of the best repertory, both contemporary and from the past. Coolidge (1864–1953) began her work in musical philanthropy only at the age of fifty-two, in 1916, when the death of her parents and her husband left her with a considerable fortune. The Sprague family wealth was made in the wholesale grocery business in post–Civil War Chicago, where Elizabeth was born and raised. She trained as a pianist and also studied composition, and although she appears not to have considered pursuing either field professionally, this background was invaluable for her later activity as a patron. During the years of her marriage to a Chicago surgeon, Coolidge fostered music through the musicales she gave in her home.

In assuming virtually a second career at middle age, Coolidge found a new significance for her life, and over the next forty years and more she combined patronage with management and performance, plus friendship with her many beneficiaries. Near the end of her career she gave a retrospective talk, in which she described how the range of her philanthropies had broadened in time. Excerpts from this speech are presented below.

Elizabeth Sprague Coolidge, *Da Capo* (Washington, D.C.: Library of Congress, 1952), pp. 1–5, 7–9. Reprinted by permission of the U.S. Government Printing Office.

Thirty-five years ago, while I was living in New York, I received a letter from a total stranger in Chicago, saying that he, as a member of the Chicago Orchestra, was playing quartets with others of the same body, and felt that, with the aid of a sponsor, they might become a first-class organization. He had been given my name as one who might possibly be interested in such a project. (In parenthesis, let me say that Chicago was my birthplace; that my father had been one of the sponsors of its orchestra; that I had played with it under its founder, Theodore Thomas, and had lately established in it a pension fund in memory of my parents, both recently dead. I suppose that these facts had brought my name to this artist's attention.)

The artist in question was Hugo Kortschak, who told me, later, that he had felt uncertain that I would even reply to his letter.

However, I was very much interested. I had been listening, with great pleasure, to the regular performance of the Flonzaley Quartet, in the New York home of Mr. Edward de Coppet, whom I envied such a privilege and whom I later consulted about such a responsibility.

I therefore replied to Mr. Kortschak that, as I was shortly going to Chicago to assist in the settlement of my mother's estate, I would be happy, while there, to listen to his quartet.

How well I remember their exciting performance of the César Franck![1] It has never thrilled me more than on that unique occasion in 1916. Before I left Chicago I had signed with these artists a three-year contract. They were to play for and with me in Pittsfield, my summer home, and at my New York apartment in winter.

So, they arrived in Pittsfield in June 1916, and played the first notes in a program which has expanded for thirty-five years, until it has long-since outstripped my original thought and has carried me with it into a wonderful experience.

I called them "The Berkshire Quartet"; (one sarcastic fiddler asked me, "why not the Park Avenue Quartet?"). On alternate Sundays we invited the neighbors to listen. In Pittsfield the experiment was entirely novel to many; there arose some comments and questions such as, "how many players are there in your quar-

---

1. Quartet in D major, M. 9.

tet?" "Will the wives join, later, as it grows?" "Are the meals included?" A [Ildebrando] Pizzetti composition was reviewed in North Adams as having been written by "an Italian named Pizzicati." But many sophisticated visitors also came to us, and by the time we left Berkshire for New York the new quartet was welcomed as a sincere and high-minded addition to our musical life.

Their agreement with me was that they should not play publicly until, by their concentrated practice, they should have reached a satisfactory level of excellence. Their rehearsals, which I regularly attended, were held in my music-room. You can imagine what an education this was for me, whose musical idiom had hitherto been so largely formed by keyboard standards. I had never before so well understood the possibilities of abstract music.

Mr. and Mrs. Kortschak, for one season, occupied an apartment communicating with mine (it had been my mother's at the time of her sudden death, and was left at my disposal). This meant very easy access, for the quartet, to my own quarters. At an early hour on the morning of one October 30th—my birthday—I was awakened by the sound of Percy Grainger's quartet arrangement of "Molly on the Shore." My rooms looked out upon a courtyard around which was built the ten-storied apartment-house. Delightful as was this early serenade, I had a few misgivings as to the reaction of my surrounding neighbor cliff-dwellers. What was my relief, at its close, to hear from the windows the sound of spontaneous applause!

And so the time went happily by; winters in New York, summers in Pittsfield. In 1917 there occurred an event which, although inconspicuous at the time, introduced a new motif into our work. Dr. Frederick Stock, the conductor of the Chicago Orchestra and one of my dearest friends, with his wife and daughter, visited me in Pittsfield, and, of course, listened to the playing of my Berkshire Quartet. Frederick had taken part in the Litchfield County Festivals in Norfolk, Connecticut. He was eager to have me see the famous "shed" in which these were held, and to meet Mr. and Mrs. Stoeckel [Carl and Ellen Battell], who had built and sponsored it and whom I had not as yet known.

So, one day, we drove over to their home and were cordially

received and personally conducted about the estate, including the vast shed.

Sitting at dinner that evening and discussing the significance of Mr. Stoeckel's work, Frederick made the casual remark that he wished my Quartet might be heard at one of those festivals. I, as casually, replied—"Why go so far? Why not have our own festival at our own home?" But the casualness was short-lived. I did not forget the suggestion and, although I only spoke very privately about it to the members of the Berkshire Quartet, I secretly pondered the idea and elaborated it in my imagination until I had secured the permission of my son to build a music hall and some artists' bungalows on South Mountain, his Pittsfield property. I then engaged an architect to design and a contractor to build the structures which are still standing and functioning on that romantic hill-top. A year later, in September 1918, we gave the first Berkshire Festival and, with it, inaugurated the main section of my "magnum opus," to which the foregoing events had been but the prelude.

It took place but two months before the armistice of 1918. All our thinking and acting had been geared to war since April 1917; it was truly wonderful to see, gathered together in peace and enjoyment, the representatives of nations still in deadly combat; Italian Ugo Ara and Austrian Fritz Kreisler, each of whom had fought against the other's country; German Emmeran Stoeber and French Georges Longy, listening in appreciation each to the other's music; Hungarian [Artur] Harmat playing Russian music; Austrian Kortschak leading his Quartet through a prize-winning Polish composition.

Our first notes, in which I joined my Berkshire Boys, were those of the Star-Spangled Banner; and then, after five highly serious concerts of classical, romantic and modern chamber music, we ended our Festival by dancing a Virginia Reel to the accompaniment of Strauss waltzes, played by Richard Epstein on an upright piano in the old bar in the Wendell basement. Epstein, by the way, was a son-in-law of Eduard Strauss.[2]

2. The brother of Johann Strauss, Jr., the "Waltz King," and also a composer.

In this way, then, we initiated, on our mountain, a series of yearly Chamber Festivals. I established prize-competitions and commissions, from which beginning scores of fine works have since resulted, among them compositions by Bloch, Loeffler, Martinů, Malipiero, Milhaud, [Ildebrando] Pizzetti, Respighi, [Albert] Roussel, Schönberg, Stravinsky and many prominent Americans, both North and South. We have presented such artists as Harold Bauer, Alfredo Casella, [Ossip] Gabrilowitsch, Myra Hess, [Georges] Enesco, [Lionel] Tertis, [Efrem] Zimbalist; the Flonzaley, London, Gordon, Kolisch, Lenox, Letz and Roth Quartets; Longy, [Georges] Barrère and [Georges] Laurent brought their wind-ensembles. For the prize competition of 1920 we received 136 manuscript entries; from America, England, Canada, Belgium, Holland, Germany, Austria, Spain, France, Italy, Poland, Czechoslovakia, Yugoslavia, Hungary, Norway, Sweden, Switzerland and Argentina. I mention these statistics in order to indicate the wide and unexpected response which, in a very short time, was evoked by my more or less unplanned project. Indeed the interest became so widespread that my good friend, Ugo Ara, urged me to extend my program beyond Pittsfield, suggesting that I repeat, in his country—Italy—some of the outstanding music that had originated on South Mountain.

With his executive help and Alfredo Casella's musical management, therefore, there began the next development in my plans for chamber music, namely the giving of Festivals both at home and abroad.

In 1923 the first foreign one was held at the American Academy in Rome and oh, what fun it was! Here, during the evenings at the old Hôtel de Russie, situated at the foot of the Pincian Hill, was often gathered a musical group comprising Malipiero, Respighi, Casella and de Falla; the first class of resident Fellows in Music,—Howard Hanson, Randall Thompson and my protégé, Leo Sowerby; my New York friends, Kurt Schindler and the Misses [Lillian] Littlehales and [Gladys] North, of the former Olive Mead Quartet; and, of course, Mr. Ara and Mr. Felix Lamond, founder and head of the Music Department. On a grand piano in my pleasant parlor, they would sometimes play over for me their recent compositions. I particularly remember de Falla, rendering with his little short hands, a very effective piano version of his "Nights in the Gardens of Spain," recently composed for piano and orchestra. Or, between rehearsals, we would drive to Frascati for lunch; or, at midnight, visit the Colosseum by moonlight. De Falla, however, was more apt to seek a church, to pray while we others amused ourselves. . . .

By 1924 Coolidge had become convinced that her aims regarding the Berkshire Festival needed to be institutionalized and impersonalized. She found such an institution in the Library of Congress, where she established the Elizabeth Sprague Coolidge Foundation in 1925.

It was following this concert [at the 1924 Berkshire Festival] that I received a suggestion which led to the solution of the problem about the future of my Festival. I had asked Frank Bridge and his wife to remain awhile in America and, for relaxation after our strenuous three days, to take a motor trip with me. After a visit to Southern Virginia, we stopped at Washington, and, as sight-seers, were invited to take luncheon at the "Round Table"—a gathering of the Chiefs of Divisions in the Library of Congress, presided over by its wonderful Librarian, Dr. Herbert Putnam. Naturally, the conversation turned to the recent Berkshire Festival. I happened to be seated next to a certain Dr. Moore [Charles Moore, Manuscripts Division], who, while chatting about my musical affairs, rather pointedly asked me if I might not consider giving some such music to the Library of Congress. The only equipment for such a prospect seemed, at that time, to be an upright piano upon which, in the basement, music might be tried out or practiced. However, when, the following Spring, I sent to the Library two chamber programs, Dr. Putnam borrowed from the Smithsonian Institution a delightful little auditorium in the Freer Gallery, and there my Pittsfield players opened a series of three concerts which, later, led to the establishment of the Coolidge Foundation and thus found a way to insure the perpetuation of my Festivals; the little Coolidge Auditorium, with

a Skinner organ, was built into a corner of one of the courts of
the Library; a fund was accepted by President Coolidge and the
Congress, and our first Washington Festival was given in October
1925. (Let me add—that both the Librarian and the Congress
had to be persuaded; the former by a warm friend of mine and
of music; the latter by the Librarian himself!) I was asked if,
according to Congressional usage, I wished the inauguration to
be opened with prayer. I replied that I felt it more impressive
to present Mr. Loeffler's beautiful setting of St. Francis's "Canticle
of the Sun," surely a more exultant hymn of praise and devotion
than would be likely to issue from the Senate or the House of
Representatives! . . .

In my opinion, the most significant—because the most constructive—work of the Foundation is its so-called extension concerts, performed at educational institutions; of these we share
the expense. Thus we not only reach and educate hundreds of
students, creating a future public for the best music, but also
enlarge the opportunities of artists and institutions. From both
these groups we have had hundreds of applications.

Another Foundation achievement which much pleased me was
the broadcasting of chamber programs at a time when the radio
stations, some of the artists and even Dr. Engel himself were
not enthusiastic. Three networks—Columbia, National and Mu-
tual—yielded to Carl's pressure, as he had yielded to what he
called my "enlightened obstinacy." This was before the habit
of broadcasting serious music, which is now so universal, had
become fashionable; and, in the year 1934/35 they gave nineteen
broadcasts which we sponsored. Some conservatives feared this
radio competition with personal appearances; but I believe that
it ultimately increased their audiences.

Still another outcome of my festivals, in both Pittsfield and
Washington, deserves mention; namely, the numbers of interesting compositions which have originated from them. These were
begun by the prize-winning or commissioned works on the Pittsfield programs; but their numbers were augmented by gifts to
me or by works written for special occasions.

Elizabeth Sprague Coolidge.

41 NADIA BOULANGER:
TEACHER OF COMPOSERS

*The French musician Nadia Boulanger (1887–1979) was
an extraordinary teacher of composers for almost seventy years,
and in this capacity she had a profound influence on American
music from the 1920s to the 1950s. Boulanger came from a family
of musicians: her father and her grandfather taught at the Paris
Conservatory; her mother was a professional singer and Nadia's
first teacher. Boulanger trained at the Paris Conservatory herself,
concentrating in organ and composition, and upon graduation
she won second place in the Prix de Rome competition in 1908.
It was in teaching, however, that she found her vocation. As
a member of the faculties of the Conservatory, the École Normale, also in Paris, and the American Conservatory at Fontaine-
bleau, Boulanger taught harmony, composition, and orchestration, and in addition she had a large class of private pupils
drawn from all over the world. One of the first Americans to
seek her tutelage was Aaron Copland, who, in 1960, wrote this
tribute.*

AARON COPLAND: "NADIA BOULANGER;
AN AFFECTIONATE PORTRAIT"

It is almost forty years since first I rang the bell at Nadia Boulanger's Paris apartment and asked her to accept me as her composition pupil. Any young musician may do the same thing today,
for Mademoiselle Boulanger lives at the same address in the same
apartment and teaches with the same formidable energy. The

Aaron Copland, "Nadia Boulanger: An Affectionate Portrait," *Harper's Magazine*,
October 1960, pp. 49–51. Reprinted by permission of the author.

only difference is that she was then comparatively little known outside the Paris music world and today there are few musicians anywhere who would not concede her to be the most famous of living composition teachers.

Our initial meeting had taken place in the Palace of Fontaine-bleau several months before that first Paris visit. Through the initiative of Walter Damrosch a summer music school for American students was established in a wing of the palace in 1921 and Nadia Boulanger was on the staff as teacher of harmony. I arrived, fresh out of Brooklyn, aged twenty, and all agog at the prospect of studying composition in the country that had produced Debussy and Ravel. A fellow-student told me about Mademoiselle Boulanger and convinced me that a look-in on her harmony class would be worth my while. I needed convincing— after all, I had already completed my harmonic studies in New York and couldn't see how a harmony teacher could be of any help to me. What I had not foreseen was the power of Mademoiselle Boulanger's personality and the special glow that informs her every discussion of music whether on the simplest or the most exalted plane.

The teaching of harmony is one thing; the teaching of advanced composition is something else again. The reason they differ so much is that harmonic procedures are deduced from known common practice while free composition implies a subtle mixing of knowledge and instinct for the purpose of guiding the young composer toward a goal that can only be dimly perceived by both student and teacher. Béla Bartók used to claim that teaching composition was impossible to do well; he himself would have no truck with it. Mademoiselle Boulanger would undoubtedly agree that it is difficult to do well—and then go right on trying.

Actually Nadia Boulanger was quite aware that as a composition teacher she labored under two further disadvantages: she was not herself a regularly practicing composer and in so far as she composed at all she must of necessity be listed in that unenviable category of the woman composer. Everyone knows that the high achievement of women musicians as vocalists and instrumentalists has no counterpart in the field of musical composition. This his-

Nadia Boulanger.

torically poor showing has puzzled more than one observer. It is even more inexplicable when one considers the reputation of women novelists and poets, of painters and designers. Is it possible that there is a mysterious element in the nature of musical creativity that runs counter to the nature of the feminine mind? And yet there are more women composers than ever writing today, writing, moreover, music worth playing. The future may very well have a different tale to tell; for the present, however, no woman's name will be found on the list of world-famous composers.

To what extent Mademoiselle Boulanger had serious ambitions as [a] composer has never been entirely established. She has published a few short stories, and once told me that she had aided the pianist and composer Raoul Pugno in the orchestration of an opera of his.[1] Mainly she was credited with the training of her gifted younger sister Lili,[2] whose composing talent gained her the first Prix de Rome ever accorded a woman composer in more than a century of prize giving. It was an agonizing blow when Lili fell seriously ill and died in 1918 at the age of twenty-four. It was then that Nadia established the pattern of life that I found her living with her Russian-born mother in the Paris of the twenties.

Curiously enough I have no memory of discussing the role of women in music with Mademoiselle. Whatever her attitude may have been, she herself was clearly a phenomenon for which there was no precedent. In my own mind she was a continuing link in that long tradition of the French intellectual woman in whose salon philosophy was expounded and political history made. In similar fashion Nadia Boulanger had her own salon where musical aesthetics was argued and the musical future engendered. It was there that I saw, and sometimes even met, the musical great of Paris: Maurice Ravel, Igor Stravinsky, Albert Roussel, Darius Mil-

1. More correctly, Boulanger finished Pugno's incidental music to Gabriele D'Annunzio's *La città morta*.
2. Although this has been a common assumption, Nadia gave Lili only a few lessons, in the summer of 1911. See Leonie Rosenstiel, *The Life and Works of Lili Boulanger* (Rutherford, N.J.: Farleigh Dickinson University Press, 1978), pp. 47–49.

haud, Arthur Honegger, Francis Poulenc, Georges Auric. She was the friend of Paul Valéry and Paul Claudel, and liked to discuss the latest works of Thomas Mann, of Proust, and André Gide. Her intellectual interests and wide acquaintanceship among artists in all fields were an important stimulus to her American students: through these interests she whetted and broadened their cultural appetites.

It would be easy to sketch a portrait of Mademoiselle Boulanger as a personality in her own right. Those who meet her or hear her talk are unlikely to forget her physical presence. Of medium height and pleasant features, she gave off, even as a young woman, a kind of objective warmth. She had none of the ascetic intensity of a Martha Graham or the toughness of a Gertrude Stein. On the contrary, in those early days she possessed an almost old-fashioned womanliness—a womanliness that seemed quite unaware of its own charm. Her low-heeled shoes and long black skirts and pince-nez glasses contrasted strangely with her bright intelligence and lively temperament. In more recent years she has become smaller and thinner, quasi nun-like in appearance. But her low-pitched voice is as resonant as ever and her manner has lost none of its decisiveness.

My purpose here, however, is to concentrate on her principal attribute, her gift as teacher. As her reputation spread, students came to her not only from America but also from Turkey, Poland, Chile, Japan, England, Norway, and many other countries. How, I wonder, would each one of them describe what Mademoiselle gave him as teacher? How indeed does anyone describe adequately what is learned from a powerful teacher? I myself have never read a convincing account of the progress from student stage to that of creative maturity through a teacher's ministrations. And yet it happens: some kind of magic does indubitably rub off on the pupil. It begins, perhaps, with the conviction that one is in the presence of an exceptional musical mentality. By a process of osmosis one soaks up attitudes, principles, reflections, knowledge. That last is a key word: it is literally exhilarating to be with a teacher for whom the art one loves has no secrets.

Nadia Boulanger knew everything there was to know about

music; she knew the oldest and the latest music, pre-Bach and post-Stravinsky, and knew it cold. All technical know-how was at her fingertips: harmonic transposition, the figured bass, score reading, organ registration, instrumental techniques, structural analyses, the school fugue and the free fugue, the Greek modes and Gregorian chant. Needless to say this list is far from exhaustive. She was particularly intrigued by new musical developments. I can still remember the eagerness of her curiosity concerning my jazz-derived rhythms of the early twenties, a corner of music that had somehow escaped her. Before long we were exploring polyrhythmic devices together—their cross-pulsations, their notation, and especially their difficulty of execution intrigued her. This was typical, nothing under the heading of music could possibly be thought of as foreign. I am not saying that she liked or even approved of all kinds of musical expression—far from it. But she had the teacher's consuming need to know how all music functions, and it was that kind of inquiring attitude that registered on the minds of her students.

More important to the budding composer than Mademoiselle Boulanger's technical knowledge was her way of surrounding him with an air of confidence. (The reverse—her disapproval, I am told, was annihilating in its effect.) In my own case she was able to extract from a composer of two-page songs and three-page piano pieces a full-sized ballet lasting thirty-five minutes. True, no one has ever offered to perform the completed ballet, but the composing of it proved her point—I was capable of more than I myself thought possible. This mark of confidence was again demonstrated when, at the end of my three years of study, Mademoiselle Boulanger asked me to write an organ concerto for her first American tour, knowing full well that I had only a nodding acquaintance with the king of instruments and that I had never heard a note of my own orchestration: "Do you really think I can do it?" I asked hopefully. *"Mais oui"* was the firm reply—and so I did.

Mademoiselle gave the world première of the work—a symphony for organ and orchestra—on January 11, 1925, under the baton of Walter Damrosch. My parents, beaming, sat with me in a box. Imagine our surprise when the conductor, just before beginning the next work on the program, turned to the audience and said: "If a young man, at the age of twenty-three, can write a symphony like that, in five years he will be ready to commit murder!" The asperities of my harmonies had been too much for the conductor, who felt that his faithful subscribers needed reassurance that he was on their side. Mademoiselle Boulanger, however, was not to be swayed; despite her affection for Mr. Damrosch she wavered not in the slightest degree in her favorable estimate of my symphony.

All musicians, like the lay music-lover, must in the end fall back upon their own sensibilities for value judgments. I am convinced that it is Mademoiselle Boulanger's perceptivity as musician that is at the core of her teaching. She is able to grasp the still-uncertain contours of an incomplete sketch, examine it, and foretell the probable and possible ways in which it may be developed. She is expert in picking flaws in any work in progress, and knowing why they are flaws. At the period when I was her pupil she had but one all-embracing principle, namely, the desirability of aiming first and foremost at the creation of what she called *"la grande ligne"*—the long line in music. Much was included in that phrase: the sense of forward motion, of flow and continuity in the musical discourse; the feeling for inevitability, for the creating of an entire piece that could be thought of as a functioning entity. These generalizations were given practical application: her eye, for instance, was always trained upon the movement of the bass line as controlling agent for the skeletal frame of the harmony's progressive action. Her sense of contrast was acute; she was quick to detect *longueurs* and any lack of balance. Her teaching, I suppose, was French in that she always stressed clarity of conception and elegance in proportion. It was her broadness of sympathy that made it possible for her to apply these general principles to the music of young men and women of so many different nationalities.

Many of these observations are based, of course, on experiences of a good many years ago. Much has happened to music since that time. The last decade, in particular, cannot have been an easy time for the teacher of composition, and especially for any teacher of the older generation. The youngest composers have taken to worshiping at strange shrines. Their attempt to find new constructive principles through the serialization of the chromatic scale has taken music in a direction for which Mademoiselle showed little sympathy in former years. The abandonment of tonality and the adoption of Webernian twelve-tone methods by many of the younger Frenchmen and even by Igor Stravinsky in his later years cannot have been a cause for rejoicing on the Rue Ballu. And yet, I have heard Mademoiselle Boulanger speak warmly of the music of the leader of the new movement, Pierre Boulez. Knowing the musician she is, I feel certain that she will find it possible to absorb the best of the newer ideas into her present-day thinking.

In the meantime it must be a cause for profound satisfaction to Mademoiselle Boulanger that she has guided the musical destiny of so many gifted musicians: Igor Markevitch, Jean Françaix, and Marcelle de Manziarly in France; Americans like Walter Piston, Virgil Thomson, Roy Harris, Marc Blitzstein, among the older men, Elliott Carter, David Diamond, Irving Fine, Harold Shapero, Arthur Berger among the middle generation, and youngsters like Easley Blackwood during the fifties.

In 1959, when Harvard University conferred an honorary degree on Nadia Boulanger, a modest gesture was made toward recognition of her standing as teacher and musician. America, unfortunately, has no reward commensurate with what Nadia Boulanger has contributed to our musical development. But, in the end, the only reward she would want is the one she already has: the deep affection of her many pupils everywhere.

Women in the Orchestral Field from the 1920s to the 1940s

42 WOMEN'S SYMPHONY ORCHESTRAS

During the 1920s and 1930s American women musicians formed organizations and became increasingly vocal about the status of women in the field. In composition, the Society of American Women Composers was founded in 1924, with Amy Marcy Beach as its first president. The society was dedicated to the advancement of music written by women, and it sponsored festivals of performances until the Depression curtailed its activities in 1929.

Among performers, an important development was the establishment of close to thirty women's symphony orchestras, which were founded to give trained women employment and professional experience, since the standard all-male orchestras continued to exclude women from their ranks.[1] Unlike the earlier lady orchestras, the women's symphonies typically had full complements of eighty or more players, and they specialized in the performance of strictly symphonic repertory. The majority of the new groups had female conductors, who also aspired to work in the symphonic field.

Conductor Frederique Petrides reported on the progress of women orchestral musicians in her newsletter Women in Music *between 1935 and 1940, when funds for publication became exhausted. In capsule form this newsletter traces the activities of women's orchestras across the United States and abroad in London, Paris, and Vienna, together with women's rising demands for the "mixed" orchestra, made up of men and women*

1. Carol Neuls-Bates, "Women as Orchestral Musicians in the United States, circa 1925–45," in *Women Making Music: Studies in the Social History of Women Musicians and Composers,* ed. Jane Bowers and Judith Tick (Berkeley, Calif.: University of California Press, 1982).

chosen on the basis of ability. Here are three representative selec-
tions from Petrides's newsletter.

CALIFORNIA CITY SPONSORS WOMEN

Long Beach, Calif., July 20 [1935]

Since the fall of 1930, the city of Long Beach has played sponsor
to its local woman's orchestra—thus winning for itself the distinction of being the first and only city in the world to support the
undertaking of musicians on the distaff side.

The Long Beach Woman's Orchestra was organized in 1925.
There are 102 experienced players in its ranks now, and plans
for the coming season include the addition of about 25 more
members to the personnel. Its record includes more than 100
public concerts; also participation in over 1000 programs through
its various ensemble units.

The group was started as a cooperative association with member-
players contributing for its maintenance. This policy was continued until the time when the City's Recreation Commission created
a special tax allotment for the support of the venture. The public
funds set aside for the orchestra take care of expenditures for
new orchestrations, the purchase of heavy instruments, rehearsal
halls, advertising, and arrangements.

Miss Eva Anderson, the orchestra's conductor, has presided over
the group for the last nine and a half years. This forceful and
gifted artist is a graduate of the Beethoven Conservatory of Music
in St. Louis. She has also studied under Dr. Howard Hanson of
the Eastman School of Music.

"BE LESS PERSONAL," CHICAGO URGES

Chicago, Ill.

"Women's orchestras must not merely play well; they must
strive to play better than other orchestras if they are going to
be successful musical ventures," says the credo of Miss Ebba Sund-

Frederique Petrides, ed., *Women in Music* 1/2 (August 1935).
Frederique Petrides, ed., *Women in Music* 1/4 (November 1935).

strom, conductor of the Women's Symphony Orchestra of Chicago. Another tenet of this credo is that women players, although patient, hard-working, and gifted, must, nevertheless, learn how to be a little less personal and emotional about their jobs.

If these days find Miss Sundstrom's orchestra in the class of the constantly developing musical groups, the answer for such growth and increasing recognition is given by its goal for the achievement of a uniform perfection.

It is an admitted fact, indeed, that this Women's Symphony Orchestra has developed a tone and that its work has a distinct individual personality. It is also a fact that a number of its players could easily stand comparison with the first class men in any good orchestra. Despite these achievements, however, Miss Sundstrom is not fully satisfied. A uniform perfection will be possible only after some of her players will no longer be new to their instruments, she has told a newspaper interviewer.

The Women's Symphony Orchestra of Chicago was founded in 1925. It is composed of 100 players, and back in 1928 had functioned for some time under the leadership of Ethel Leginska. It plays regularly during each successive season. It goes frequently on the air, an activity which probably makes it the best known of all women's orchestras in America.

"NO GOOD REASON" FOR BAN ON WOMEN

Like a good many other American writers on music and musicians, William J. Henderson, the Dean of New York music critics, who died last month, was in favor of including women in orchestras. His authoritative voice was raised more than once in behalf of women as conductors and orchestral players. The following comments on the subject were printed in his *New York Sun* column on Saturday, November 16, 1935. Quoted in parts they read:

"There is no good reason why women should not be employed in orchestras. The chief question to be asked is whether they can play as well as men. After that other considerations may be

Frederique Petrides, ed., *Women in Music* 3/1 (July 1937).

taken up. Can a conductor enforce discipline among the women as well as he can among the men, or will they have recourse to the defense of tears when the hard-hearted one addresses the instrumental body in merciless rebuke? Can women endure the severe strain of long and repeated rehearsals? These as well as other questions become individual rather than general. All a conductor needs to know is not whether women can fill all of the requirements, but whether the particular woman can, whom he contemplated engaging.''

"Are there female performers on all kinds of instruments? Certainly. . . . Now there must have been a fine spirit of enterprise in the soul of a woman who took up the study of the tympani. How many jobs are there for the female tympanist? What is the outlook for the female bassoonist? Does anyone wish to see a woman playing the bass drum or an E-flat tuba? . . .''

"Well it is all a matter of custom. Students in such institutions as the Juilliard School of Music see women playing in their orchestra continually and think nothing of it.''

43   AMERICAN WOMEN DEMAND "MIXED" ORCHESTRAS

By the late 1930s American women orchestral players had found some acceptance in secondary-level orchestras and in the free-lance groups that were on the rise in major centers. This success, coupled with the fact of having proved themselves through the women's symphonies, prompted some women players to go on the record demanding that all orchestras—especially the major orchestras—be mixed institutions. In Chicago and New York, organizations were formed in 1938 to publicize the need for better professional opportunities for women. The New York Times *report about the first open meeting of the New York group constitutes this short reading. Ultimately, it was the draft during World War II that depleted the ranks of men and thereby made possible the entrance of female players of all instruments into the major symphony orchestras and orchestras in opera, radio, and the movie and recording industries. Once the mixed orchestra became the rule, there was less need for the all-female group, and most women's symphonies did not survive the war years.*

May 19, 1938, *New York Times*

WOMEN MUSICIANS URGE EQUAL RIGHTS

Full Opportunity for Jobs is Asked at Rally of New Organization Here

Full opportunity of employment for professional women musicians was proclaimed as a right yesterday morning at the first

---

"Women Musicians Urge Equal Rights," *New York Times*, May 19, 1938, p. 24.

mass meeting of the six-week-old Committee for the Recognition of Women in the Musical Profession. Nearly 125 women musicians heard invited speakers and officers of the group discuss organizational plans and programs to combat "an unjust discrimination" for which, according to one speaker, "there was absolutely no reason except habit."

The first speaker, Antonia Brico, conductor of the New York Women's Symphony Orchestra, protested against the existing prejudice as regards engaging women in leading musical organizations.

"The law, medicine, economics, politics, and many other professions are open to women," she said. "Why then should not music be equally open to them? There is no lack of opportunity to study, what with tuitionless schools, music colleges, private teachers. And the union admits us to its ranks. But what after that? Where shall we work, when so many organizations will not only not accept us, but not even give us auditions?"

Jean Schneider, the committee's director of organization, stressed that the group's two main present considerations were the recognition of women's rights within the Musicians Union and the bringing of the problem to the attention of the public.

As to the first, she proposed the resolution, which was unanimously passed, that women take a greater active part in the union.

It is to the second consideration, Ruth Wilson, director of public relations, reported that various clubs and societies that have been informed of the committee's grievances have offered support. . . .

44 THREE MUSICIANS RECALL THEIR CAREERS: ANTONIA BRICO, FREDERIQUE PETRIDES, AND JEANNETTE SCHEERER

Antonia Brico, Frederique Petrides, and Jeannette Scheerer are three musicians who made important contributions to the advancement of American women in the orchestral field from the 1920s through the years of World War II: Brico and Petrides as conductors, and Scheerer as a clarinetist and for several years also as a conductor. Women, of course, were active as conductors of the Damen and lady orchestras of the nineteenth and early twentieth centuries—for instance, Caroline B. Nichols, who is a subject in Reading 31. The emergence of women conductors of symphonic and chamber orchestras, however, was a new phenomenon that occurred in the United States beginning in the 1920s.

Not surprisingly, the new group of women conductors found more opportunities in conducting women's symphony orchestras than standard all-male groups. Being a conductor and directing large numbers of people in one's own interpretation of great artistic works is an authoritative and prestigious position to say the least, and even today the number of female conductors is small. When she began, in 1930, Antonia Brico obtained a string of guest conducting dates with major all-male orchestras in Europe as well as America, but she enjoyed her longest tenure in the period under discussion as head of the New York Women's Symphony Orchestra. Petrides and Scheerer worked solely with the women's groups they founded, also in New York. Scheerer was active chiefly as a clarinetist, and when she began the instrument was considered unusual for women. She was an early con-

*tender in the mixed orchestra, where she typically occupied
the first clarinetist's chair.*

Antonia Brico: Conductor

*This interview with Antonia Brico took place at the time of
her May 1976 appearance with the American Symphony Orchestra at Carnegie Hall. The engagement was one of many that
resulted for her after the 1974 documentary about her career
entitled* Antonia: Portrait of the Artist, *which was made by Judy
Collins, a former piano student of Brico's, and Jill Godmillow.
As interviewer, I was particularly interested in events the film
didn't document—above all, why and when Brico left New York
and relocated in Denver, where she still teaches and conducts
the Brico Symphony Orchestra, a semiprofessional group. For
as the film indicates, with the disbanding of the New York Wom-
en's Symphony Orchestra, Brico no longer had a regular show-
case, and in general the demise of the women's orchestras during
and after World War II meant fewer and less prestigious opportunities for women conductors, since they were* not *typically hired
to conduct mixed groups.*

*Antonia Brico was a 1923 graduate of the University of Califor-
nia at Berkeley in piano, and she subsequently played in orchestral and chamber ensembles on radio in the San Francisco area.
After further piano studies with Sigismund Stojowski in New
York from 1925 to 1927, she received a fellowship that enabled
her to realize her youthful ambition to train as a conductor
in Berlin.*

In all I spent six years in Germany, from 1927 to 1932, although
I came back to the States in 1930 to make my American debut
at the Hollywood Bowl. I was the first American to graduate from
the [Staatliche] Hochschule für Musik in Berlin. As I recall
twenty people applied to the Hochschule in conducting when I

Antonia Brico and Carol Neuls-Bates, Interview May 15, 1976. Used by permission
of the interviewee.

did, and two of us were accepted on the basis of competitive exams—a young man and myself. . . .

The whole German conducting field was based on the premise that once you completed your training you would embark on the "route" through the different opera houses, and this route called for you to play for rehearsals at the piano and to coach the singers. A conductor would progress, say, from being the third conductor in a small opera house to the second conductor in a larger house, then perhaps back to a small house as first conductor, and so forth up the ladder. I am quite sure I could have followed that route if World War II had not intervened.

I returned to the United States in September 1932 for the simple reason that all the foreigners were booted out of Germany by the Hitler business, which was getting very serious. I was very poor at the time, and I remember that Iris Pactrez was one of the people who sent me money to buy my passage home. And so I arrived in New York in the height of the Depression with thousands of musicians out of work! I had spent years and years training; I had conducted in Berlin, Hamburg, Hollywood Bowl, San Francisco, Warsaw, Lodz, Posnan, and Riga; and yet I had no opportunities forthcoming to me at that time. I even owed money for the trip back.

I went to [the offices of] *Musical America*, just to ask questions. There was a wonderful person working there at the time by the name of Ludwig Wielich, and I came in very shyly and told Mr. Wielich that I had some press notices from Berlin, Riga, and cities in Poland that I wanted to have translated. Well, he started to read the reviews, and then he said, "Something should be done about you." "Yes, what?" I answered.

I don't believe things happen by accident; there *is* a scheme behind events, I think. I asked Ludwig Wielich why I couldn't become one of the conductors then being featured in a series of orchestral concerts at the Metropolitan Opera House sponsored by the Musicians Emergency Fund. He told me that Mrs. Olin Downes handled the concerts and that Mrs. Sidney Prince, the wife of the then-current head of the New York Stock Exchange and many times a millionaire, would be a good person from whom

to seek help. Would I come back in a week's time after he had
had a chance to talk with Mrs. Prince? Well, of course I went
back, and then at Mrs. Prince's invitation I visited her at her
Park Avenue apartment (fifteen rooms and all very spacious!)
to tell her of my pressing need to obtain one of the concerts
with the Musicians Symphony Orchestra.

*Mrs. Prince guaranteed Brico $500, provided that Brico match
the amount, and as a result Brico was able to conduct the Musicians Symphony for two concerts. She was denied a third concert
because John Charles Thomas, the baritone who was already
scheduled, would not perform under a female conductor.*

In those days wealthy people often took on protégés, and I
was Mrs. Sidney Prince's protégée for the year 1933. Naturally
I worshipped her, and why shouldn't I have done so under the
circumstances? She took me to concerts, insisted that I come to
her apartment for meals on occasion because she worried that I
wasn't eating sufficiently, and she bought me a dress to wear
for my appearances with the Musicians Symphony. I remember
the first concert particularly, for I conducted Tchaikovsky's fourth
symphony from a score containing annotations by the composer
himself. The score was lent to me by my piano teacher, Mr.
Stojowski.

In the mid-1930s I was engaged by the WPA to conduct three
concerts a week in the New York City area, and this was thrilling
for me—three concerts a week! On Wednesday afternoons I conducted at the Museum of Natural History here in Manhattan,
and then on Saturdays I had a children's concert in the morning
at the Brooklyn Museum followed by a concert for an adult audience in the afternoon. There was a man in the WPA management
who was not well disposed toward me, and he would program
works for me that were extremely difficult to conduct. I remember
one and that was Debussy's *Ibéria*.

I founded the Women's Symphony [Orchestra of New York]
in mid-1934: "If nine women can play together, then why not
ninety?" That's my line from the film, no? I feel as though I

know *every* line of that movie! The women who made up the orchestra were all well trained. Some were young, and some had played a lot like Betty Barry [first trombone] and Muriel Watson [tympani], both of whom had done a considerable amount of work in Boston. Lois Wann [first oboe] was a phenomenal oboe player who has since taught just about everywhere, and my concert master, Elfrieda Bos Mesteschkin, was an excellent violinist. So many women in the orchestra were very fine players, but they had limited opportunities for good engagements. . . .

Once I turned the Women's Symphony into a mixed orchestra [for the 1938–39 season], the board of directors wasn't interested any more. The board felt that the "female aspect" of the orchestra was the interesting feature, and since the orchestra had no other capital than the board's backing, that was that! I had to look elsewhere.

I had a manager, so-called, but he really didn't do a thing for me. All managers had a star and lived off that star; my manager's ace card was Georges Enesco, the Rumanian violinist, composer, conductor, and pianist. Now, in 1940 Hitler wouldn't let Enesco out of his own Rumania, and as my manager stood to lose a tremendous income from Enesco's dates he tried to substitute other people, me included. He wanted to fit me into a conducting engagement with a semiprofessional orchestra in Denver in December 1940, but the Denver people said, "Antonia Brico instead of Georges Enesco? How horrible!" And they turned him down flat.

Because of the interest of the head of the board of directors of the Denver Symphony, whom Brico described as a "determined and willful" woman, Brico conducted the orchestra on December 10, 1940, in a program that included Enesco's Rumanian Rhapsody, op. 11, no. 1.

The board was so enthusiastic that they engaged me for two concerts for the following season, one of which was to be the Brahms Requiem [op. 45] with the University [of Denver] chorus. As plans developed, it seemed that I would have to be in

Denver for a period of seven months in order to prepare the
chorus for the Brahms, and I could hardly afford to maintain
an apartment in New York in addition. Also, at that time I was
experiencing frightful sinus problems, and Denver's climate was
good for me. (Now we have smog just like everyone else, but
then, no.) And finally, a number of different people on the board
of the Denver Symphony told me that they were about to make
the orchestra a professional one, and that if I came to Denver
they would see that I got the conductorship. Well, that was just
what I wanted—a professional orchestra.

I pulled up stakes in New York, and everyone in Denver was
so glad to see me for the two guest concerts [during the 1941–
42 season]. But when I said wasn't it wonderful that I am going
to live here now, all their faces froze. It became clear that some
people thought that as a permanent resident I would be a great
threat to the local music teachers.

Of course it was difficult to become established in Denver,
but I had burned *all* my bridges in New York, and I had no
money. I managed though, and some people gave me students
and lecture dates. Yet when it came to the conductorship of the
Denver Symphony, there was no way the board would accept a
woman conductor. I think that's the first time I realized I was
thoroughly *persona non grata* as a conductor. That's when I hit
the lowest of lows.

Then the conductor[1] the board chose came to Denver, and
he fired three-quarters of the orchestra and brought in his own
friends from New York and Philadelphia. The orchestra members
who were left out went to the Musicians' Union and said, "We
want to form a nonprofessional orchestra with both union and
nonunion members, for if we don't continue to play we won't
be able to keep our hands in for even an occasional orchestral
job." And so this nonprofessional orchestra came to me, and it
is the orchestra [later named the Brico Symphony] that I have
been conducting for twenty-eight years, with some changes in
personnel, of course. . . .

1. Saul Caston, an American-born trumpet player, who played with the Philadelphia Orchestra from 1918 to 1945 and also served as assistant conductor.

*Brico remains active at the head of the Brico Symphony Or-
chestra, and she travels widely for guest conducting dates.*

Frederique Petrides: Conductor

*Frederique Petrides came to the United States from Belgium
in 1923 on a visit, and she liked it so much that she stayed.
Miss Petrides trained originally as a violinist, and she studied
theory and composition with her mother, who had been active
in the 1890s as a concert pianist, composer, and teacher at the
Royal Conservatory of Antwerp. This young woman of the 1890s
was preparing to compete for the Belgium Prix de Rome in composition until dissuaded by her conventional parents, and after
her marriage in 1901 she abandoned her professional career altogether. It was the waste of her mother's fine talent, Petrides
believes, that motivated her to work for the advancement of
women musicians as she did in the 1930s and 1940s.*

Did you decide to become a conductor at an early age?

Oh yes, but first I became a violinist. I studied with Matthieu
Crickboom, who was an assistant to Eugène Ysaÿe and the second
violinist in Ysaÿe's famous string quartet. I played a good deal
of chamber music and heard many great orchestral concerts, and
as a child of nine or ten I played often in the hospitals in Antwerp
for the wounded of World War I. When I came to New York I
taught the violin. My great desire, however, was to become a
conductor, and what a conductor needs is an orchestra to work
with. This I found at New York University, where for several
summers I took a conducting course with a charming man who
had been a pupil of Felix Weingartner. He taught us many of
the things that the great master had told him.

The musicians that took this course made up the orchestra.
Some of them were extremely good players, men from the New

Frederique Petrides and Carol Neuls-Bates, Interview Sept. 2, 1981. Used by permission of the interviewee.

York Philharmonic and other fine groups, who wanted to get degrees. Julia Smith, who was studying piano and composition at Juilliard, was in the class. We became friends, and together we made plans for an orchestra of women—the Orchestrette of New York—that would demonstrate the fine capabilities of women musicians. That was in 1932.

How large was the Orchestrette, and from where did you draw the musicians?

It numbered between thirty and forty players, depending on the work I wanted to program. When we began we had about twenty-two players, all from Juilliard, and in fact the violin sections were made up entirely of pupils or former pupils of Louis Persinger. As the orchestra grew we added players from the Curtis and Eastman schools.

I never was interested in promoting a women's orchestra per

Frederique Petrides and the Orchestrette of New York.

se. Rather, I saw the Orchestrette as a stepping stone to the mixed orchestra. It was important to me to show that women could do fine orchestral work! I wanted also to show that women could do more than just teach, because teaching at that time was the major means of livelihood for women instrumentalists [other than solo work], and if you didn't like teaching, well, that was just too bad! There simply wasn't any other choice! The one exception was the female harpist. She could gain entrance to male orchestras, and it seemed that as long as a conductor could point to the presence of a woman harpist among his players, he felt he had done all he should for women.

You received considerable praise in the press for the Orchestrette's programs. Would you comment on your intentions?

For one thing, I wanted to promote American music, and you have to remember that in those days very little new music by Americans was being performed. The Orchestrette premiered and played works by David Diamond and Norman Dello Joio, Aaron Copland's *Quiet City*, Samuel Barber's *Adagio for Strings*, and works by Julia Smith, Ulric Cole, Gian Carlo Menotti, and others. We also did the first American performance of a beautiful work by Ralph Vaughan Williams that I discovered: *Flos Campi* for orchestra, solo viola, and chorus.

Then there was Paul Creston. He was a fine artist and very interested in what we were trying to do. Toscanini believed very much in Creston and played many of his works with the [New York] Philharmonic. . . . I had a timpanist, Ruth Stuber, who played her instrument very beautifully. She also played the marimba, and one day she asked me to come and hear her: Mozart, Bach, violin concertos by Henri Vieuxtemps—all sorts of things! She made the marimba a beautiful singing instrument! I felt that this instrument should be heard and have works written for it. I asked Paul Creston to go and hear her play. He did and was as impressed as I was, and as a result I commissioned Paul to write the Concerto for Marimba and Orchestra (1940), which I premiered with Ruth and the Orchestrette, and which is dedicated to me. It has been widely performed over the years. Another fine work that Paul wrote for the Orchestrette was for our tenth anniversary, *The Chant 1942*. When Ormandy went to Russia for the first time with his Philadelphians he took our *Chant* and performed it there.

I also did a lot of research. I practically lived at the library, and I found many things by great composers such as Haydn and Mozart that were rarely played. So the Orchestrette did these too.

How did you manage to run an orchestra successfully in the middle of the Depression?

We had five or six concerts a season, which was quite a lot for those times. And there weren't any foundations or government agencies to help. Our tickets, as I recall, sold for $1.25, which was substantial for the Depression. But ticket receipts hardly defrayed a major part of the orchestra's expenses. Really my husband and I underwrote the orchestra. My husband Peter was a writer, and I was teaching. You know, I made a great mistake in not finding outside backing for the Orchestrette at the very beginning. Because three or four years later—after the orchestra had a fine performance record and excellent reviews—I did seek support, and I met with the response that I had carried on thus far without assistance, so why not longer?

We filled the hall [Carnegie Recital Hall] for every concert because we had an audience that was really interested in what we were doing. We had wonderful soloists, such as Lonny Epstein, who was Carl Friedberg's assistant at Juilliard. She played Mozart piano concertos with us that had not been played here. She was a well-known Mozart player in Europe. William Masselos, the pianist, and Frances Magnes, the violinist, also performed with us.

Meanwhile, weren't you studying conducting by observing Dimitri Mitropoulos?

Yes, I met Maestro soon after he came to the [New York] Philharmonic, and I asked him if I could attend his rehearsals.

So for years every week I was there, with my scores. The only way to learn to conduct, I think, is to observe a great conductor, and Mitropoulos certainly was that. He had a photographic memory that was phenomenal! I profited no end from following his interpretations and from observing the way in which he related to the men in his orchestra. His example as an interpreter of all great works—contemporary and classical—was a great inspiration to me.

Would you comment about some of the outstanding players in the Orchestrette of New York?

Well, Lois Wann, the oboist, should certainly be singled out. When Mitropoulos heard her play he said, "What a pity you aren't a man, for I would pick you for my orchestra." Hinda Barnet was our fine concertmistress, Eleanor Kovar our equally fine bassoonist, Helen Enser, horn, and Eugenie Limberg-Dengel, viola—just to mention a few. All the women in the orchestra were such good players that when the war came many found first-desk positions with major orchestras, replacing men who had left because of the draft.

Is this why the Orchestrette disbanded in 1943?

Yes, I didn't want to stand in the way of the girls' advancement, and it would have been difficult to find replacements for them right away. Besides, at the time the idea of preserving and fighting for a women's orchestra seemed so insignificant in the face of a world war and the daily reports of the many terrible tragedies.

Several questions come to mind about your family. You have mentioned your husband's interest in the Orchestrette. Would you comment further? Second, as I recall, your daughter was born in the late 1930s. How did you combine her advent with your work?

My husband Peter was wonderful and the right man for me. He was completely supportive in everything I did or tried to do.

He was a newspaper man with a fine publicity sense, and he
managed all the business details of the Orchestrette. Our daughter
Avra was born in 1938, and it was a great joy for both of us to
have this beautiful baby. It was not easy to combine being a
parent and a conductor, but I was fortunate in having a marvelous
Greek woman to look after Avra when she was little.

Would you comment on your newsletter Women in Music,
*which you published between 1935 and 1940? I am impressed
with the extent of your coverage on the activities of women
orchestral musicians, both in the women's orchestras and elsewhere.*

The conductors of the women's orchestras of the time were
all in touch with me, and I would include information about
what they were doing and about the general interest in orchestras
made up of both men and women. We sent the newsletter to
many, many conductors, major orchestras, to libraries—both here
and in Europe—so as to keep everyone we could informed about
our activities and the need for the mixed orchestra. I was especially
gratified that the newsletter was so widely quoted during its existence.

But another important purpose of the newsletter was to report
on the history of women as musicians, a history that goes back
as far as Ancient Egyptian times. I wanted women to feel a sense
of pride in that they had a special tradition. I also wanted to
tell women to keep on working, to assure them they would move
ahead.

*Frederique Petrides was encouraged by some to revive the Or-
chestrette of New York after the war had ended, but she felt
that the women's groups had proved their point: "women could
work well in orchestras and deserved a place alongside of men."
Petrides went on to conduct several all-male orchestras and then
mixed groups, notably in summer concert series in New York.
From 1961 to 1977 she was director of the West Side Orchestral
Concerts, Inc.*

Jeannette Scheerer: Clarinetist

At the age of nine, in Cedar Falls, Iowa, Jeannette Scheerer began piano study with her uncle. She "hated it," although she later came to appreciate his thorough approach to scales and other fundamentals. Instead she was enchanted with the clarinet, which her neighbor was practicing, and she taught herself to play his instrument before her parents bought her one of her own. Scheerer's first playing job was in a small orchestra at the local movie theater, two nights a week. She also played as soloist with the Cedar Falls concert band but was not allowed to join the band because of being female. Upon her graduation from high school her family expected Scheerer to attend Iowa State Teachers' College, but she was determined to study music, and with moneys saved from her third summer playing the Chautauqua circuit she struck out for Chicago in the fall of 1918.

One of the first things I did in Chicago was to go to hear the orchestras in all the movie theaters. These theaters were palatial—some could seat 1000 people—and the orchestras played through the entire film. So I went to hear them all, and I found a job with one. Next I registered with Joseph Schreurs, who was first clarinetist with the Chicago Symphony Orchestra, and *so* famous! I started lessons with him, together with classes at the American Conservatory.

Was this, then, your first formal training as a clarinetist?

Yes, my first formal training. I had played clarinet like a fish swims, but the first lesson I ever had was with Schreurs. He helped me right away, and when he saw my wrong fingerings for the high notes, he said, "What are you doing there?"

Jeannette Scheerer and Carol Neuls-Bates, Interview July 9–10, 1978. Used by permission of the interviewee.

You had devised the fingerings by yourself?

Yes, and Schreurs said: "That's funny, that [fingering] actually comes off. How do you get that?" And so he started me out so that I could obtain perfection as a clarinetist for the first time, and here I had already played for years in orchestras!

Then I tried out for the Civic Orchestra,[1] which was conducted by Frederick Stock, also the conductor of the Chicago Symphony Orchestra. I was in that orchestra from 1920 to 1924, and by the second season I got the first clarinet chair. Mr. Stock seemed interested in me; he liked my tone.

Were there many women in the Civic Orchestra?

There were about seven of us in the beginning I think, and in my fourth year the concertmaster was a concertmistress, Mildred Brown. . . .

Was the Civic Orchestra a good experience for you in terms of training?

Oh! There was no training in the world like playing in that orchestra. In the first place, Frederick Stock—and I've played with many conductors in my life—there was no one who had an ear like he did. He would give out a chord—for the string sections, for example—and he would have them hold it at an even dynamic level; and he could always hear which players varied the loudness of the tone. In our choir [the woodwinds] he would try us out on transpositions. And he always made *all* of us concentrate on the sound of the *whole* orchestra because then we would play with one another in tune. He was the likes of a teacher I've never met again.

---

1. The Civic Orchestra of Chicago was founded in 1919 as a graduate-level training orchestra with the aim of enabling more Americans to secure positions with major orchestras, which were then dominated by European musicians.

What did you do when you finished your studies at the American Conservatory and left the Civic Orchestra?

Stock got me a post with a friend of his, Theodore Spiering, another German conductor, in Spiering's Portland Symphony Orchestra. I was to be in Portland in September, and so with a journalist and a painter-friend from the University of Chicago I took a leisurely trip west. We fished, we went to Yellowstone [National] Park—a wonderful trip. And in Coeur d'Alene, Idaho I had a telegram from Mr. Stock that Theodore Spiering had died in Berlin of a heart attack, and that plans for the next Portland season had stymied. Stock said maybe I should come back to Chicago.

But I didn't want to go back to a movie theater orchestra! That was [supposed to be] my first post in symphony work, and Mr. Stock had always said I must play in a symphony— that "Oh! it was so hard for him to get a place for a girl." That was true: he had trouble finding positions for all the women in the Civic [to move on to]. And he often wrote to newspapers saying that all orchestras should be opened to women. It was such a waste of fine talent and training, he said.

Eventually Scheerer decided to go to San Francisco.

I had written to my folks to send my trunk, and the day the trunk came I finally had some decent clothes to wear; so I went into the city to look for work. We went to this cafeteria that had an orchestra, and I set my tray down in front of the group. They were playing a potpourri of light classical things, and [when they had finished] I clapped and said, "Fine, but you need a clarinetist, don't you?" This is how I met Mary Passmore,[2] a fine violinist, who was the orchestra's conductor. So, I got a good

2. Mary Passmore and her sister Dorothy Passmore, a cellist, were among the four female string players who joined the San Francisco Symphony Orchestra with the 1925–26 season, thus becoming the first women to be hired by a major American orchestra.

job right away at $60 a week and two meals a day. Like everything else it came from the sky, and I never questioned.

After a year or so Mary and I joined the newly organized orchestra at CBS radio, Station KFRC, where I was first clarinet. . . . By the late 1920s everyone was playing the Böhm clarinet, while I was a little behind this new mode with the old-fashioned Albert system. [I decided to make the change] and while I was waiting for my new instruments to come from Paris—it took about six months—I made a vacation trip to visit my parents. And of course I went on to Chicago to see Frederick Stock, and he said: "Jeannette, you still have *five months free!* Why don't you go to Europe? I've always said you should *hear German orchestras.* You must go to Berlin, and I'll give you letters of recommendation."

Scheerer personally picked up her new clarinets in Paris and then traveled to Berlin.

To whom were Stock's letters of recommendation for you addressed?

One was to a conductor and one to just a friend, about me and how I played wonderful clarinet. The one to the conductor said that I should get acquainted with people with whom I could go to all the operas and hear everything I wanted to hear. The other to the friend asked that person to find me a pension near the Hochschule [für Musik] and to "keep Jeannette away from any place where English was spoken."

I went to the Hochschule, got the two letters out, and made apologies for my faulty German. They were very nice, and they liked me at the Hochschule. I sat in on some classes, and I went to all the operas and the theater—all week, every week I was busy. I got acquainted with Professor [Alfred] Richter [clarinetist at the Hochschule], and he said: "You should keep your old German clarinet." "Well, I know that," I said, "but in America you are out of date if you don't have a Böhm." Richter asked me why I didn't stay on at the Hochschule, and I told him that

I had to be back in San Francisco at a certain date, and besides I didn't have a lot of money. "You should take the entrance examination," Professor Richter said. "The Hochschule costs only 150 marks each semester, and the experience might be very interesting for you." In the end I stayed, until 1932.

Were you working for a degree?

No, I didn't have to any more [after the American Conservatory]. I played a lot of chamber music—especially Hindemith; I played soloist a lot, but being a foreigner I couldn't get into an orchestra. I did play first clarinet in the Hochschule orchestra, though.

It was while you were at the Hochschule that you studied conducting, wasn't it?

Professor [Julius] Prüwer, the head of the Conductor's Studio, thought that I should pursue conducting, and I was suggested for a scholarship. But I had been at the Hochschule for such a long time already, and the conducting course took six years to complete. So I didn't want that. I studied conducting for fun, though, on the side, with Robert Robischeck, the founder and director of the Berlin Bach Choir for many years. I played chamber music with him, and I studied conducting with him. Studying conducting was fun!

What happened next? Did the Hitler business send you home?

Yes, things were getting pretty hot in 1932. So I came back to New York, and what did I see? I didn't know anything about this [the Depression]. I had never written many letters and kept in touch with people in the States. The Germans were badly off, but I had had enough money to get along while I was there, so I guess I didn't notice more. Now that I was back in New York—with all my savings used up—I was suddenly in the same boat.

I didn't want to stay in New York; I had every intention of

returning to San Francisco, since that's where I knew everybody. Well, on the first night I was in New York, a violist friend whom I had met on board ship said, "Come with me tonight and go to a very interesting place, the Leventritts' house." Do you know the Leventritts?

I know of the Leventritt competition.

Mr. [Edgar] Leventritt was a great lover of music, and he played very good piano. He always had a houseful of the best players, such as Ernest Silverstein, Legara, Joseph and Lillian Fuchs, Lily Kroll, Arthur Balsam, Erica Morini, William Kroll and his quartet, the Musical Art Quartet, Maria Roemaet-Rosanoff, Sascha Jacobsen. It was a beautiful house!

I stayed in New York because every Sunday I went to the Leventritts' to play. He gave all sorts of music there. I remember I played the second Weber [clarinet] concerto [in E-flat major, op. 74] and also the Weber [clarinet] quintet [in B-flat major, op. 34], the Brahms clarinet quintet [in B minor, op. 115], and so much more. The Leventritts insisted, "You can't go to San Francisco. New York is *the* market place for music. You must stay here." So, what could I do? They got me engagements on the radio. I played solos; I played everything there was to play. But still I was a woman.

You must be referring to orchestral jobs. Did you try to join a symphony orchestra in New York?

Oh, I tried. But there really wasn't anything open. . . .

And despite the hard times of the Depression you were able to put together a salary?

It was so. I have never liked to teach, but I went to the City and Country School and taught clarinet there a bit. . . . Then President Roosevelt [i.e., the WPA] started two symphonies here

New York: the Civic and the Federal. I played first clarinet in the Civic.

How often did a WPA orchestra like the Civic play?

We played two concerts every week, and we had conductors from all over the world. The one I liked most was from Leningrad, Eugene Plotnikoff. The Civic was a pretty good orchestra.

Meanwhile, didn't you help Antonia Brico to organize the New York Women's Symphony Orchestra?

Brico came back from Germany in 1932, a little before I did, I think. Soon after, she conducted a concert or two with the Musicians Symphony Orchestra at the Metropolitan [Opera House], in which I played first clarinet. There were maybe five women in that orchestra—Francis Blaisdell was first flutist, I recall—but the work was not permanent.

Brico told us that if she could get a women's orchestra together [as she planned], it would be the first time in New York that a women's group could depend on a stable contract for a season's work. But oh!, did that ring a bell with every woman musician in New York. It was easy to get players for the orchestra. . . . But with such great demands as ''Carnegie Hall only,'' the largest possible orchestra, extensive publicity and all, the expenses for the orchestra *must* have been very high at that time, because Brico had to tell her board of directors that the girls would be ''content'' if only they could earn $10 a concert! Several of us lost interest and quit after three concerts.

What about your own orchestra, the New York Women's Chamber Orchestra, which you started and conducted in 1937?

Yes, I think it was 1937. My idea was that we might eat a little better, and that a small orchestra of twenty-eight players and myself, with less expenses [than the New York Women's Symphony Orchestra] would be viable. We just got together; they were the best musicians, so we didn't have to rehearse very much. . . . We made our debut in Town Hall on October 12, 1937, with success!—and no agents or advertising, so to speak. Thanks to Mrs. H. A. Guinzberg, the small deficit of $387 was paid, and the hall was filled. The Leventritts' friends were all there, and many others, and we all thought that the orchestra would be offered a radio or recording job very shortly. But the best thing we got were the two tours of eastern colleges that Arthur Fiedler couldn't play [with his Boston Pops Orchestra] in the 1939–40 season. When we came back, my wealthy aunt, who owned one of the largest pharmaceutical firms in Iowa, wanted to help me, and so we were able to give a concert in Carnegie Recital Hall [on November 28, 1940].

Tell me about some of the players in the orchestra. As I recall, many in your group broke into the major orchestras in the late 1930s through World War II. I know some of their names.

I hope you *do* know their names. Ellen Stone was a great horn player, and she went to Pittsburgh. The timpanist, Muriel Watson, went to New Orleans, and the head of the second violins, Gertrude Buttrey—she played a lot in New York and with the Stuttgart ballet. They were all fine players: Elfrieda Bos Mesteschkin, our concertmistress; Francis Blaisdell and Ruth Freeman, flutists; Jean Schneider, a cellist.

I thought the orchestra could get more dates than it actually did. But then, I'm not the best person when it comes to day-to-day business details. I thought the manager I picked was wonderful, but that proved not to be the case. . . . My aunt said I had to get this conducting bug out of my head.

In 1941 Jeannette Scheerer joined the New Orleans Symphony Orchestra as first clarinetist, the first woman to hold such a post with a major American symphony orchestra. She also played with the New Jersey Symphony Orchestra and the Kansas City Symphony Orchestra before relocating permanently in Germany in 1953.

An American Pioneer for Minorities

45   MARIAN ANDERSON: CONTRALTO

Reading 21 traces the concert career of the black American soprano Sissieretta Jones in the late 1880s and 1890s, a career that was necessarily brief, since the novelty of black performers among white audiences faded within several years. When contralto Marian Anderson (born 1908 in Philadelphia) began to seek recognition, in the 1920s, her situation was somewhat different: black musicians were associated with jazz and not thought capable of excelling in art music. Anderson broke down this prejudice and, by her example, paved the way for younger generations of black artists, notably as singers. Anderson used income from church jobs to pay for voice lessons, and her early professional engagements were at black colleges in the South. She won a vocal competition against 300 contestants that awarded her a debut with the New York Philharmonic at Lewissohn Stadium in 1925, but despite the favorable reviews she received on this and other occasions, it was not until she returned from successful concert tours in Europe in 1935 that she was generally acknowledged as a major talent in the United States.

In 1939 the Daughters of the American Revolution refused Anderson's request to hire Constitution Hall because of her color. In protest, a distinguished group of citizens headed by Eleanor Roosevelt sponsored a concert for Anderson at the Lincoln Memorial, which was attended by 75,000 people. Anderson describes this momentous event in the following excerpt from her autobiography. Only in 1955 did she make a Metropolitan Opera debut, the first ever by a black.

From *My Lord, What a Morning*, by Marian Anderson (New York: Viking Press, 1956), pp. 187–91. Copyright © 1956 by Marian Anderson. Reprinted by permission of Viking Penguin Inc.

The excitement over the denial of Constitution Hall to me did not die down. It seemed to increase and to follow me wherever I went. I felt about the affair as about an election campaign; whatever the outcome, there is bound to be unpleasantness and embarrassment. I could not escape it, of course. My friends wanted to discuss it, and even strangers went out of their way to express their strong feelings of sympathy and support.

What were my own feelings? I was saddened and ashamed. I was sorry for the people who had precipitated the affair. I felt that their behavior stemmed from a lack of understanding. They were not persecuting me personally or as a representative of my people so much as they were doing something that was neither sensible nor good. Could I have erased the bitterness, I would have done so gladly. I do not mean that I would have been prepared to say that I was not entitled to appear in Constitution Hall as might any other performer. But the unpleasantness disturbed me, and if it had been up to me alone I would have sought a way to wipe it out. I cannot say that such a way out suggested itself to me at the time, or that I thought of one after the event. But I have been in this world long enough to know that there are all kinds of people, all suited by their own natures for different tasks. It would be fooling myself to think that I was meant to be a fearless fighter; I was not, just as I was not meant to be a soprano instead of a contralto.

Then the time came when it was decided that I would sing in Washington on Easter Sunday. The invitation to appear in the open, singing from the Lincoln Memorial before as many people as would care to come, without charge, was made formally by Harold L. Ickes, Secretary of the Interior. It was duly reported, and the weight of the Washington affair bore in on me. . . .

. . . I studied my conscience. In principle the idea was sound, but it could not be comfortable to me as an individual. As I thought further, I could see that my significance as an individual was small in this affair. I had become, whether I liked it or not, a symbol, representing my people. I had to appear.

I discussed the problem with Mother, of course. Her comment was characteristic: "It is an important decision to make. You are

Marian Anderson.

in this work. You intend to stay in it. You know what your aspirations are. I think you should make your own decision.''

Mother knew what the decision would be. In my heart I also knew. I could not run away from this situation. If I had anything to offer, I would have to do so now. It would be misleading, however, to say that once the decision was made I was without doubts. . . .

We reached Washington early that Easter morning and went to the home of Gifford Pinchot, who had been Governor of Pennsylvania. The Pinchots had been kind enough to offer their hospitality, and it was needed because the hotels would not take us. Then we drove over to the Lincoln Memorial. Kosti was well enough to play,[1] and we tried out the piano and examined the public-address system, which had six microphones, meant not only for the people who were present but also for a radio audience.

When we returned that afternoon I had sensations unlike any I had experienced before. The only comparable emotion I could recall was the feeling I had had when Maestro Toscanini had appeared in the artist's room in Salzburg. My heart leaped wildly, and I could not talk. I even wondered whether I would be able to sing.

The murmur of the vast assemblage quickened my pulse beat. There were policemen waiting at the car, and they led us through a passageway that other officers kept open in the throng. We entered the monument and were taken to a small room. We were introduced to Mr. Ickes, whom we had not met before. He outlined the program. Then came the signal to go out before the public.

If I did not consult contemporary reports I could not recall who was there. My head and heart were in such turmoil that I looked and hardly saw, I listened and hardly heard. I was led to the platform by Representative Caroline O'Day of New York, who had been born in Georgia, and Oscar Chapman, Assistant Secretary of the Interior, who was a Virginian. On the platform

---

1. Kosti Vehanen, a Finnish pianist, was Anderson's accompanist for many years. Initially her manager, Sol Hurok, had strong reservations about the appropriateness of Anderson's having a white accompanist in the United States.

behind me sat Secretary Ickes, Secretary of the Treasury [Henry] Morgenthau [Jr.], Supreme Court Justice [Hugo] Black, Senators [Robert] Wagner, [James] Mead, [Alben] Barkley, [D. Worth] Clark, [Joseph] Guffey, and [Arthur] Capper, and many Representatives, including Representative Arthur W. Mitchell of Illinois, a Negro. Mother was there, as were people from Howard University and from churches in Washington and other cities. So was Walter White, then secretary of the National Association for the Advancement of Colored People. It was Mr. White who at one point stepped to the microphone and appealed to the crowd, probably averting serious accidents when my own people tried to reach me.

I report these things now because I have looked them up. All I knew then as I stepped forward was the overwhelming impact of that vast multitude. There seemed to be people as far as the eye could see. The crowd stretched in a great semicircle from the Lincoln Memorial around the reflecting pool on to the shaft of the Washington Monument. I had a feeling that a great wave of good will poured out from these people, almost engulfing me. And when I stood up to sing our National Anthem I felt for a moment as though I were choking. For a desperate second I thought that the words, well as I know them, would not come.

I sang, I don't know how. There must have been the help of professionalism I had accumulated over the years. Without it I could not have gone through the program. I sang—and again I know because I consulted a newspaper clipping—"America," the aria "O mio Fernando,"[2] Schubert's "Ave Maria," and three spirituals—"Gospel Train," "Trampin'," and "My Soul Is Anchored in the Lord."

---

2. From Donizetti's *La favorita*.

The "Woman Composer Question" Revisited

46   ETHEL SMYTH: "FEMALE PIPINGS IN EDEN"

On the occasion of Ethel Smyth's seventy-fifth birthday in 1933, plans for a festival of her works were announced, and Smyth, quite delighted with this recognition, responded with the essay Female Pipings in Eden, *in which she analyzed the difficulties confronting the female composer of her time. While she was, of course, influenced by her friend Virginia Woolf's* A Room of One's Own *(1929),[1] Smyth was no newcomer to feminism. Throughout her career she championed the needs of women to aspire and achieve, and from 1911 to 1913 she devoted her total energies to the suffrage movement. This experience had a profound influence on her life, as the excerpts from* Female Pipings, *below, indicate. Her song "The March of the Women" was the trademark of the English suffrage movement, which proved successful in 1918.*

Smyth's vantage point in Female Pipings *is England early in the twentieth century, where she felt that the lack of a rich musical life and the absence of a native tradition of great composers posed still greater problems for the aspiring composer than elsewhere in Europe. Her premise that women must have access to musical institutions and the machinery of the music world, however, applies to all geographical locales and time periods.*

Ethel Smyth, *Female Pipings in Eden* (London: Peter Davies, 1933), pp. 3–5, 7–12, 14–16, 19–20, 24–29, 31–32. Reprinted by permission of the publisher, William Heinemann Ltd.

1. Correspondence between Woolf and Smyth in March through August 1933, Berg Collection, New York Public Library.

FEMALE PIPINGS IN EDEN

Chapter I

(a) Introductory

Lecturing the other day at King's College, London University, on what will turn out to be the theme of this study, I had the pleasure of introducing to a young and learned audience a hitherto unedited legend. I am a little vague as to its exact provenance, but what matter, when authenticity is so triumphantly established by internal evidence?

The legend relates that one afternoon while Adam was asleep, Eve, anticipating the Great God Pan, bored some holes in a hollow reed and began to do what is called 'pick out a tune.' Thereupon Adam awoke; 'Stop that horrible noise,' he roared, adding, after a pause, 'besides which, if *any one's going to make it, it's not you but me.'*

Here the cuneiform inscription, or palimpsest, or whatever it is rather gives out, but among still decipherable words are 'unwomanly' . . . 'sex-appeal' . . . and (this almost illegible) 'L-l-th.' Whence one gathers that Eve's refusal to stop the noise drove Adam to set up a second female companion.

If this story shows what kind of encouragement women musicians met with when the world was in its swaddling clothes, the following pages will prove that all down the ages every possible facility for pursuing music as a career has been withheld from us; not so much by malice prepense (though in latter days there has been some of that too!) as by the turn our civilisation seemed bound to take . . . anyhow *did* take. Yet in spite of this, the fact that up to now there have been no great women composers has often been commented on with surprise. Indeed I myself am perpetually being asked how I account for it.

Now the reply is so closely connected with the nature of the musical world—a matter about which general ignorance is peculiarly dense—that I shall presently jump with both feet plumb into the centre of the subject and endeavour to show what a complicated art music is, and what difficulties the study of it involves. I think any one will then be able to make a shrewd guess as to the fate of such foolish women as dare to set sail on these troubled waters, more especially as creators, and will also understand one's despair when for the millionth time the old, old question is propounded—with an air, too, of being such a facer that you are evidently expected to retire from the field in disorder!

Occasionally I have put the true answer in a nutshell by retorting: 'There are no great women composers for the same reason that there are no female Nelsons!' whereupon the interlocutor says no more but looks both puzzled and unconvinced. I hope to prove this is no mere verbal flourish, but a sober, reasoned reply to a natural, but, given the circumstances, rather provoking question.

(b) The Main Thesis

My main argument is, that as things are to-day it is absolutely impossible in this country for a woman composer to get and to keep her head above water; to go on from strength to strength, and develop such powers as she may possess. But first I should like to define my attitude towards this state of things, and explain that if I deserve an encomium recently handed me in the Press of being an ardent but *good-natured* fighter in the cause of women, it is not owing to kindliness but to reason. The situation appears to me quite inevitable, given, firstly, an ingrained racial conservatism that enabled parliamentarians to persist in the criminal injustice of taxing the voteless more than sixty years after John Stuart Mill had pointed out that thereby one of the most fundamental principles of our constitution was being violated;[2] given, secondly, the fact that unlike Germany and Italy, England has had no great line of composers during the last two centuries, and consequently is bereft of a musical tradition that nothing but abundance of creative genius in a people can beget; and,

2. Mill introduced the first petition in favor of women's suffrage to the English Parliament in 1867.

thirdly, given very elementary facts of human nature which will be discussed in a later section of this study.

I am convinced too that few men realise how differently from themselves women are placed in the musical world, which is not surprising. How many of us are capable of profound X-ray insight on any question whatsoever, let alone on one that doesn't interest us? I could name one or two men who know the truth, but these discreetly keep their knowledge to themselves, for, after all, can you expect males to fight and suffer all the results of unpopularity for a cause that does not affect one single man; or rather, which, if successful, might affect some of them rather unpleasantly?

●　　●　　●　　●　　●　　●　　●

Chapter II: Women's Training Hitherto

To begin at the beginning. Nowadays, in all departments of human effort, the first necessities are, a thorough training, followed by untrammelled opportunities for exercising the trade you have learned. In the past, now and again a situation could be rushed by unskilled individuals of genius, but in the twentieth century Joan of Arc could hardly have superseded Marshal Foch; nor will any contend that holiday canoeing on the South Coast, or even lifelong practice in rowing and punting on the Thames, is sufficient to turn out a female Drake or Cook.

Now up to quite recent times the excursions of women into the world of music have not been much more extensive than the above seafaring operations. To-day there are as many fine violinists of one sex as of the other; but in the latter part of the nineteenth century I can recall only one eminent woman fiddler, [Wilma] Norman-Neruda; and I doubt if her brilliant progress round Europe would have been a certainty if [Joseph] Joachim had not been big enough and shrewd enough to see the spectacular advantage of playing Bach's double concerto [in D minor, BWV 1043] with a violinist of genius who was also a very graceful woman. As for the professional female orchestral player, the idea of such a being had hardly risen above the horizon in the early years of this century; and I well remember that no one looked on Lady Folkestone's String Band of women-amateurs as an outlet for serious musical energy and passion, but merely as an aristocratic fad;[3] a resource for such bored and elegant ones as to-day eke out the hours with feeble bridge.

By and by, students at our musical colleges began clamouring to learn stringed instruments, and presently half the string band consisted of girls. Later on the mouthpiece of certain wind instruments was permitted to insert itself between feminine lips, and, to cut a long story short, to-day there is not an instrument in the orchestra that is not taught to female musical students. Some of the best wood-wind players in the country are women, though horns and the bass-brass are still unpopular, perhaps because these are rather *damp* instruments. But the big brass is always placed well at the back of the orchestra, and as women cough and sneeze with less *abandon* than men (which is a mercy, for otherwise this planet would be uninhabitable), so my sex may find a way of blowing down tubes more dryly than males seem able to do. Anyhow, if Dame Clara Butt and other fine broad-chested contraltos one could name had taken to orchestral playing, what wonders they might have done on the Bass Tuba!

I cannot remember at what exact moment this important new move in our training was inaugurated, though of course the war interrupted it. But in order to master music *as a trade* more than that is necessary; you have to be right down in the rough and tumble of music life, and no sooner did a woman leave college than she became aware of men's firm intention to keep her out of that arena. It was too late, of course, to prevent her from training as an orchestral player; if she wanted to go on with it, let her supply hotels and restaurants with jazz and sob-stuff, but sit on equal terms with them in a first-class orchestra? . . . Never!

Unfortunately to play in a first-class band is one of the main entrances to that delectable land of rough and tumble where alone

3. Since Lady Folkestone's lady orchestra raised money for the establishment of the Royal College of Music in the 1880s, its performances must have been creditable at least.

salvation is to be found. There's education for you, if you like!
Just think of it! All the best music, ancient and modern, passes
in procession across your desk; here as nowhere else can you
learn instrumentation, phrasing, conducting, rhythm; here the
beautiful workaday part of your vocation gets into your blood
automatically and gratis. Then, as regards material issues, you
command a good salary, and get innumerable chances of engagements at Chamber Concerts and private houses, not to speak of
lucrative provincial tours with your band. Finally, as member
of a first-class orchestra you can ask good fees for giving lessons.
Having said which, you will understand why, until a year or
two ago, the men's unions, backed by popularity-hunting and
perhaps honestly prejudiced conductors, contrived to keep women
out of their bands—as some do still.

Needless to say, such training as an incipient woman composer
could squeeze out of teaching school children their notes has
never been begrudged her by men. Nor, since God had made
the initial mistake of creating women as well as men, since great
composers have written for mixed voices, and since men unfortunately can't sing soprano (except in Italy, where the Pope's band
takes advantage of a peculiar but time-honoured receipt for getting
round this difficulty),[4] no one tried to stop women singing in
choruses. Moreover choruses are generally voluntary, and in no
case demand the large fees of orchestral players. But alas! chorus
singing and teaching children their scales is not a very advanced
form of 'education.'

In the days when Henry Wood was a free man and had his
own orchestra, he at once set himself to the task of breaking
down the cruel man-erected barrier between us and orchestral
playing; an act of moral courage for which we can never be grateful
enough.[5] I myself have always concentrated on that point, because, belonging to the unfortunate class styled by critics 'lady
composers,' I burned with curiosity as to whither woman's wings

4. Smyth seems to refer here to the practice of employing castrati in the papal
choir, which was, in fact, banned by Pius X in 1903.
5. Wood hired women players into his Queen's Hall Orchestra during World
War I and retained them after the war because of their fine performance record.

will carry her once she is free to soar, and had grasped that here lay the first step towards the liberation of a creative spirit. Few deny that the Brontës and Jane Austen brought a new note into our literature. Why then should not our musical contribution be equally individual and pregnant?—and O I wish I were as sure of heaven as I am that so it will be! . . .

Little by little the doors of this Hall of Initiation began to open, and if there was a good deal of creaking, diversified by a sharp slam now and again worked by those inside, one bore in mind a dictum of Mrs. Pankhurst's to the effect, that if any Government were willing to give the vote only to women with red hair whose name was Eliza, the offer should be jumped at.[6] One was ready to take an instalment; content for the time being if two or three women were to be descried sitting at the last desks of the 2nd violins, and of course on the *inside row* so as not to obstruct the audience's view of the male who shared her desk (also perhaps that his shame might be concealed). But as the season went on (I am speaking of only two or three years ago) a metamorphosis such as we read of in V. Sackville-West's *Orlando* took place, only the other way round.[7] By degrees these female back-benchers turned into men; and as in the 'Orlando' business it seemed impossible to learn how and when and why the change had come about. This, although no one attempts to deny that women players are as efficient as men, and often far keener! Mozart even declared that they have more natural gift for stringed instruments than males; and one reason he gave was their greater delicacy of touch, another the readier access of a conductor to their emotions.

Since the war the female taboo in orchestras has fluctuated like the money market and exhibits equally baffling features. For instance the B.B.C. has plenty of women in its fine band— probably from motives of policy. For in such matters the musical

6. Emmeline Pankhurst was a militant leader in the women's movement in England.
7. Vita Sackville-West provided the inspiration for Woolf's character Orlando in her 1928 novel of the same name. Orlando begins life as a male and then changes to the female sex.

colleges have a say, and apart from the Directors of our two leading educational institutions being conspicuously honourable men, the fee of a female student is as good money as that of a male. Moreover a *quasi* State affair like a Corporation has to avoid 'unpleasantness.'

But here's a strange thing; in that orchestra women 'cellists are banned! Why, I cannot conceive! If it is a question of physical strength I can crush adherents of the brute force school by telling them how Joachim once laughed at me for enquiring if tone depended on muscle. Of course I knew it didn't, but was setting a little trap for him into which he obligingly walked; and when I went on to ask why, if that was so, women were kept out of orchestras (this was in the 'nineties) he stared, and then said slowly: 'Well! I never thought of that point!'

As regards the B.B.C. band, perhaps the *attitude* of the 'cello player is considered an unseemly one for women? The B.B.C. is nothing if not proper, and once men's vicarious sense of modesty gets to work you never know where it will break out next. In my youth they strained at that harmless gnat, a girl on a bicycle; since then they have had to swallow something far worse than camels—horses with girls riding them cross-legged! To-day, engulfed by the rising flood of woman's independence, perhaps they are clinging to the violoncello as the drowning cling to a spar.

In the other London orchestras, the L.S.O. [London Symphony Orchestra], the Philharmonic, and also the Hallé band, whose conductor is that admirable musician and professed anti-feminist Sir Hamilton Harty, not a woman is to be seen, unless occasionally plucking the strings of the 2nd Harp. The harp being a cumbrous and rather unlucrative instrument, woman has been permitted by ancient tradition to play it. Indeed I think her colleagues rather cherish this solitary white-armed presence in their midst, much as the men in the Welch regiment cherish the regimental goat.

In the meantime, our sex being admitted only on sufferance as it were to the outskirts of the musical scene, all the really interesting and educative jobs in our institutions, such as the training of choruses, stage management, conducting, the manipulation of the electric light, etc., etc.—exercising which people

286   WOMEN IN MUSIC

learn the meaning of the word authority and how best to use it—all these jobs, I say, fall automatically into the hands of youthful males. Now and then, favoured by the god of chance, some woman of quite exceptional gifts, an Ellen Terry, or a Lilian Baylis, achieves a commanding position;[8] but Edith Craig, perhaps our greatest producer, has still to explain to casual stage hands who work under her that she really *does* know something about electricity! And it is only in a later section of this study that we may be able to guess how it comes that London managers have not been tearing each other to pieces for years in order to secure the services of this supreme artist, while a Russian producer is over-lord *pro tem.* at Stratford-on-Avon!

.   .   .   .

And now, the most elementary part of this paper, the matter of training, having been dealt with, prepare for a statement which may cause readers to stretch their eyes but which is none the less an incontrovertible fact. Face this truth; that because of what has been our position hitherto in the world of music, *there is not at this present moment (1933) one single middle-aged woman alive who has had the musical education that has fallen to men as a matter of course, without any effort on their part, ever since music was!*

Imagine then our feelings when people whip out their binoculars, sweep the landscape, and announce that so far, strange to say, no advancing army of eminent women composers is to be descried on the horizon. As if a pack of girls who had never handled a golf club nor been permitted to set foot on the links are likely to turn out even *one* Joyce Wethered! And golfers start early, whereas few composers get into their stride much before thirty!

So much for the training of musical maidens who fondly believe they have something worth saying to say, and ask but one thing: a chance of hearing their work in public and finding out whether or no they are harbouring illusions. For until a work is publicly

8. Terry, the noted actress, was also a manager. Baylis was an administrator of the Old Vic Company in the 1930s.

performed, it is impossible even for the composer to form a true judgment on its merit.

Chapter III: Literary and Musical Careers Contrasted

I often think the happiest bit of a composer's life is the moment when, fortified by his instructor's blessing, rich in the faith of his friends, and buoyed up by a secret belief in his own power, he is about to set sail for the first time on what will turn out to be the most treacherous of seas. But before following the fortunes of a musical maiden who has arrived at that moment, I should like to deal with a misleading analogy which is often drawn between the musical and the literary careers.

Most of us have heard friendly commentators remark, that though the liberal education of women is only in its infancy, we have already made a distinct mark in literature. If, then, nothing of the sort seems happening in music, surely it must be owing to some congenital defect in the female brain—some mysterious recalcitrancy to musical creation?

I would like to invite these logicians to begin at the beginning and see what a relatively simple matter it is to become a writer. You can teach yourself to write by reading, by watching life, by taking flights on your own and inflicting the result on such of your friends as have patience and discrimination. Even in the ladylike nineteenth century, nobody could prevent women from writing novels on the sly, as did Jane Austen, the Brontës, Mrs. Gaskell,[9] and others. And mark that nearly all of these thought it wisest to adopt either male or non-committal names. Books on philosophy, astronomy, physics, mathematics, and other so-called 'serious' subjects they of course could not write, having had no opportunity of studying such high matters; and as regards medicine, from the earliest times the Faculty had wisely discouraged competition by causing herb-healing women to be burnt alive as witches. But in novel writing self-expression was possible, and to-day, though all-round emancipation of the female spirit

9. Elizabeth Gaskell.

is only in its initial stages, it has been a comparatively easy matter to consolidate and extend the victories won in the eighteenth and nineteenth centuries, thanks to the divinely simple nature of the machinery of the book trade, and the comfortable *start*, at least, in the world of literature that almost any book can hope to compass. For instance: (1) there is only one person between you and the public, a publisher; (2) book-printing is a relatively cheap matter, hence book publishers are willing to take a risk; (3) by issuing your book you are standing in no one else's way, for in that world there is room for all; (4) if the critics dislike your book, there is nothing to hinder people from ordering it and judging for themselves.

And now observe what difficulties confront even a composer of the favoured sex when it comes to making an effort to get at his public. I will merely indicate them in shorthand: reams upon reams of closely scored, very complicated manuscript, the parts of which have to be drawn out by copyists who, even when not slightly inebriated, are but human, and whose mistakes it takes weeks and weeks to correct. Music engraving is a very costly process, and if your trend happens to be choral writing—an excusable trait surely in Handel's England?—a choral work cannot well be performed at all till it is printed. And unless it achieves what is called a huge success the publisher has no chance of getting his money back.

But I anticipate; before that stage is reached a tyro must cope with the difficulty of awaking the interest of a conductor, and the uncertainty (nowadays) of the outcome of that conductor's interviews on the subject with his Committee—the Committee being a group of thirty or forty gentlemen, mostly tradesmen, who consider themselves musical because year after year they have sung in 'The Messiah' (some not having missed a single performance in forty years); who know that new music doesn't pay, and whose private feeling is that all this damned modern stuff ought to be put down by the police. And seeing that it is among their duties to provide the cost of orchestral rehearsals, the fees of soloists, the hire of halls, the advertising, and so on;

and being well aware the while that as a rule the audience really wants to hear old favourites only, it is not surprising if their abiding instinct is to fight shy of the works of unknown composers.

Given all the lions in the path, I think even laymen must by now grasp how hard it is for a tyro to bring his work and the public together. Nor is there any parallel in any other department of artistic achievement for the tragic fact, that owing to the cost and cumbrousness of the musical machine and the smallness of the English market, it is more than likely that failing the miracle of an overwhelming triumph (a miracle that not even artificial boosting can always secure), a work of very great value, that has cost its creator months and months of labour, may go back, *after one performance*, into the composer's cupboard, practically without a soul outside that concert hall having even heard of its existence!

·   ·   ·   ·   ·   ·   ·

Chapter IV: The Difficulties of Women Musicians

At the outset of this chapter let an appeal be made to all the intelligence, all the large-mindedness of which readers are capable, coupled with a special request to women to fight down the natural bitterness which certain reflections can but raise in one's heart. The only weapons that are of the slightest use in such cases are the above two, coupled with patience and almost unlimited courage; and meanwhile the whirligig of time is on our side.

To me one of the curious facts in life is how slowly things move. Think how long it took the powers that were, including even a shrewd woman like Queen Victoria, to understand that by and by women would have to be reckoned with. In literature, in state-craft, in travel, and, with John Stuart Mill to jog their unwilling attention even in politics observers might have seen what was coming. But they didn't; and when I am inclined to be impatient or unjust about what women are up against in music, it calms and steadies me to think about the golf course at Cromer.

Let me explain. The golf course runs along the beautiful cliffs above the sea, and all that coast is a prey to erosion, so that ages ago it must have been obvious to the meanest intelligence that certain holes were, so to speak, getting nearer and nearer to the cliff edge. But successive Committees clung obstinately to the attractive ideal that Cromer was, and should ever remain, a purely seaside links, and refused to consider the taking in of some flat-lying inland meadows, whereon three or four new and relatively ignoble holes—'Votes for Women Holes' they might have christened them—would have to be laid out.

In the end their minds were made up for them by the North Sea, and this almost in my time. A very old former caddy told me how an uncle of his had been conveying a cart-load of turf along a track on the seaward side of the high-lying fourteenth hole, when cart, horse, and driver suddenly sank out of sight, and, together with a large portion of the cliff, only came to a halt half-way down between the cliff top and the sea. 'Were they all buried?' I asked. 'No,' he said, 'at least not that time; and if you believe it, my uncle just unharnessed the horse and led him home, and there wasn't a scratch on either of them! But,' he added, *they had to shift the fourteenth hole then!*'

Now if this story is as veracious as it is arresting, the incident must have happened, I calculate, about the year 1840, and all that time the cliffs had gone on slipping into the sea, but such was the optimism (shall we call it?) of successive golf committees that the remoulding of the course only took place, so to speak, yesterday. And now you will understand how it comes, that when anger or impatience at the snail-like progress of ideas as regards matters connected with women threaten to take the upper hand, even as in the past certain people used to say to themselves that blessed word 'Mesopotamia,' so do I say to myself, 'The Golf Course at Cromer.'

To take the bull by the horns, the chief difficulty women musicians have to face is that in no walk of life do men like to see us come barging in on their preserves. Every woman who has to work for her living in trades that once were male monopolies knows this, and luckily a good many feel with me that after all it is only natural; consequently that it is as foolish of us to resent the inevitable as it is of men to deny the obvious. But whether we take it philosophically or resentfully, this is the determining factor in the position of Women in Music.

.   .   .   .

To resume. Quite apart from men's natural dislike to seeing women cut a dash on fields hitherto sacred to their own exploits, innocent clannishness plays a great part in this matter, as it does in many others. The present Lord Birkenhead tells us that though his father never made a bad appointment, he was inclined 'to give an immediate preference to a Wadham man, or to a member of the Northern Circuit.' You can't get rid of the colleague element, nor deny that men are nearer to other men than they can ever be to women. I once heard a lady who has the reputation of having loved pretty liberally in her time make a memorable remark. 'Surely,' she murmured, smiling the dreamy, disarming smile of one who has dined extremely well: 'surely it is a *Law of Nature* that the nearest should be the dearest?' Quite so! I quite agree! and an exceptionally honest conductor once told me that nine out of ten of his tribe would rather give a desk in their band to a Grade B male than to a Grade A woman . . . and often did! (One was aware of the fact but liked to hear it confirmed.) Cross-questioned further, he denied ever having gone such lengths himself, 'but between a man and woman player of equal capacity,' he said, 'I should unhesitatingly choose the man!' And if I had expressed to him my private conviction that the majority of conductors would rather produce a boring piece of male music than score a resounding success with a work by a woman, I believe that truth-loving man would have said 'Yes! that is so!' This sort of thing does not simplify a woman's journey towards a musical goal!

When it comes to the Lords of Creation considering the *creative* work of women on a field that has not yet become, willy-nilly, one of their recognised provinces, many other factors besides clannishness come into play; for instance prejudice, including a certain secret disinclination to take an ultra-favourable view; and, more subtle still, until the male eye has been broken in, an honest incapacity to understand what women are driving at. I fancy that on the whole this is what the authors of '1066 and All That' would call *a good thing*, proving the present writer's eternal contention that the male and female brains being differently constructed, an important contribution by a woman ought to be on every field a *new* contribution, an element necessary to an all-round vision of things human. I once heard Lord Robert Cecil, as he then was, elaborate this idea with relation to legal matters, and add 'that's why I am so keen on woman suffrage.'

These darkeners of counsel, clannishness, prejudice, subconscious *a priori* inclination not to think very highly of a woman's work, and, lastly, a natural difficulty in focussing it correctly, play in and out over the whole field of women's fortunes in music, and can be sorted out and applied as the reader pleases to incidents that will turn up in the further course of this study. And once more be it said (since this is the all-important point and so very few people seem capable of grasping it) that if this male recalcitrancy takes time to wear down in all departments of female activity (Mrs. Swynnerton had to wait for her R.A. till she was over seventy!) it is absolutely devastating on the field of music: because the machine is cumbrous, costly, and complicated; because it is entirely in the hands of *groups of men*, not of isolated individuals, as in the book publishing business; and finally for the reason that if put in motion for a woman, it is for the time being unavailable for fifteen furious male composers who are on the waiting list!

Among quotable incidents take the following—a curious one mentioned in my Autobiography.

Years ago that great Wagner paladin, Hermann Levi, referring to the work of a girl of his acquaintance remarked: 'It is almost impossible to believe it is by a woman!' And I, knowing that the composer had left Munich, and that her score was to be sent after her that very night, said, 'Yes! and in a week's time you *won't* believe it!' Levi stared at me . . . saw my point, and said slowly: 'By heaven! it's quite possible!' Now such a posthumous doubt could not have risen up out of the floor and automatically unsettled a judicial mind had the composer been a young man.

If I repeat this story, which I will call for reference 'the Levi incident,' it is because if a man of notoriously noble character (see various lives of Wagner) and superb musicianship can be assailed by 'posthumous' doubts concerning a work which had bowled him over—doubts born of the hard fact that up to then no first-rate women composers had darkened the pages of history—surely other men need not be affronted if one imputes to them a like mentality, more especially in these days of industrialised music?

Levi was a German, a Jew (that is an idealist), and also a man of exceptional honesty and brain power, so after that remark of his we discussed the whole matter; and he agreed with me that it requires great detachment, great independence of thought, and a degree of insight that almost amounts to genius for one of the musical faculty to *see* a woman's work at all until the psychological moment has arrived; that is, until, as eventually happened in literature, prejudice has been broken down, twig after twig, by ever-recurring evidence to the worth of something one thought negligible simply because, as it says in the Bible, one's eyes were not opened.

Chapter V: Further Difficulties for Women

My fundamental proposition was that given the lines on which music is run in this England of ours—a country which in some ways has more, and in others less, sense of chivalry and fair play than any other country in Europe—women are practically outside the pale of musical civilisation. This can easily be proved, but as some of the proofs are autobiographical and will be dealt with (sparingly) in another chapter, will the reader assume, just for the sake of argument, that things are as I say, and quietly consider the impossibility of getting rid of inherited pariahdom in England thanks to a matter so irrelevant as your calibre as artist.

Note for instance how differently the Press reacts in the case of men and of women. Once I had grasped that it would take all one's courage to keep going at all, I gave up reading Press notices. 'Why court depression needlessly?' I said to myself (and say it even to-day both to myself and others), 'don't think about it at all.' Hence for aught I know reviewers are not more unsympathetic to our work than they are to men's. But the reaction on the composer's future is different. If you are going *with* the stream, as men do, and barge up against an obstacle, very often the impact will shoot you right out into the current and actually help you on your way. But if you are swimming *against* the stream, which is the privilege of the female, such an impact can but send you spinning back . . . back . . . yards and yards in the wrong direction.

One of the greatest spiritual difficulties we have to contend with, the responsibility for which lies mainly with the elementary condition of musical culture in England, is the extreme isolation of the woman composer, an isolation none save those who have endured it can imagine. Any on-coming young fellow, be his music ever so hideous, or on the other hand ever so obviously of the flash-in-the-pan order, can count on a bodyguard of enthusiastic contemporaries. Of course the less momentum there is in a stream, the more inevitable are silly little backwaters of clique and sex-uppishness, and it goes without saying that on a talented girl composer the backwater frequenters will turn an indifferent, a patronising, and perhaps an inimical gaze.

.   .   .   .

My point is this. The hatred and enmity excited by every great innovating genius is one thing; this damping down *on principle* of feminine efforts is another. Great innovating geniuses are few and far between, but there are plenty of composers who earn a nice little income and give a good deal of pleasure. It is this possibility that is denied to women; for among the consequences of exclusion from the ranks of the performed are: no royalties, no performing fees; unwillingness of publishers to act for you (which means you pay for your own MS. if you can afford it, and forgo all chance of getting known even at home, let alone abroad); resultant unwillingness of gramophone companies to make records of works that are never performed, and so on and so on.

And there is a worse consequence than all this. To quote my own remark made elsewhere, you cannot get giants like Mt. Blanc and Mt. Everest without the mass of moderate-sized mountains on whose shoulders they stand. It is the upbuilding of this platform that is impossible so long as full music life is denied to women, and I suppose it is unnecessary to say that conductors and Committees are generally of one mind about keeping us out of Parnassus, Committees being, as I have hinted, the most hidebound bodies on earth. (I am talking of London and the big choral and orchestral forces at places like Sheffield, Liverpool, etc., and have not forgotten the splendid pioneer work for women composers done by people like Sir Dan Godfrey and other conductors of small but admirable municipal bands.)

'But,' I hear an objector say, 'those conductors whose field of action is in London, or in one of those big northern music centres you speak of . . . do you really mean to tell me that men like A. or B. could not put through anything they choose?'

A few years ago, yes; but things have changed a good deal, and the day is past when a conductor was able and willing to override his Committee. The competition is great, his seat in the saddle less secure, perhaps, than people imagine, and by performing a woman's work he cuts no ice. Now if a man is going to make himself a nuisance to his masters, it will either be for something he is passionately interested in, or something to produce which will bring him *Kudos*—an end he will therefore pursue with so much energy that opposition wilts. I have so far not met a single English conductor who would feel or act thus for the work of a woman. It is not in the breed. Such a thing could have happened in the past in Germany where music used to be religion, but not here where it is more than half business. Indeed the only case of passion I know of is Sir Thomas Beecham's stand for Delius, and Sir Thomas being a man of genius, rich, and with rich backers, he can put things through. And then there is Donald Tovey; but he has educated his public and his orchestra up to his own high level, so the question of suffering for his faith may perhaps not arise.

As for the ordinary conductor, lacking passionate conviction, can you wonder if in the case of a woman's work he recalls the proverb about driving a nail where it will go, and gets sick of vain hammerings that make his wrist ache? Whereupon follows what I called a 'Levi incident.' If only to excuse himself for luke-warm advocacy, he reverts to what is still a natural male instinct, slips off the spectacles that made him consider this a fine work which ought to be produced, shrugs his shoulders and pitches the opus on to the pile of rejected MSS.; with a sigh perhaps, but rather a perfunctory one.

Of all this the public knows nothing, and mildly says from time to time: 'Strange that there are no great women composers!'

47   CARL E. SEASHORE: "WHY NO GREAT WOMEN COMPOSERS?"

The "woman composer question" cast a long shadow. While Ethel Smyth, in Female Pipings in Eden *of 1933 (Reading 46), decries the "general damping down on principle on feminine efforts" that she feels prevailed for composers of her generation, declarations about the innate inferiority of women as composers persisted, despite the activity of notable women. Psychologist Carl E. Seashore's essay* Why No Great Women Composers? *is included here as an example of a negative assessment of women's creativity from the mid-century period.[1] Seashore's approach is modernized over that of George Upton and others, reflecting the improved status of women through time. Women are considered by Seashore to be equal to men in talent, intelligence, and education for composition; they do not create, however, because they are by nature passive.*

How many names of women composers have appeared on programs of great and lasting music? Their absence is conspicuous. David Ewen in his recent volume, *Twentieth Century Composers*, presents biographies of seventeen of the world's outstanding composers of the last century, and among these there is not one woman. Claire Reis, in the 1932 edition of *Composers in America*, sketches the lives of 200 composers who have written "in the larger form" and of these only 5.5 per cent are women. The same author gives a supplementary list of 274 composers, presumably of the second order; of these, 11 per cent are women.

Carl E. Seashore, "Why No Great Women Composers?," *Music Educators Journal* 25/5 (March 1940): 21, 88. Reprinted by permission of the journal.

1. Seashore reprinted the essay in his 1948 collection entitled *In Search of the Beautiful in Music* (New York: Ronald Press).

Many explanations of this disparity have been offered and argued vigorously. There is no single or simple explanation that holds universally; history, science, sociology, anthropology, and the arts are involved. The problem is, however, fundamentally a psychological one and calls for analysis, although as a psychologist I cannot offer a full or authoritative explanation. Let me list without elaboration some of the issues involved, proceeding by a process of elimination.

Native Talent

Great composers must be born with musical talent. Nature is prolific in this respect, but individuals, society, and environment are wasteful with such resources. It is only rarely that such seed which nature has implanted comes to full fruition in creative music. Indeed such fruition is especially rare among women. But from all evidence now available it appears that boys and girls inherit musical talent in approximately the same degree, of the same kind, and equally diversified. Therefore, we cannot attribute differences in the inheritance of musical talent to the sex difference.

Intelligence

Of all musical pursuits, composition demands the highest order of intelligence—both native capacity and cultivated power. This intelligence is fundamentally of the same order as scientific, philosophical, or esthetic intelligence in general, but its content is dominantly musical. Given artistic talent and a musical constitution, a good general intelligence may become a great musical intelligence. Girls tend to average better than boys in public school subjects. While inheritance may be developed in diversified types, present evidence indicates that boys and girls are approximately equal in this endowment. Therefore, the explanation cannot lie in the lack of native resources for musical intelligence.

Musical Temperament

Great composers are born with certain mental and nervous, often psychotic and neurotic, dispositions which, when cultivated, take on marked forms of artistic license, sometimes beneficent, sometimes noxious. To favor creative work, the composer must cultivate the beneficent aspect of temperament. It is now generally recognized that artistic temperaments—the musical in particular—are inherited approximately in the same way and to the same extent by boys and girls. Women therefore cannot find an alibi in the supposed lack of this endowment.

Creative Imagination

Composition is an act of invention or creative imagination on a large scale and in diverse forms. It is admitted that women have rich and free imagination, but it is said to be of a less sustained order, while men's achievement in creative work is often attributed to greater native capacity for creative power. For this there is no clear support in genetics. The difference is probably due to environmental influences and should not be attributed to heredity.

Musical Precocity

The great composers as a rule have been precocious, often musical prodigies. Countless potential musical prodigies have been born, probably boys and girls in equal number, but only the "ships that come in" count for much in history and tradition. Since the great musicians as a rule have been men, memories and records of their childhood tend to live. The girl prodigies are forgotten.

Education

Composition in the larger forms demands a high and intensive order of education. But most of the great composers have been self-educated, often, especially at the higher levels, in the face of most adverse circumstances. The power of genius for outstanding achievement cannot be taught. Teachers of great composers take but little credit for their prodigies. Throughout modern history music has been considered a feminine accomplishment. Many more girls than boys study music. As compared with the useful arts, the fine arts have for the most part been a realm open to women. Musical environment, criticism, and admirers are among the most formative musical influences. These have been equally available for women and for men.

Recent Emancipation of Women

It is often said that until recently women have not had a chance; that they have not been free; that modern women will come to the front in this field. Yet, in the Victorian period and later, women were the influential patronesses and promoters of music. They were in search of genius wherever it could be found. The salon was open to men and women on equal terms, and the outcropping of genius is above social considerations. Will the emancipated woman who smokes, dons mannish attire and manners; takes marital obligations lightly, is athletic and competes freely with men in business, politics, and professions, pave the way for great composers?

Marriage

In the graduate school I have observed that when a woman of marked achievement and fine personality is invested with the doctor's hood, there is a young man around the corner: we hear the wedding march, love's goal is reached, and the promising Ph.D. settles down and gets fat. We find no fault with that; but to the career-minded woman, it is often a tragedy. Yet it need not be and should offer no true alibi. The bearing of one or more children should add to normal development of a woman, and marriage under favorable circumstances occasionally brings to the wife more freedom for self-expression in achievement than the husband—the breadwinner—enjoys. A woman skilled in music is, as a rule, especially admired and sought in marriage; and marriage, as a career in itself, then invites music as an avocation and not as a fierce, all-demanding, time-consuming goal of composition. Seldom is either the husband or the woman willing to make marriage the secondary career. Married women may not have produced great compositions, but they have produced great composers.

Endurance

The achievements of great geniuses came from work, work, work, according to Edison. It often involves excessive, even pathological strain. When we speak of the male as the stronger sex, we usually refer to muscular strength. The passionate intellectual and emotional drain and suffering undergone by the great composers is of a different order. Women can bear, suffer, and sacrifice in such respects fully as much as men.

Summing up the above observations, we may say that the real explanation for the absence of women from the higher fields of achievement in creative music does not lie in any form of limitation by heredity, nor does it lie to any great extent in present limitations of opportunity, environment, or woman's peculiar obligations. Woman is born with many distinctive feminine traits, but it is doubtful if we shall find any of these of critical significance in the present issue. Environmental factors of all sorts often determine types of development and achievement, but each of these may be laid to some other and more fundamental cause.

Theories of Urges

Woman's fundamental urge is to be beautiful, loved, and adored as a person; man's urge is to provide and achieve in a career. There are exceptions; but from these two theories arise the countless forms of differential selection in the choice and pursuit of a goal for life. Education, environment, motivation, obligations, and utilization of resources, often regarded as determinants in themselves, are but incidental modes for the outcropping of these two distinctive male and female urges. They make the eternal feminine and the persistent masculine type. It is the goal that accounts for the difference. Men and women both have their choice and both can take pride in their achievements.

Three Composers

48   RUTH CRAWFORD-SEEGER

When Ruth Crawford-Seeger (1901–53) wrote this letter to Nicolas Slonimsky early in 1933, shortly after her marriage to Charles Seeger, she was at the threshold of a major career, an acknowledged member of the American avant-garde. Crawford-Seeger was eagerly awaiting the premiere of her String Quartet (1931), and she anticipated returning to sketches for two orchestral works she had begun in Paris during her year abroad on a Guggenheim fellowship—the first ever awarded to a woman in composition. Despite this highly promising start, Crawford-Seeger abandoned composition in the same year, with the birth of the first of her four children. The possible reasons for this move will be discussed, but first consider Crawford-Seeger's description for Slonimsky of her formative years.

294½ West 13th Street
New York City
January 29, 1933

Dear Nicolas Slonimsky:

How nice you want to write me up in the [*Boston Evening*] *Transcript.*[1] I have thus far not been much good when it comes to giving autobiographical data, even for such an inviting prospect. I usually get no further than a few bare facts. But I'll see if I can help you out less barely than usual.

My father was a minister (Methodist) with a fine sense of humor; he was of Scotch-Irish-English ancestry, and was born in a cabin off in the hills of West Virginia, the oldest of six

---

Letter from Ruth Crawford-Seeger to Nicolas Slonimsky, January 29, 1933, Ruth Crawford-Seeger Collection, Music Division, Library of Congress. Used by permission of Michael Seeger.

 1. The editor was unable to determine whether the article was published.

children. My mother, youngest of six, was born in Illinois, of New England parents of English ancestry who had gone west from their Vermont homes during the 1840s. (Her father was also a Methodist minister.) I was brought up till I was twelve in Ohio, Indiana, Missouri, and Florida parsonages; after my father's death we stayed on in Florida. I had had lessons in piano since my sixth birthday, but until I was sixteen or seventeen [. . .] (I at this time worked with a very fine and beloved, but much feared, Leipzig-trained Norwegian teacher, [Madame] Valborg Collett.) From seventeen till twenty I taught piano at the School of Musical Art in Jacksonville, Florida (my home since twelve); then at twenty it was made possible for me to achieve Chicago with enough money for one year's study in my pocket. Till then I had never, with the exception of a concert by a travelling chamber music group, heard any ensemble music—not even string quartets, to say nothing of symphony orchestras. I knew, and had heard of, piano music only—and songs. My concert experience consisted of one concert each of [Percy] Grainger, Paderewski, and [Josef] Hofmann. I had written a few little bits of piano music, and had four dry lessons from [George W.] Chadwick's harmony book.

Sprinkling sevenths and ninths plentifully and insistently, and observing or breaking the solemn rules of harmony with equal regularity, I was guided with great understanding during the next years by Adolf Weidig of the American Conservatory in Chicago, who seems to me to have had an unusual balance between necessary discipline and necessary allowance for individuality. The two years following my first financially free year, I made my way by ushering and checking coats in the "Loop" theaters of Chicago; after that, by teaching. Contact in 1925 with Djane Lavoie-Herz, with whom I studied piano, and with Dane Rudhyar, and later with Henry Cowell, established a definite turning point in my work, and enabled me to see far along the way toward which, in my student compositions, I had been groping. I discovered Scriabin at this time; the music of Schönberg and Hindemith I did not hear until later; Stravinsky's *Sacre* and *L'Oiseau de Feu* came to me too about this time. During practically all my years in Chicago, my weekly and often bi-weekly climbs to the top gallery of Orchestra Hall (my plan in the hearing of the same program on consecutive days called for score reading at one performance and absence of score at the other) continued; and for further saturation in the orchestral manner I adorned also the percussion section of the Civic Orchestra for part of a season, counting, not too successfully, measures by the hundred behind a triangle. During these years I was, of course, teaching piano and harmony, and doing most of my composing at nights and on Sundays.

In 1929 came an invitation from Mrs. [Blanche] Walton for a year in New York; I accepted with alacrity. The summer was spent at the MacDowell Colony in Peterboro [New Hampshire], then to New York. Then too to the second and still more vital turning point—a year's study with Charles Seeger in New York, who shared with me his conception of the innumerable aspects and yet untried possibilities, both in form and content, of a new music, and his views as to various means of bringing some organic coordination out of the too often chaotic superabundance of materials in use at present. As a result of this study, my work began at last to take a "handleable" shape, to present itself in some sort of intelligible continuity. The Guggenheim Fellowship came to me in the spring of this year (1930), and I sailed for Berlin in August.

In Europe I studied with no one, composed assiduously with interspersed periods of idleness, during which I investigated a few museums and many winding streets (of which America has all too few) and a considerable number of concert halls (though I gave these up almost entirely after a few months' experiment, becoming discouraged by the programs usually given). I am sure that the work I did during this time was by far the best I had done—a fact which I attribute not so much to Europe itself (though the experience abroad was invaluable to me in a general sort of way) as to the financial freedom to work, and to the natural course of my growth. I spent seven months in Berlin; a too-short while in Vienna, where I had the pleasure of long talks with Berg, [Egon] Wellesz, and [Josef] Hauer; and then to Budapest to gain some idea through talks with the young group of

Ruth Crawford-Seeger.

the trends in new music there; then to Munich for a week's festival of new music; and the rest of the time in Paris. My *Chants for Women's Chorus*[2] were the first work[s] completed in Berlin; a quartet (to be played on March 6th at the Pan Americans) was written partly in Berlin and partly in Paris; "In Tall Grass" was written in Berlin, and "Prayers of Steel" later in New York. Other smaller works were written in Berlin also.

From the new music which I heard in Europe I brought back two lasting impressions: the greater, *Wozzeck* of Berg, which I felt to be the most towering of a very few master works in Europe today (or are there any others at all?); the lesser, that of a choral work with orchestra by Werner Egk of Munich, which contained for me great virility and sensitiveness.

The rest of my history you know. Since returning to New York I have busied myself with the orchestral ostinati superimpositions to the two songs you know, and the composition of the third one you don't know; to the unspeakable and exacting copying of these for photographic publication, and the copying of numerous other things, the quartet included. (What is the ratio of a composer's hours of copying to his minutes of composing?) As soon as I finish some songs for soprano which have recently been asked for, I hope to get at the sketches for two orchestral pieces begun in Paris—they have waited long enough through this siege of copying.

And of course—my marriage (October 1932). That is more important than all these two pages put together.

. . . Thanks for the suggestion about a new work for percussion and string quartet! I'd have done it if I hadn't this one, which I am extremely anxious to hear.

Ruth Crawford

Raising four children, who were born between 1933 and 1944, certainly must have made great demands on Ruth Crawford-Seeger's energy and precluded the possibility of large blocks of time for composition. Nevertheless, there were other factors that

2. Crawford-Seeger wrote three chants. The two utilizing women's chorus have not yet been published.

seem to have influenced her cessation as a composer. The eco-
nomic realities of the Depression were especially hard on the
avant-garde, and then in 1935 Crawford-Seeger left the new-mu-
sic circles of New York, relocating with her family in the Wash-
ington, D.C., area. Once in Washington she combined her need
to contribute to the family income and her developing interest
in folk music by transcribing field recordings of American folk
songs from archives at the Library of Congress and publishing
many of the songs. With the general interest in American folk-
lore during the Depression, her work thus allowed her to make
a connection between music and the current economic-political
life.

The 1948 letter from Crawford-Seeger to Varèse that follows
includes one of the numerous mentions she made about return-
ing to classical composition and provides insight into her hetic
schedule as well as to the value she accorded her transcription
work. She did resume composition with her Suite for Wind Quin-
tet, which in 1952 won first prize in a competition sponsored
by the Washington, D.C., chapter of the National Association
for American Composers and Conductors. Shortly thereafter she
was stricken with cancer and died untimely in 1953, at the
age of fifty-two.

> May 29, 1948
> 7 West Kirke Street
> Chevy Chase 15
> Maryland

Dear Edgard Varèse:

Your first letter saying you wanted to include me in your course at Columbia was dated January 8. I ought to wait ten more days to make it exactly five months. I hope my lateness has not inconvenienced you too greatly. It seems that everything has combined to make this spring full. Teaching at two schools, plus a full private-teaching schedule (including an 8 till 6 Saturday), plus

Letter from Ruth Crawford-Seeger to Edgard Varèse, May 29, 1948, Ruth Crawford-Seeger Collection, Music Division, Library of Congress. Used by permission of Michael Seeger.

work on a book which is coming out this fall, plus proof on the Lomax book which came out this spring, plus four healthy children-and-a-house, have combined to emphasize my natural indolence as to letter writing.

One reason I have been late in answering is, that you asked for a kind of "credo." I found that a little hard, for I am still not sure whether the road I have been following the last dozen years is a main road or a detour. I have begun to feel, the past year or two, that it is the latter—a detour, but a very important one to me, during which I have descended from stratosphere onto a solid well-traveled highway, folded my wings and breathed good friendly dust as I travelled along in and out of the thousands of fine traditional folktunes which I have been hearing and singing and transcribing from field-recordings, for books and for pleasure. Until a year or so ago I had felt so at home among this (to me) new found music that I thought maybe this was what I wanted most. I listened to nothing else, and felt somewhat like a ghost when my compositions were spoken of. I answered no letters pertaining to them; requests for scores and biographical data were struck in drawers. There were, of course, occasional periods during which I returned to composition, as for instance when CBS wanted works for orchestra utilizing folk material for performance on the "School of the Air." Charlie and I were among those commissioned, and his *John Henry* and my *Rissolty Rossoltry* were performed there in 1941. But for years the only instrument in the house was a guitar, a modern dulcimer, and a special slow-speed phonograph for transcription of folk recordings.

Whether I ever unfold the wings and make a start toward the stratosphere and how much of the dust of the road will still cling to me, is an interesting question, at least to me. If I do, I will probably pull the road up with me.

As for a "credo" typifying my music of the type of [the] String Quartet (1931) and Three Songs for Contralto and Orchestra, which ISCM[3] chose for [the] Amsterdam festival back in 1933, I could mention a few points about which I felt strongly. And

3. International Society for Contemporary Music.

I still feel strongly about them. I believe when I write more music these elements will be there, or at least striven for:

Clarity of melodic line
Avoidance of rhythmic stickiness
Rhythmic independence between parts
Feeling of tonal and rhythmic center
Experiment with various means of obtaining, at the same time, organic unity and various sorts of dissonance.

As to works which I consider most representative, I am inclined to choose the String Quartet (1931). It is the slow movement of this quartet which was recorded on New Music Recordings, a copy of which Mrs. Varèse says you have. I am sending the score of this quartet, with the third and fourth movements analyzed as to tone, rhythm, form, and dynamics. I would like to mention that the recording was made at rather short notice, and that therefore the counterpoint of the crescendos, mentioned in the analysis, is not well heard on the recording.

A few of the things Charlie and I have been doing since 1935 may be of interest as a backdrop. We have four children, said by our friends to have both charm and good looks, born in 1933, '35, '37, and '44: Michael, Peggy, Barbara, and Penelope. When Barbara went to co-operative nursery school in 1941 I went with her, and a book, *American Folk Songs for Children*, grew out of the experience (to come out this fall, Doubleday). Previous to this I worked as music editor on the Lomax *Our Singing Country*, which involved transcription to musical notation of several hundred traditional songs, and the listening to many hundred more in [the] process of choosing these for publication. In connection with this I worked on a sixty-page treatise on the music of these songs, [which was] never quite finished nor published. This work really grew out of Charlie's activities as technical advisor in the Special Skills Division of the Resettlement Administration, and our close acquaintance with the music we heard everywhere during our travels among and to and from the resettlement colonies.

We have acted as consultants for several publishing houses,

in American folk music for children. I also planned and chose the music for the State Department for a series of radio broadcasts, "Music in American Life." Last summer Charlie and I, with Dr. Emrich of the Archive of American Folklore, Library of Congress, completed a book of 900 American traditional songs, to be published by Dial Press; half of them we transcribed from field recordings. And this spring another Lomax book, *Folksong: USA*, was published by Duell Sloan Pearce, with 111 accompaniments by us.

Charlie joins me in warm good wishes from us both. Perhaps next time I come to New York I can know far enough in advance to be less spontaneous in getting in touch with you.

Cordially,
Ruth Crawford-Seeger

49   ELISABETH LUTYENS

The English composer Elizabeth Lutyens (b. 1908) has been radical and prolific, cultivating all genres and many different media. In the 1930s she developed her own dodecaphonic procedures based on her study of Purcell's fantasias, before she had any contact with the works of Schönberg and Webern. Serial writing was looked upon with disfavor in England through the 1950s, however, and as a result Lutyens' music was neglected for many years. In order to survive financially and provide for her four children in this period, Lutyens wrote a good deal for film and radio. The last twenty years have brought recognition, including many commissions.

In the first of the four selections from her autobiography presented in this reading, Lutyens recalls her growing commitment to music at about age fifteen. Her father was the celebrated English architect Sir Edwin Lutyens, and her mother, Lady Edith Lytton, was active in the Theosophical Society. Her sisters and brother, who also figure in the excerpts, are Barbara, Ursula, Mary, and Robert.

My absorption in music was growing, involving a struggle to gain the family's and especially Mother's recognition of its importance to me as compared to other, earlier, passing phases of the engine-driver genre. It was not so much a struggle against opposition as against apathy, not being taken seriously, and ridicule, so painful to the young. It was my effort to prove that music for me was not just a phase but my profession, that gives significance to these years.

Elisabeth Lutyens, *A Goldfish Bowl* (London: Cassell, 1972), pp. 16–19, 59–62, 225, 267–68. Used by permission of the publisher.

I do not know who had first introduced Marie Motto, the violinist, to my mother. She had apparently been teaching Robert the
violin for some years but only now in 1921 were his interest in
and gift for music, of which I had hardly been aware, used to
demonstrate to me my lack of talent and the foolishness of my
ambition. Undeterred, I now studied the piano, wrote secret compositions and took violin lessons with Miss Motto.

Marie Motto was of Italian parentage, a fine violinist and pupil
of [Enrique] Arbós. She also had her own string quartet, in which
Frank Bridge was at one time the viola player, and it was from
her quartet concerts, given mostly at friends' houses, that I first
heard, learnt and loved the string quartet repertoire.

She was living in Scarsdale Villas, where I went for my lessons.
I think she must have been terribly poor, but in her case poverty
took the form of great austerity. The contents of her room, of
which she was obviously proud, consisted, at least in my memory,
only of a grand piano, a beautifully polished table on which was
a bowl of fruit, and a wooden violin stand. Conscious good taste,
achieved by the minimum of everything, but that minimum exquisite in its simplicity. It produced the restful effect of a monk's
cell. She was an ardent Roman Catholic but used no proselytism
on me. She designed her own rather eccentric clothes of the black
cape variety, which became her. She had a mostly beautiful face
and a short plump body.

Learning the violin was a slow, salutary process for which I
remain unforgettably grateful. There was none of the hurried,
superficial get-on-quick careerism of the jungle musical world
of today. Every lesson was as quiet and difficult as a prayer.

However quiet and austere the room and lessons, and however
embryonic I remained as a student, the impact of the music I
was now hearing for the first time was violent and exciting, as
this extract from a letter to my mother shows:

On Friday night Nannie and I went to the last of Miss Motto's concerts.
This is about the third time I have gone in Robert's place and I always
feel that Miss Motto resents my going when she loves Robert so. However,
it was *so* wonderful that I care not—not exactly true—what she

thought. I nearly burst I adored it so, especially the Schubert quintet which so thrilled me with joy-madness that I nearly burst my stays.

What student of fifteen would now go to a concert in a private house protected by a Nannie and stays? But, as Harry Graham says, 'It's better to have stayed too long than never to have worn stays at all.'

Marie Motto introduced me to the friend she had made whilst a student at the Royal College of Music, a pianist, Polyxena Fletcher, with whom she advised me to study the piano.

Polyxena Fletcher was the daughter of a German mother, a professional pianist and pupil of Clara Schumann, and a father who had been a violinist. She herself had been a pupil of [Theodor] Leschetizky. She was a very strange character and my first impression was of a weird, grey, spinsterish figure, grey hair, grey dress, in a grey room. Her face was of a peculiar yellowish hue from which a prominent aquiline nose loomed as a sort of antenna. She had an amused and rather malicious twinkle in her black eyes, and in many ways resembled a witch. She also, in spite of a pathological fussiness about tidiness in her room and person, exuded a peculiar and very strong musty smell, as of something kept too long in a box. She had a tremendous and easily provoked sense of humour in strong contrast to Marie Motto's prim and self-conscious 'artistic' behaviour. She was intensely volatile in mood which was expressed in her mobile face. One moment she would be leeringly giggling at something and the next, at a turn of the conversation to music, or the beauty of some work or performance, tears would stream unheeded down her yellow face.

Her playing was a revelation to me and I don't know why she had retired from the concert world. I have no idea of her age at this time, but to my extreme youth she seemed an old woman like Mother. But, oh the difference! She was passionately interested in all the things to which Mother and the family seemed totally indifferent, though it was to Mother, as usual, that I wrote this adolescent effusion:

Oh, Mummy darling I'm so happy in my music. I love it oh, oh, so much. It is both thrilling and interesting, so much so that I sometimes

feel as if I'll burst or something and I feel that at last I've found happiness
in myself, that whether I live here or there with this person or that I
shall be happy.

Polyxena Fletcher had genius, compared to Marie Motto's talent, and became the greatest single influence in my life. Music,
life and people were inseparable to her, and our lessons, which
lasted hours and seemed timeless, were occupied as much with
talk and discussion as piano playing. When the talk was of music
it was from the widest and most all-embracing point of view and
she became to me the yardstick by which to measure all my
new intellectual and musical experiences and values of life.

At this time, though I composed in secret I wanted most to
be a pianist and would practise for hours a day, to the exasperation
of the family and disapproval of Nannie, who thought it 'unlady-
like' to work so hard. Alas, it was to no avail, for no amount of
work has enabled me to play the piano better than a typist using
one finger.

It was to Miss Fletcher that I showed my two books of early
compositions and when she discovered my interest in composing
she started to teach me harmony. I have only a vague remembrance
of how she went about it, except for a correction of some exercise
where she wrote, 'trap fallen into.'

I now started attending the Proms[1] and Queen's Hall concerts
whenever I could. I was always accompanied by Annie, who had
been our nursery maid and stayed with us until Ursula's marriage
to Matt Ridley (Viscount Ridley), when she followed her as a
lady's maid. She was very musical; a fluent pianist who accompanied my violin playing and played for our children's parties and
later thés-dansants. She had inherited her talent, which she had
not had the opportunity to develop, from her father, who had
been a clarinettist in the Guards' Band.

Standing with Annie on many nights at the Proms, I had my
first experience of orchestral music, the classical repertoire and
the exciting flavour of the new music from France—Debussy and

1. The famous Promenade Concerts, which Henry Wood gave with his Queen's
Hall Orchestra.

Ravel—that was just beginning to filter through the fog of English programmes. More and more the desire possessed me to go to Paris to study music professionally, and from then on I started badgering Mother for the necessary permission. She was, understandably, reluctant to let me give up general education and wanted me to wait until I was eighteen and then go to be 'finished.'

I was adamant. I wanted to go then, at sixteen, and to study seriously. I even went the length of practising the violin in the early morning, well in earshot of her bedroom. I had my way at last.

The only condition was that I stay with Marcelle de Manziarly, a daughter of a Theosophical friend of Mother's. Our families had already spent some holidays together and I had conceived a great admiration for Mar, who was an excellent pianist and talented composer. I therefore jumped at the idea and in the New Year after my sixteenth birthday, I went to Paris to share Mar's flat and study at the École Normale. This was the beginning of my own life in my own world.

Although Lutyens has withdrawn all of her music written before 1937 because of its Romantic leanings, her account of her first major performance in 1932 remains worthy of consideration because it attests so well to the importance of such an event for the aspiring composer. The work performed was her ballet The Birthday of the Infanta, *based on Oscar Wilde's story of the same name. The program included two other contemporary works: Constant Lambert's* Adam and Eve *and a ballet based on a score by Frank Bridge.*

In 1932 I had the most important opportunity and experience of my budding professional career. The score of my ballet, *The Birthday of the Infanta*, was suggested by Penelope Spencer, who had choreographed it for her ballet class at [the Royal Musical] College, when offered a production by the Camargo Society, precursor of the Royal Ballet. I was introduced, for the first time, to the goldfish bowl of the ballet world; 'Darling, aren't you a *tiny* bit too old for Giselle?'

Now my first and only conflict with Father arose. *After* the choice of my ballet had been made, Maynard Keynes (husband of Lydia Lopokova, star of the Diaghilev Ballets Russes and an influential member of the Camargo Society) approached Father, at the club, and asked him to contribute £100 towards mounting my work. I was quite adamant in refusing to allow him to do this, knowing that my name would be mud amongst my musical colleagues. It was going to be quite difficult enough to make good as a composer, being a woman and daughter of a famous man and titled mother. Lopokova was furious with me, telling me that *she* had accepted help from her brother. This argument didn't move me. It was harder to stick to my guns when I found to my surprise that Father, who I had thought would be pleased at not having to cough up £100, was cross with me too. Maynard Keynes was a very influential man, especially in Cambridge where Father had many commissions. After all his kindness and generosity I hated crossing Father but it appeared to me then as if my whole professional life was at stake. I offered to help raise funds for the Camargo Society in any other way but this. I did help by introducing them to Rex Whistler, a friend of Barbie's and now mine, who offered to do the décor and costumes for my ballet—his *first* stage work—for free.

Then came a rather difficult lunch to be lived through with Lopokova still pressurizing me and Constant Lambert, the musical director, who had to pass as well as conduct the score. I had only met Constant once before—beautiful and disdainful—coming from the library at College, where he had been searching for the original—*not* the Rimsky-Korsakov—edition of *Boris Godunov*. I disliked him as heartily at this lunch as I was beginning to dislike the once so adored Lopokova. He was extremely arrogant and patronizing for someone only a year older than myself, proclaiming, didactically, that the *only* ballet requiring a chorus was the *Rio Grande*.[2] (Never having expected my ballet to be performed, still less staged, I had used chorus, large orchestra—the lot!) First impressions can be misleading; Constant became

2. Lambert's ballet of 1927.

one of the very best friends I ever had and the musical world shrank for me at his death.

Rex came up with splendid ideas and beautiful sketches for the ballet, but he had at that time no experience of materials, so that the dresses of the Infanta and her ladies, which should have been on hoops or, at least in buckram, hung flat in limp sateen. Of course, there was a shortage of money. My friends and I were helping Rex with the painting of the scenery up till the last moment. One of Rex's designs [Tamara] Karsavina refused to accept. For the dance of the Funambulist (a tightrope-dancer) he had drawn a nun holding an umbrella, precariously poised. This shocked her. In the event, the dance was disastrously reconceived to suit Eve, a contortionist from a Cochran revue, who was available and might be a draw. Wendy Toye, aged fifteen, was the Infanta and Hedley Briggs, the Dwarf. Being young and a tyro in the theatre, I listened to all opinions; changing the score, inserting new dances, or whatever was required of me. But they were all wrong. I should have stuck to my original dramatic conception. It was a poor score, now scrapped and forgotten, but not forgotten is the experience gained. I am grateful to Lopokova for her decision—without consulting me, of course—that I was to be 'Elisabeth.' To the family I was always Betty (a name I detest). I had tried, for a spell, 'A.E.' at concerts to avoid the sex war; to my old school friends I had been B'lutty; to friends, in other future worlds, I would be Liz, or Lizzie, and to Mother alone Tinka (short for Betinka). Now Madame L. decided I was to be Elisabeth to the public and so it has remained.

A letter from my aunt, Betty Balfour, as usual written in transit, not only shows the family support I had for, at least, this one early event of my musical life (if seldom afterwards) but admirably introduces that overwhelming character, Dame Ethel Smyth:

In the train going home

Betty darling,

Ethel Smyth came with me to the Savoy—sandwiched between a hunt after a good wireless set at Kilburn, and a treatment by her osteopath.

We had excellent places in the front row of the upper circle. She joined me in time for the *Casse Noisette* Ballet, which bored her stiff—

'How I hate ballets—How I hate amusements—What are they doing?—
Why are they doing it?' . . . Half-way thro' she went out to read the
'Argument' . . . Here a strange female querulously accosted her . . .
How was she to get in? 'Go down and buy a ticket' sd. E. 'I can't, the
house is sold out!' (How splendid, B.B.) . . .

. . . During the Romance of the Rose, Ethel was entirely happy. . . .

At last the exciting moment for the beginning of The Infanta's Birthday
came. Over the introduction Ethel murmured 'Good'—'I like that'—
Then the curtain rose on the enchanting Infanta. The scene did look
like a Velazquez picture. All the incidents of the Ballet Ethel praised—
'What good *gesture* music it is'—specially liked the Moorish Prisoners
& their music. Then entry of the Dwarf and his dance—supremely good.
The interval between the end of his capers and the exit of the Infanta
Ethel thought too long—this is her only criticism. But from the moment
the Dwarf reappears to the end, she was enthusiastic—& thought the
Dwarf played his part supremely well.

When all was over my Dame shouted herself hoarse 'Bravo—Bravo.—
Author—Author' and because the rest of the audience did not follow
her lead, she became equally violent. 'What an audience! What are they
made of—Don't they realize this is an achievement—This counts. This
is something vital—alive—They are dead. They are fools—oh these English!'

With that she flung out of the theatre—I breathlessly following. In
again she went by the STAGE DOOR. . . . Here we began to jostle
against half-dressed men & ballet dancers to their obvious annoyance
and inconvenience. . . . So I dragged Ethel away—& outside we fell
upon Mary—whom I called 'Barbie' & we poured into her ear all we
felt about the young composer—& then went to drown our feelings in
tea in a Lyons shop.

*Finally, here are two descriptions by the composer about how
she has worked in the past, the first dating from the death of
her friend Dylan Thomas in 1953.*

Dylan's death had occurred on the heels of my finishing the
Motet [op. 27][3] and I now attempted to take it easy for a few

3. *Excerpta tractatus—Logico philosophici*, op. 27.

days, shattered as I was by the terrible news. But, for me at least, a finished work produces a stimulation and desire for further work immediately. It is interrupted work which induces musical constipation.

I have often been accused, in a derogatory way, of working quickly. This may be true if only the time of actual notation is considered, but ideas simmer for weeks, months and even years. On the writing down of the first sound I become totally obsessed until the work is finished; compressing in a short time the number of hours some composers spread over months. Afterwards I have little interest in the work beyond assessing from the first performance to what extent I have succeeded in achieving what I intended. (Luckily, I love my children—after birth!)

In my attempt at 'taking it easy' I was snoozing one afternoon when I was kicked violently awake by a musical idea. With Dylan's death so much in mind the character of the musical idea became identified with a lament. I originally heard a wordless voice but singers without words generally produce a monotonous 'Ah!,' so I looked at Shelley's translation of 'Fragment of the elegy on the death of Adonis' from the Greek of Bion. The idea was appropriate but the words themselves in no way matched the sound of that first vocal entry.

Before I had written down a note I received a phone call from Georgina Dobrée, the clarinettist and daughter of my good friends and Blackheath neighbours, Bonamy Dobrée and his wonderfully gifted wife Valentine, asking me to write her a piece for clarinet and piano. So I transposed my new idea, still, luckily, in embryonic form, to the desired combination, thereby solving the problem of the unwanted words and wrote my *Valediction* [op. 28] (*Dylan Thomas 1953*).

In this last selection, Lutyens reflects on the year 1960.

I remember nothing of 1960 but the works I wrote, the conditions under which I wrote them and what initiated the writing of them.

The first was the Wind Quintet [op. 45] that William Glock

asked me to write for an Invitation Concert (works were not
commissioned for these concerts then) for the newly formed
B.B.C. Chamber Music Ensemble, now the Leonardo Ensemble.

I know that a wind quintet was the *last* thing I was wishing
to write at the time, being immersed in a piece of different character—*Catena* [op. 47] for Soprano, Tenor and Instruments. However, I had to put this to one side and it took me three days to
transform my aural reluctance into the one and only thing I
wanted to do—a metamorphosis that must take place. I even
looked up the movement of Beethoven's String Quartet [no. 16
in F major, op. 135] with its prefaced motto theme: 'Muss es
sein?—Es muss sein! Es muss sein!' which so expressed my mood
that at one stage I contemplated taking these notes as my *donné*
for the quintet. I discarded this tentative idea as other ideas,
shapes and sounds began to emerge and my initial indecision
became transformed into an opening, a kernel of deliberate and
definite decisiveness.

Shape and form remain my major preoccupation, before I even
begin the writing of a piece, to ensure that the initial basic cell,
however small, contains the possibilities within it for change and
development in various proportions, tensions, relaxations, speeds,
etc., in relation to each other.

Once I have got my cell—probably but a few notes scribbled—
the aural and formal possibilities grow in my mind: the why,
wherefore, character and gesture of the whole work. Eventually
I begin the writing down of the piece (alongside it any serial
arrangement to be called upon). Or so it was with the quintet.

Each work I write—and this, no doubt, applies to most composers—has a different starting point, more often than not outside
music: some thing, some object, some word, some line of thought,
something visual. For instance, sitting at my desk one summer's
day overlooking the garden I became absorbed in watching a poplar
tree. Though with roots fixed in one place, wind, air currents
and light all coming from the same direction, every one of the
myriad leaves was moving and turning at different speeds, which
produced shifting shadows, light and colour. This was the stimulus of one work. I think most works are written on the razor-

edge between the arbitrary/intuitive and principle/constructive—
both elements welded in a piece. Use of principles automatically
involves the arbitrary; the arbitrary leads to the discovery of principles. At least, this is my experience.

50   NANCY VAN DE VATE

As an undergraduate in pursuit of both conservatory and liberal arts training, Nancy Van de Vate studied at the Eastman School of Music, majoring in piano, and Wellesley College, where she majored in music theory. She decided to become a composer only at age twenty-four, but she does not regret the latish start because of her strong background as an instrumentalist. She holds master's and doctoral degrees in composition from the University of Mississippi and Florida State University, and she has taught on college and university faculties in various parts of the United States. In 1975 she founded the International League of Women Composers, which she chairs.

In your opinion what have been the chief problems confronting women composers in achieving recognition in recent years?

I think the stereotype of woman as amateur is still highly detrimental to us as professionals and aspiring professionals. Women amateur composers, of course, have been and still are very plentiful. Each little town has its local piano teacher who writes teaching pieces or church anthems. To move up a notch, there are amateur women composers whose chamber and vocal works are performed by local music clubs. In general, amateur music is conservative; it's based on one's performing experience, largely of the standard repertory. But amateur women can also reach a very high level of competence, and their work is accepted. Society seems to think it is all right for them to be creative because they are using their education, for which a financial investment has been made. We've

Nancy Van de Vate and Carol Neuls-Bates, Interview Oct. 7, 1981. Used by permission of the interviewee.

all heard the comment, "Oh, isn't it nice you are using your music." Now by contrast, music composition has not been a hobby among men. I don't know of any dentists who come home and write chamber music. Men may have hobbies, but not music composition.

It seems to me that the notion of woman as amateur has had two profound effects on the role of the professional woman composer in American society today. First, we all tend to be tarred with the same brush, and people—especially those outside the music field—make no distinction between the "housewife amateur" and the serious woman professional. They have no idea that professional women are holding their own. Also many men in the music field itself regard all women composers as amateurs or possibly upgraded amateurs, with a few startling exceptions such as Barbara Kolb, the first woman to win the Rome Prize. What I am talking about has regional implications too. Around New York and on the East Coast in general, women can claim to be professional composers with much more credibility than elsewhere in the country, except possibly on the West Coast.

Secondly, the stereotype of woman as amateur affects those women who want to make the step up from amateur to professional. Consider, for instance, a woman who has raised children and during those years couldn't claim to be a full-time professional, or a woman who is middle-aged and wants to go back to graduate school in composition, or say a woman who had full professional training but for years accepted amateur status: even if these women are poised for a change they do not yet have complete credentials to be professional, and frequently they are pushed back into the category of amateur. This wouldn't happen to a man because no such category exists. He can't be pushed back into the circuit of women's clubs. He's either a student, a developing composer, or a professional. And if he's a student university faculties are interested in him rather than in the older woman, who is sometimes regarded as a bit of a nuisance.

A few words more about the female amateur and women's music clubs, if I may. The amateur base is important, and probably if it didn't exist—or hadn't existed in the past—we wouldn't have as many professional women today as we do. Also, the music clubs support a lot of good music making at the local level, and they've done a great deal to foster American music and American professional composers—both women and men.

What about the impact of the new wave of the women's movement in the last ten years for professional women composers? Surely the movement has helped!

Yes, absolutely, the climate *is* changing! Women composers are becoming more assertive about themselves all the time, and are receiving more performances of their works. We still, however, lag very much behind men in the important areas of orchestral performances, commissions and grants, competitions, and recordings. We still need to fully integrate ourselves into the musical mainstream.

Male composers today in the United States typically hold academic positions, while women do not: am I correct?

Most women composers certainly do not hold academic positions! In 1975 the College Music Society conference on the status of women reported only sixty-seven women teaching composition in the entire United States,[1] and my impression is that the situation isn't any better now. But the astonishing thing is that the number of women as composition students—both undergraduate and graduate—has increased immensely. I don't have definite figures, but I can say that through its Search for New Music by women student composers in the age category of eighteen through twenty-eight, the League [of Women Composers] is receiving a great number of superior entries, and not just superior on musical grounds: the level of calligraphy and presentation, the sophistication of tape techniques, are all light-years ahead of ten or even five years ago. These women have had their expectations raised.

1. Adrienne Fried Block, "Women in Composition," in *The Status of Women in College Music: Preliminary Studies*, ed. Carol Neuls-Bates (Binghamton, N.Y.: College Music Society, 1976), pp. 27–28.

They expect to function as professionals, but it's my feeling that faculties in academe are no more willing to absorb them than they were ten or fifteen years ago. I suspect the situation is even more difficult for women outside the United States.

How do women composers exist outside of academe? Are there any advantages in not having to teach on a college faculty?

Other than having more time for one's own composing, there are no advantages. Most important, the college or university position validates your credentials as a professional composer and gives you all kinds of professional contacts. And in college teaching you often have a whole range of facilities at your disposal: recording studios, recital halls, electronic studios, and much more. Some of your expenses are absorbed.

For you see, composition is such an expensive and complicated business. You have to have your scores bound, and perhaps a copyist to do parts. You need to have tapes reproduced, and if you start producing recordings—as a total you can spend between $5,000 and $15,000 a year promoting your music. To go back and answer your first question of these two, a great majority of women composers earn the major share of their income by giving private piano lessons, which can be a reasonably lucrative pursuit.

Are there problems in being classified as a "woman composer"? What about the women who don't want this classification?

I personally don't think there are problems. If we all banded together and were classified as women composers, we would have a much stronger case than we now have. But yes, women who *don't* want to be associated with an organization for women have posed a problem for the League. Usually they raise the charge of separatism: "If you are really good you don't need to be identified as a woman composer."

When I applied to college, I could not have attended Harvard, Princeton, or Yale because of being female, and so I went to one of the Seven Sister colleges, Wellesley. No one then suggested there was anything ignoble about separatism, or anything ignoble about women doing things for themselves, or anything inferior about the caliber of education we were receiving at a women's school. These questions were never raised, and it bothers me very much that *now* people think there is something wrong with women composers acting as advocates in their own behalf—which is what the League is doing. As women we simply have not had access to the same opportunities as men. And advocacy is a fine old American tradition.

Last August I attended a conference on string quartets by women composers in San Francisco that was exceedingly well done and cheered me more than any other event has in years. The music was picked by an outside committee that included Lou Harrison, the composer, and Daniel Kobialka, the principal second violinist with the San Francisco Symphony Orchestra, and other unbiased persons. Two superb string quartets performed at the conference: the Aurora and the Ridge. The opening concert was on Friday evening, and the next morning during the panel discussions there was not a single mention of the fact that this was a women's conference, as far as I can recall. The discussion focused on programming contemporary music and contemporary composers in general. Why was this the case? Because, I think, if the quality of the music is high and the performances are good, people forget, and they stop treating women as curiosities.

What were the events that triggered your founding the League of Women Composers in 1975?

International Women's Year in 1975 triggered the founding of the League, but there were other contributing factors. For some time I had been involved in the Southeastern Composers' League: as executive secretary—writing the newsletter and running the organization for six years—and as president for two years. It was a lot of hard work for an organization that gave me no real return for my own compositions. Then I was also active in founding the Knoxville, Tennessee, chapter of the National Organization for Women. It was my husband who suggested that I should found a new organization just for women composers and devote my time to it instead of to the SCL.

Another factor was that through my newsletter work for the SCL I became known as a composer who could write articles, and in the mid-seventies I was commissioned to write about women for *Symphony News*, *Musical America*, and *International Musician*. When the *Musical America* query came through I realized what a marvelous opportunity for publicity it offered. So I wrote the article in which I announced the League's formation, and then I went out and organized the League in January 1975, well before the article was published.

Our goals then are what they are now: to open up those areas that have been insufficiently accessible to women, namely orchestral performances, grants and competitions, and recordings. We have the most stringent eligibility requirements of any composers' organization in the country. This is not an attempt on my part to be elitist but reflects the realization that if we are to have real clout we need maximum credibility. The League has tried to emphasize activities that are not duplicated by other groups, because there is no need for just another group of composers. And all of our members are eligible to belong to the American Society of University Composers, the National Association of Composers, U.S.A., the American Music Center, etc.

In the League we have produced a radio series of sixteen programs that have been heard all over the country, we've published a directory about the members and sponsored chamber music programs of their works, and we've passed around a lot of information about career opportunities and where to find music by women. I think we have helped women create visibility for themselves, and the sense of collegiality we've generated has enabled some women to apply for grants, competitions, etc. for which they might not otherwise have put themselves forward.

The organization is growing by leaps and bounds with members in fifteen countries and more and more projects. This isn't good for me personally, and I am always trying to pass the job along. But no one else has been willing to do the work that I do on a, frankly, unpaid basis. Also, one problem I wasn't aware of when

I began the League was that since most women do not hold academic positions, they are not typically involved in professional societies and must therefore learn how to work together in these particular circumstances.

Would you comment on other organizations of women composers in the United States and elsewhere?

There is only one other group here, the American Women Composers, Inc. They have a rather different thrust than the League. They are exclusively American, and they admit anyone in sympathy with their aims. In Japan a federation of women composers has been formed, and they regularly translate our League's newsletter. There are a number of exceedingly well-qualified, ambitious, and stylistically progressive women composers in Japan today. They are not quite the Polish avant-garde, but almost! A Canadian federation has been organized, and in Germany Frau und Musik admits both performers and composers. There is no federation in Italy yet, although Italy has produced two superb festivals of women's music. A number of composers have approached our League about forming chapters in their own countries, but with our volunteer staff we couldn't handle this. We would like to see an international confederation of organizations of women composers, though, and I think all of us are moving in that direction.

In recent years the "blind audition" behind a screen has enabled increasing numbers of women instrumentalists to gain positions with orchestras. What about the case for "blind competitions" in composition?

Anonymity in competitions is of crucial importance and something women should insist upon. I think it is a disgrace that the National Endowment for the Arts does not have anonymous submission of scores for its Composer/Librettist fellowships. I now personally limit my entrance to competitions to anonymous ones, and that means I don't enter many competitions. But in those I do enter, I've had remarkable success. This means that the judges are reacting to the music and not the name on the score. I might mention that when I started composing, before the new women's movement, I sent off my compositions under my first initial and last name. I remember the very first was an orchestral work that a major symposium accepted, and were they amazed when I showed up for the performance! I followed the same procedure several times, always with an orchestral work, but Van de Vate is a distinctive name, and after I became known a little I couldn't do this any more.

That recollection brings up another idea I have been tossing around lately. There comes an awkward stage in a composer's career regarding critical response. This is true for both men and women, I think, although women maybe more responsive to it than men because their position in the field is less secure. When you are young and unknown you don't get knocked down by the press, and of course you have all sorts of hopes. On the other end of the spectrum, if you are well established, the critics are very chary. But in between there is a middle ground of which I am especially conscious, perhaps because I seem to have reached this point. You may have a lot of works circulating, and you are getting a good number of performances and reviews. But you don't have a big enough name yet that critics feel they have to treat you with any particular respect. So the increased attention not only is sometimes uncomfortable, it can even be devastating. You may decide it was better being anonymous. And I really do think there is still some residual tendency among critics to judge women's music more harshly than men's.

You have lived and worked in a number of different areas of the country. Would you care to comment on "regionalism"?

Yes, I resent the seeming domination of the field by composers in the New York–Boston area, and I think the Northeastern stylistic bias should be protested by regional composers! I don't even like the word "regional": it suggests we are rural, whereas most of us live in cities. The Eastman alumni magazine recently did an article about Dominick Argento and asked him how he, a Pulitzer Prize winner, survived in Minneapolis, and he answered to the effect: "Exceedingly well, thank you."

I noticed when I was living in the South that composers would send a work north to a conference and perhaps be thoroughly snubbed by the New York establishment, only to nurse their bruised feelings for the next twenty years. If they start feeling provincial and cut off, pretty soon they aren't heard from any more. It's a self-fulfilling prophecy.

Do you think the climate is more open to different musical styles at the present time? What about your own work and stylistic changes over the years?

In the last three to five years things have definitely opened up, and the so-called New York School of serial composition is no longer the only acceptable route. Ever since George Rochberg, among others, abandoned writing dodecaphonic music to be eclectic, it's been all right to be eclectic. And a composer, like myself, who has a strong lyric bent is now allowed to be fashionable. Regarding my own music, I completed an orchestral work—*Dark Nebulae*—in March of this year, and I've just now finished the revisions for it. And I've begun another orchestral piece, as yet untitled, which I have wanted to do for a long time. It's in the Lutoslawski-Ligeti-Takemitsu tradition. Not so far out as Penderecki. I think it has some of the tone color and sound of Varèse.

My whole style changed when I discovered Varèse, and that was late, in 1972. I also found out about electronic music only in 1972 when I had a fellowship from the National Endowment for the Humanities to attend an eight-week summer symposium at Dartmouth and the University of New Hampshire. That summer certainly opened my eyes to timbral and temporal composition. I had been trained in the old pandiatonic contrapuntal Eastman style, and I never was very comfortable with it. The only compromise I could make with it was a type of Bartókian chro-

matic contrapuntalism. I find myself so much more at ease in
the new, freer climate, and I love to write for orchestra. The
big palette fascinates me.

How do you compose? On a schedule?

I certainly would like to write on a schedule, every day. But
I find—and I feel sure this is true for most composers—that 90
percent of one's time is devoted to circulating one's works. You
have to duplicate tapes, send out scores with cover letters, etc.
Also I revise a lot based on performance, and if you change one
chord cluster in an orchestral piece, possibly as many as twenty-
four to twenty-six parts will have to be changed. Or suppose
you take out a beat: that's even more time-consuming, since *all*
the parts must then be changed. The proportion of time composers
spend on actual creative work is surprisingly small. But you must
keep your works circulating! There comes a point when you can
no longer stockpile.

Typically I work in desparation. Some days I just make up
my mind I am going to write and I do. Yesterday, for instance,
I did and composed five measures. That is actually a lot for an
orchestral work, if you think about it. My last piece was eleven,
twelve minutes, or 150 measures. If you average four measures
a day in full score, that makes twenty-eight measures a week,
and thus only about five weeks to turn out a full score.

Are you sanguine about the future for women composers?

I would have to say that the future of women in composition
depends very much upon the future of the overall women's movement. But beyond that, I think the future of women in composition is as promising as women themselves choose to make it.

Selected Bibliography

With a very few exceptions for major items, this bibliography does not relist the sources of readings in the anthology or any publications appearing in the footnotes. Rather it aims to introduce the reader to additional sources of information, chiefly in English: reference works, general studies and histories, and other writings about and by the individual women represented in the anthology. Works concerning other prominent women and topics have also been included, with an emphasis on European women, since the literature on Americans has been covered in several recent bibliographies about women in American music listed below.

The reader should also consult articles about individuals in *The New Grove Dictionary of Music and Musicians,* edited by Stanley Sadie (London: Macmillan, 1980) and, when appropriate, *Notable American Women, 1607–1950: A Biographical Dictionary,* edited by Edward T. James, Janet Wilson James, and Paul S. Boyer (Cambridge, Mass.: Harvard University Press, 1971). The latter has a supplement, *The Modern Period,* edited by Barbara Sicherman and Carol Hurd Green (1980).

Bibliographies and Other Reference Works

"Available Recordings of Works by Women Composers." *High Fidelity/Musical America* 23/2 (February 1973): 53.

Block, Adrienne Fried, and Carol Neuls-Bates, comps. *Women in American Music: A Bibliography of Music and Literature.* Westport, Conn.: Greenwood Press, 1979.

Bowers, Jane. "Teaching About the History of Women in Western Music." *Women's Studies Newsletter* 5/3 (summer 1977): 11–15. Includes discography.

Cohen, Aaron I. *The International Encyclopedia of Women Composers.* New York: R. R. Bowker, 1981.

Green, Miriam. *Women Composers: A Checklist of Works for the Solo Voice.* Boston: G. K. Hall, 1980.

Hixon, Don L., and Don Hennessee, comps. *Women in Music: A Biobibliography.* Metuchen, N.J.: Scarecrow Press, 1975.

Mitchell, Charles, comp. *Discography of Works by Women Composers.* Paterson, N.J.: Paterson Free Public Library, 1975.

Pool, Jeannie G. *Women in Music History: A Research Guide.* Ansonia Station, P.O. 436, New York: Author, 1977. Includes discography.

Skowronski, JoAnn. *Women in American Music: A Bibliography*. Metuchen, N.J.: Scarecrow Press, 1978.

Smith, Julia, comp. *Directory of American Women Composers*. Chicago: National Federation of Music Clubs, 1980.

Stern, Susan. *Women Composers: A Handbook*. Metuchen, N.J.: Scarecrow Press, 1978.

Williams, Ora. *American Black Women in the Arts and Social Sciences: A Bibliographic Survey*. Rev. ed. Metuchen, N.J.: Scarecrow Press, 1978.

Women and Folk Music: A Select Bibliography. Washington, D.C.: Archive of Folk Song, Library of Congress, 1978.

Zaimont, Judith Lang, and Karen Famera, comps. *Contemporary Concert Music by Women: A Directory of the Composers and Their Works*. Westport, Conn.: Greenwood Press. 1981.

General Studies and General Histories

Ammer, Christine. *Unsung: A History of Women in American Music*. Westport, Conn.: Greenwood Press, 1981.

Arnold, Dennis. "Instruments and Instrumental Teaching in the Early Italian Conservatories." *Galpin Society Journal* 18 (1965): 72–81.

———. "Orphans and Ladies: The Venetian Conservatories (1680–1790)." *Proceedings of the Royal Musical Association* 89 (1962–63): 31–48.

Bagnall, Anne D. "Musical Practices in Medieval English Nunneries." Ph.D. diss., Columbia University, 1975.

Borroff, Edith. "Women Composers: Reminiscence and History." *College Music Symposium* 15 (spring 1975): 26–33.

Bowers, Jane, and Judith Tick, eds. *Women Making Music: Studies in the Social History of Women Musicians and Composers*. Berkeley, Calif.: University of California Press, 1982.

Daughtry, Willa E. "A Study of the Negro's Contribution to Nineteenth Century American Concert and Theatrical Life." Ph.D. diss., Syracuse University, 1968.

Driggs, Frank. *Women in Jazz: A Survey*. New York: Stash Records, 1977.

Drinker, Sophie Lewis. *Music and Women. The Story of Women in Their Relation to Music*. Washington, D.C.: Zenger Publishing, 1975. A reprint of the 1948 edition.

Elkins-Marlow, Laurine. "Have Women in This Country Written for Full Orchestra?" *Symphony News* 27/2 (April 1976): 15–19.

Elson, Arthur. *Woman's Work in Music.* Portland, Me.: Longwood Press, 1974. A reprint of the 1903 edition.

Elson, Louis Charles. *Woman in Music.* New York: Gordon Press, 1976. A reprint of the 1918 edition.

Jackson, Irene V. "Black Women and the Afro-American Song Tradition." *Sing-Out!* 25/2 (July–August 1976): 10–13.

Le Page, Jane Weiner. *Women Composers, Conductors, and Musicians of the Twentieth Century.* Metuchen, N.J: Scarecrow Press, 1980.

Lerner, Gerda. "Placing Women in History: Definitions and Challenges." *Feminist Studies* 3/1–2 (fall 1975): 5–14.

Neuls-Bates, Carol. "Sources and Resources for Women's Studies in American Music: A Report." *Notes: The Quarterly Journal of the Music Library Association* 35/2 (December 1978): 269–83.

———, ed. *The Status of Women in College Music: Preliminary Studies.* Binghamton, New York: College Music Society, 1976.

Nochlin, Linda. "Why Are There No Great Women Artists?" *Women in Sexist Society.* Ed. Vivian Gornick and Barbara K. Moran. New York: Basic Books, 1971, pp. 480–510.

Oliveros, Pauline. "And Don't Call Them 'Lady' Composers." *New York Times,* Sept. 13, 1970, Section 2, pp. 23, 30. Includes discography.

Pool, Jeannie G. "America's Women Composers." *Music Educators Journal* 65/5 (January 1979): 28–41. Issue on women.

———. *Women Composers of Classical Music: A Research Guide.* Boston: G. K. Hall, 1982.

Quasten, Johannes. "The Liturgical Singing of Women in Christian Antiquity." *Catholic Historical Review* 27/2 (July 1941): 149–65.

Rieger, Eva. *Frau und Musik.* Frankfurt am Main: Fischer Taschenbuch Verlag, 1980.

Riley, Joanne M. "The Influence of Women on Secular Vocal Music in Sixteenth Century Italy." Master's thesis, Wesleyan University, 1980.

Rosen, Judith, and Grace Rubin-Rabson. "Why Haven't Women Become Great Composers?" *High Fidelity/Musical America* 23/2 (February 1973): 46–52. Includes discography.

Rossi, Alice S. "Introduction: Social Roots of the Women's Movement in America." *The Feminist Papers.* Ed. Alice S. Rossi. New York: Bantam Books, 1974, pp. 241–81.

Shapiro, Marianne. "The Provençal Trobaritz and the Limits of Courtly Love." *Signs* 3/3 (spring 1978): 560–71.

Tick, Judith. "Towards a History of American Women Composers Before 1870." Ph.D. diss., City University of New York, 1979.

———. "Why Have There Been No Great Women Composers?" *International Musician* 79/1 (July 1975): 6, 22.

———. "Women as Professional Musicians in the United States, 1870–1910." *Yearbook for International Music Research* 9 (1973): 95–133.

Van de Vate, Nancy. "The American Woman Composer: Some Sour Notes." *High Fidelity/Musical America* 25/6 (June 1975): 18–20. Includes discography. Issue on women.

WOMEN IN MUSIC. *Heresies* 3/2 (summer 1980). Issue on women.

"Women of Music." *Music Journal* [New York] 30/1 (January 1972): 9–24, 55, 58–59.

Wood, Elizabeth. "Review Essay: Women in Music." *Signs* 6/2 (winter 1980): 283–97.

Works By and About Individual Women

Barth, Prudentia, et al. *Hildegard von Bingen: Lieder.* Salzburg: Otto Mueller, 1959.

Bates, Carol Henry. "The Instrumental Music of Elisabeth-Claude Jacquet de La Guerre." Ph.D. diss., University of Indiana, 1975.

Bonime, Stephen. "Anne de Bretagne (1477–1514) and Music." Ph.D. diss., Bryn Mawr College, 1975.

Bradshaw, Susan. "The Music of Elisabeth Lutyens." *Musical Times* 112 (July 1971): 653–56.

Chauvin, Marie-José. "Entretien avec Betsy Jolas." *Le Courier Musical de France* No. 27 (1969): 163–72.

Citron, Marcia J. "The Lieder of Fanny Mendelssohn Hensel." *Musical Quarterly* (forthcoming in 1983).

Dale, Kathleen. "Ethel Smyth's Prentice Works," *Music and Letters* 30/4 (October 1949): 329–36.

Daughtry, Willa E. "Sissieretta Jones: Profile of a Black Artist." *Musical Analysis* 1/1 (winter 1972): 12–18.

Du Moulin-Eckart, Richard M. F. *Cosima Wagner.* Trans. Catherine Alison Phillips, intro. by Ernest Newman. New York: Knopf, 1930.

Elkins-Marlow, Laurine. "Gena Branscombe, American Composer." Ph.D. diss., University of Texas at Austin, 1981.

Friedland, Bea. *Louise Ferranc, 1804–75: Composer, Performer, Scholar.* Ann Arbor, Mich.: UMI Research Press, 1981.

———. "Louise Ferranc (1804–75): Composer, Performer, Scholar," *Musical Quarterly* 60/2 (April 1974): 257–74.

Gaume, Mary Mathilda. "Ruth Crawford-Seeger: Her Life and Work." Ph.D. diss., Indiana University, 1973.

Glackens, Ira. *Yankee Diva: Lillian Nordica and the Golden Days of Opera.* New York: Coleridge Press, 1963.

Handy, D. Antoinette. "Conversation with Mary Lou Williams." *Black Perspective in Music* 8/2 (fall 1980): 194–214.

Henderson, Robert. "Elisabeth Lutyens," *Musical Times* 104 (August 1963): 51–55.

Jepson, Barbara. "American Women in Conducting." *Feminist Art Journal* 4/4 (winter 1975–76): 13–18, 45.

———. "Looking Back: An Interview with Doriot Anthony Dwyer." *Feminist Art Journal* 5/3 (fall 1976): 21–24.

———. "Ruth Crawford-Seeger. A Study in Mixed Accents." *Heresies* 3/2 (summer 1980): 38, 40–43.

Kerr, Jessica M. "Mary Harvey—The Lady Dering." *Music and Letters* 25/1 (January 1944): 23–33.

Kupferberg, Herbert. *The Mendelssohns: Three Generations of Genius.* New York: Scribner's, 1972.

Lerner, Ellen. "Music of Selected Contemporary American Women Composers: A Stylistic Analysis." Master's thesis, University of Massachusetts at Amherst, 1976.

Mahler, Alma. *And the Bridge Is Love.* New York: Harcourt, Brace, Jovanovich, 1958.

Merrill, Lindsey. "Mrs. H. H. A. Beach [Amy Marcy Beach]: Her Life and Works." Ph.D. diss., University of Rochester, 1963.

Milinowski, Marta. *Teresa Carreño: "By the Grace of God."* New York: Da Capo Press, 1979. A reprint of the 1940 edition.

Myers, Roland. "Augusta Holmès: A Meteoric Career." *Musical Quarterly* 53/3 (July 1967): 365–76.

Neuls-Bates, Carol. "Five Women Composers, 1587–1875." *Feminist Art Journal* 5/2 (summer 1976): 32–35.

Raney, Carolyn. "Francesca Caccini, Musician to the Medici, and her *Primo libro.*" Ph.D. diss., New York University, 1971.

———. "Francesca Caccini's *Primo libro.*" *Music and Letters* 48/4 (October 1967): 350–57.

———. "Vocal Style in the Works of Francesca Caccini." *Bulletin of the National Association of Teachers of Singing* 23/3 (February 1966): 26–29.

Reich, Nancy B. "Louise Reichardt." *Ars Musica, Ars Scientia: Festschrift Heinrich Hueschen.* Köln: Gitarre & Laute Verlag, 1980, pp. 369–77.

Rosand, Ellen. "Barbara Strozzi, *virtuosissima cantatrice:* The Composer's Voice." *Journal of the American Musicological Society* 31/2 (summer 1978): 241–81.

Rosenstiel, Leonie. *The Life and Works of Lili Boulanger.* Rutherford, N.J.: Fairleigh Dickinson University Press, 1978.

———. *Nadia Boulanger: A Life in Music.* New York: W. W. Norton, 1982.

Roxseth, Yvonne. "Antonia Bembo, Composer to Louis XIV." *Musical Quarterly* 23/2 (April 1937): 147–69.

Scott, Marian. "Maddalena Lombardini, Madame Syrman." *Music and Letters* 14/2 (April 1933): 149–63.

Silbert, Dorris. "Francesca Caccini, called "La cecchina." *Musical Quarterly* 32/1 (January 1946): 50–62.

Smyth, Ethel. *A Final Burning of Boats.* London: Longmans, Green, 1928.

———. *As Time Went On.* London: Longmans, Green, 1936.

———. *Streaks of Life.* New York: Alfred A. Knopf, 1922.

———. *What Happened Next.* London: Longmans, Green, 1940.

Sollins, Susan. "Interview with Betsy Jolas." *Feminist Art Journal* 2/3 (fall 1973): 16–17, 22.

St. John, Christopher. *Ethel Smyth: A Biography.* With additional chapters by V. Sackville-West and Kathleen Dale. London: Longmans, Green, 1959.

Stookes, Sacha. "Some Eighteenth-Century Women Violinists." *Monthly Musical Record* 84/1 (January 1954): 14–17.

Tuthill, Burnette. "Mrs. H. H. A. Beach [Amy Marcy Beach]." *Musical Quarterly* 26/3 (July 1940): 297–306.

Ullrich, Hermann. "Maria Theresia Paradis (1759–1824) als Musikpädagogin." *Musikerziehung* 14/1 (September 1960): 9–15.

———. "Maria Theresia Paradis and Mozart." *Music and Letters* 27/4 (October 1946): 224–33.

Werner, Jack. "Felix and Fanny Mendelssohn." *Music and Letters* 37/4 (October 1947): 303–37.

Index

Numbers in italics denote illustrations.

Abbey, Henry Eugene, 136, 139
Academic careers, 325–326
Accademia Filharmonica, Verona, 44n, 45
Accomplishment, social, music as, 73–79, 179–183, 300
Alfonso II d'Este, Duke of Ferrara, 50–51
Allen, Lew, 136
Amateur musicians, 179–183, 282; composers, 206, 323–324; female stereotype, 282, 323–324; medieval, 28–29; Renaissance, 37, *40–42*
American Academy in Rome, 235
American Conservatory, Chicago, 265, 269, 304
American Conservatory, Fontainebleau, 239, 240
American Folk Songs for Children (Crawford-Seeger), 310
American Music Center, 328
American Society of University Composers, 328
American Symphony Orchestra, 254
American Women Composers, Inc., 329
Anderson, Eva, 248
Anderson, Marian, 273–274, *275,* 276–277
Ara, Ugo, 234, 235
Arbós, Enrique, 313
Archive of American Folklore, 308, 311
Argento, Dominick, 331
Artusi, Giovanni Maria, 43
Association for the Advancement of Women, 188
Auric, Georges, 243
Aurora String Quartet, 327
Austen, Jane, 73, 74, 284, 287

Bach, Johann Sebastian, 150, 209, 281
Balfour, Betty, 318
Ballard, Christophe, 64
Balsam, Arthur, 270
Barber, Samuel, 261
Bargiel, Woldemar, 100
Barnet, Hinda, 263
Baroque, xii, xiii, 55–69; Venetian conservatories, 65–69; women composers, 55–56, 60–64
Barrère, Georges, 235
Barry, Betty, 257
Bartók, Béla, 240, 331
Bartolozzi, Francesco, 75
Bassoon, 66, 250, 263
Bauer, Harold, 235
Baur, Clara, 184
Bayadère, La (Candeille), 88
Baylis, Lilian, 286
Bayreuth, Germany, 124, 176
B.B.C. band, 284, 285
B.B.C. Chamber Music Ensemble, 321
Beach, Amy Marcy, 223–225, 247
Beecham, Sir Thomas, 295
Beethoven, Ludwig van, 91, 208, 209, 218
Beethoven Conservatory, St. Louis, 248
Belari, Emilio, 125, 126
Berg, Alban, 305, 307
Bergen, Flora Batson, 136
Berger, Arthur, 246
Berkshire Festival, 234–235, 236
Berkshire Quartet, 232–234
Berlin, Germany, 170–171, 268; Hochschule für Musik, 254, 268–269; Sing-Akademie, 115–116
Berlin Conservatory, 109, 111, 112–113
Berlioz, Victor, 208
Bernacchi, Antonio, 81, 81n
Beständig, Otto, 171

Bethune, Thomas Greene, 135
Bigot, Marie, 144
Birthday of the Infanta, The
   (Lutyens), 316–319
"Black Patti's Troubadours," 141–142
Black women concert artists, 135, 273
Blackwood, Easley, 246
Blaisdell, Francis, 271, 272
Blake-Alverson, Margaret, 131–134
"Blind" competitions, 329–330
Blitzstein, Marc, 246
Block, Ernest, 235
Boccaccio, 31, 199
Book of the Courtier, The
   (Castiglione), 37
Bosse, Abraham, 58
Boston, 194; Handel and Haydn
   Society, 131, 224
Boston Fadette Lady Orchestra, 194–
   197
Boston Symphony Orchestra, 223
Bottrigari, Hercole, 43–49, 50
Boulanger, Lili, 242, 242n
Boulanger, Nadia, 239–240, *241*, 242–
   246
Boulez, Pierre, 246
Bousquet, Georges, 149, 149n
Brahms, Johannes, 91, 100, 101, 105–
   106, 157, 163, 164, 257;
   correspondence with Clara
   Schumann, 104–107
Brass instruments, 192, 282; women
   excluded from, xiii, 192, 193, 203
Breitkopf and Härtel, 165, 165n
Brico, Antonia, 252, 253–259, 271
Brico Symphony Orchestra, 254, 258–
   259
Bridge, Frank, 236, 313, 316
Briggs, Hedley, 318
Brontë sisters, 284, 287
Brower, Edith, 211, 212
Brown, Lew, 136
Brown, Mildred, 266
Bruch, Max, 106
Bülow, Hans von, 175–176
Bunbury, H., 75
Burney, Charles, 66, 68, 80
Butt, Dame Clara, 282
Buttrey, Gertrude, 272

Caccini, Francesca, xiv, 55–56, 60–61
Caccini, Giulio, 55
Camargo Society, 316–317
Candeille, Julie, 88
Cantatas, 62, 64, 80, 85, 214
Carnegie Hall, New York, 254, 271
Carnegie Recital Hall, 262, 272
Carreño, Teresa, 226–227
Carter, Elliott, 246
Casella, Alfredo, 235
Casino Filharmonico, Venice, 67
Castelloza, 22, *23*, 26–27
Castiglione, Baldesar, 37
Caston, Saul, 258n
Castrati, xii, 283n
Casulana, Maddalena, xiv
Catena, op. 47 (Lutyens), 321
Catherine, ou La belle fermière
   (Candeille), 88
Catherine de Medici, 199, 199n
CBS radio, 268, 309
Cecil, Lord Robert, 292
Cello, 66, 267n, 272, 285
Cephale & Procris (La Guerre), 64
Chadwick, George W., 219, 304
Chamber ensembles, 253; all-female,
   xiii–xiv, 271–272; Berkshire Quartet,
   232–234; exclusion of women from,
   xiii. *See also* Instrumental ensembles
Chamber music, 231–237; female
   composers of, 62, 85, 327, 328
Chaminade, Cecile, 226
Chant 1942, The (Creston), 262
Chants for Women's Chorus
   (Crawford-Seeger), 307
Chapman, Oscar, 276
Chappell, S. Arthur, 103, 159
Chatterton, Charles F., 139
Cherubini, Maria Luigi, 209
Chiabrera, Gabriello, 61
Chicago, 198, 226, 232, 248, 251;
   American Conservatory, 265–269,
   304; Civic Orchestra, 266, 266n, 305;
   Women's Symphony Orchestra, 249
Chicago Symphony Orchestra, 232,
   233, 265, 266
Chickering, George H., 194
Chopin, Frédéric, 91
Choral singing, xii–xiii, 3–10, 283

Chrétien de Troyes, 28–29
Christian antiquity, 3–10
Church: choirs, xiii, 3–5; exclusion of women from music, xii–xiii, 3, 6
Civic Orchestra of Chicago, 266, 266n, 305
Civic Orchestra of New York, 271
Clarinet, 253–254, 265–272, 320
Clarke, Helen J., 211–213
Classic period, 73–88; composers, 80–81, 83–88; "feminine" instruments of, xiii, 192; instrumentalists, 80–81, 83–86, 88; singers, 80–86, 88
Clef d'amors, La (ed. Doutrepont), 28
Cleveland Gazette, 141
Club movement, xv, 188–191, 324–325
Cole, Ulric, 261
College Music Society, 325
Collett, Mme. Valborg, 304
Collins, Judy, 254
Colored American, The, 141
Committee for the Recognition of Women in the Musical Profession, 252
Competitions, 325, 328; blind, 329–330
Composer-performer, roles linked, xiv
Composers, 167, 208–209, 215, 218, 288
Composers, female, xiv–xv, 11, 206, 247; amateur, 206, 323–324; Beach, 223–225, 247; Boulanger (Lili), 242; Boulanger (Nadia), 239, 240, 242; Caccini, 55–56, 60–61; Candeille, 88; Crawford-Seeger, 303–311; Daniels, 219; Hensel (Fanny Mendelssohn), 143, 147–151, 165; Hildegard of Bingen, 14, 16–20; La Guerre, 62–64; Le Beau, 167–174, 206; Lutyens, 312–322; Martinez, 80–84; obstacles, xiv, 87–88, 144, 146–147, 167–168, 170, 206, 211–218, 278, 286–288, 291–296, 323–330; obstacles in getting published, 143, 148–149, 165–166, 167–168, 294–295; Paradis, 85; Renaissance, 43; Schröter, 87; Schumann (Clara), 92, 96, 153–155, 165; Smith (Alice Mary), 214; Smith

Composers, female (*cont.*)
(Julia), 261; Smyth (Ethel), 156, 162–166, 206, 225–226, 278; supposed innate inferiority of women, xiv, 153, 206–218, 223–226, 242, 291–292, 297–302; Van de Vate, 323–332
Composers in America (Reis), 297
Concert artists, 85, 179, 192; acceptance of women as, xii, xiii, 192, 205; blacks as, 135, 273; management of, 188. *See also* Instrumentalists; Pianists; Singers; Violinists
Concertmistress, mixed orchestra, 266
Concerto delle donne, 50–52
Concerts, early, 43–49, 63, 65–68
Conductors, female, xiv, xv, 46, 194, 247, 248, 249, 253; Brico, 252, 253–259; Petrides, 253, 260–264; Scheerer, 271–272
Conservatories, xi, xiv–xv, 184; sex discrimination in, xiv–xv, 211, 220; Venetian, xiii, 65–69, 192, 199n
Convents, xi, xii, xiii, xiv; early Christian, 6–10; medieval, xiv, 11, *12*, 13, 14–20; Renaissance, xiii, xiv, 43–49, 192
Coolidge, Elizabeth Sprague, 231–237, *238*
Copland, Aaron, 239–240, 242–246, 261
Coppet, Edward de, 232
Cornet, 43, 48, 203, 204
Cosa, Francesco del, 40
Counterpoint, 223, 331–332; study of, 207, 211, 220–221
Counter Reformation, xii, 43–44
Court musicians, female: bar against, xiii; Baroque, 55–56, 60–64; Classic period, 87; medieval, 22, 28, *33*; Renaissance, 37–39
Cowell, Henry, 304
Craig, Edith, 286, 286n
Cramer, Carl Friedrich, 87
Cramer, J. B., 113, 146
Crane, Julia Ettie, 184
Crawford-Seeger, Ruth, 303–305, *306*, 307–311; her "credo," 309–310

Creativity, musical, sex-prejudiced
    view of, xiv, 153, 206–210, 211–213,
    242, 291–292, 297–302
Creston, Paul, 261–262
Crickboom, Matthieu, 259
Cubli, Antonia, 68
Curtis School of Music, 260

D'Agoult, Countess Marie, 175
Damen Orchester, 192–193, 253
Damrosch, Walter, 240, 244–245
Daniels, Mabel, 219–222
D'Arco, Livia, 50, 52
Dark Nebulae (Van de Vate), 331
Davidson, Harry, 161
De Ahna, Heinrich, 114
De Brosses, Charles, 65–66
Debussy, Claude, 240, 256, 315
De Falla, Manuel, 235, 236
Dello Joio, Norman, 261
Delsarte, François, 123, 125, 126
De Manziarly, Marcelle, 246
Denver Symphony, 257–258
DeWolf Sisters, 136
Dia, Countess of, 21–22, 23
Diamond, David, 246, 261
Dieppe, Ludwig, 109
Dietrich, Albert and Clara, 106
Dobrée, Georgina, 320
Douglass, Fred, 139
Downes, Mrs. Olin, 255
Drouais, François Hubert, 82
Drums, 29, 250
Dugasseau, Charles, 149, 149n
Dulcimer, 33
Dunger, Charles, 138

Eastman School of Music, 248, 260,
    323, 331
Egeria, Abbess, 4
Egk, Werner, 307
Ehlert, Louis, 111, 112, 113
Eliot, George, 159
Elizabeth I, Queen, 199, 199n
Emma (Austen), 74, 77–79
Enesco, Georges, 235, 257
Engel, Carl, 237
Enser, Helen, 263
Epstein, Lonny, 262

Epstein, Richard, 234
Etude magazine, 179, 184
Ewen, David, 297
Ewing, Alexander, 156, 157
Excelsior Quartette, 136

Fadette Lady Orchestra, 194–197
Favart, Marie Justine Benoit, 82
Fay, Amy, 109–110, 184; Etude article
    of, 184, 184n, 185–187; letters of,
    110–121; Music article of, 217,
    217n, 218
Female Pipings in Eden (Smyth), 278–
    296, 297
"Feminine" forms of music, 223
"Feminine" instruments, xiii, 192
Ferrara, 40, 43, 47; concerto delle
    donne, 50–52
Fiddle, 28–29
Fiedler, Arthur, 272
Fine, Irving, 246
Fiorino, Hippolito, 47, 49
Fischhof, Josef, 95, 95n
Fletcher, Polyxena, 314–315
Flonzaley Quartet, 232, 235
Flute, 41, 66, 192, 271, 272
Folk music, American, 308, 309, 310–
    311
Folksong: USA (Lomax), 311
Folkstone, Lady, 282, 282n
Françaix, Jean, 246
Frank, Nathan, 203
Frari, Giacoma, 68
Freeman, Ruth, 272
French horn, 68
Frieberg, Carl, 262
Friedländer, Thekla, 157, 159, 161,
    162, 163
Fuchs, Joseph and Lillian, 270

Gabrilowisch, Ossip, 235
Gadski, Johanna, 203
Gaelic Symphony, in E minor, op. 32
    (Beach), 223–225
Gaskell, Elizabeth, 287
Georgia Minstrels, 136
Gernsheim, Friedrich, 170
Gilmore, Patrick, 122, 127
Giralda, Signora, 56, 60

Gliewmeden vs. *gligmann,* 28
Glock, William, 320
Godfrey, Sir Dan, 295
Godmillow, Jill, 254
Gordon Quartet, 235
Görger, Theodor, 173
Gounod, Charles, 149, 149n
Graham, Martha, 243
Grainger, Percy, 233, 304
Grants, competition for, 325, 328
Grau, Maurice, 136
Grove, George, 103
Guardi, Francesco, 67
Guarini, Anna (La Guarina), 50, 52
Guglielmi, Maria, 69, 69n
Guinzberg, Mrs. H. A., 272
Guitar, 73; judged a "feminine"
  instrument, xiii, 192

Hadumoth (Le Beau), 167–174
Hale, Philip, 223–224
Hallé Band, London, 285
Hamley, Barbara (Lady Ernle), 160
Handbells, *29–30*
Handel, George Frederick, 208
Handel and Haydn Society, Boston,
  131, 224
Hanson, Howard, 235, 248
Harmat, Artur, 234
Harmony, 223; study of, 207, 211, 220;
  teaching of, 239, 240
Harp, 28, *31,* 73, *76,* 88; double, 43;
  a "feminine" instrument, xiii, 192,
  202; ten-string, 19–20
Harpists in orchestras, traditionally
  female, 192, 201, 202, 261, 285
Harpsichord, xiii, 43, 62, 64, 68, 81
Harris, Roy, 246
Harrison, Lou, 327
Harty, Sir Hamilton, 285
Hasse, Johann, 65
Hauer, Josef, 305
Haydn, Franz Joseph, 80, 218, 262
Hein, Paul, 172
Heinemann, Ada, 204
Henderson, William J., 249
Henschel, George, 157, 162–163, 164–
  165

Hensel, Fanny Mendelssohn, 143–144,
  145, 146–152, 156; as composer, 143,
  143n, 147–151; discouraged by
  family from publication, 143, 148–
  149; as pianist, 143, 148, 149, 150–
  151; publication of compositions,
  148, 151, 165
Hensel, Wilhelm, 147–152 *passim*
Herzogenberg, Heinrich von, 162
Hess, Dame Myra, 235
Hildegard von Bingen, 11, 13, 14, *15*
Hiller, Johann Adam, 87
Hindemith, Paul, 269, 304
Hitz, Luise, 168
Hoch Conservatory, Frankfurt, 107
Hofmann, Josef, 304
Holler, Wenceslaus, 57
Holmes, Augusta, 224, 226
Honegger, Arthur, 243
Horn, 68, 263, 272, 282
Hummel, Johann Nepomuk, 151
Huneker, James, 179, 182
Hurok, Sol, 276n
Hymns, 3, 4–5, 9–10

Ickes, Harold L., 274, 276–277
Instrumental ensembles: San Vito
  Convent, Ferrara, 43; Venetian
  conservatories, 65–66, *67,* 68, 192.
  See also Chamber ensembles;
  Orchestras
Instrumentalists, xiii–xiv, xv, 192,
  281–282; Baroque, 62–64, 66; blind
  auditions, 329; classical period, 80–
  81, 83–86, 88; demands of opera vs.
  concert orchestra on, 203–205;
  medieval, 28, *29–33;* 19th into 20th
  century, 192–205; obstacles for
  women, xiii, 192, 198–205, 247,
  251–252, 261, 263, 265, 267, 270,
  282–285, 291, 325, 328; Renaissance,
  40–42, 43; 20th century, 247–250,
  257, 261, 265–272. *See also* Pianists;
  Violinists; *and see other specific
  instruments*
Instrumental music: first female
  composer of, 62–64; medieval
  convent, 17. *See also* Chamber
  music; Concerts

Instruments: in liturgical music, 18, 19–20; sexual stereotyping of, xiii, 37, 39, 192, 200, 202–203, 204
"In Tall Grass" (Crawford-Seeger), 307
International League of Women Composers, 323, 325, 326–329
International Musician, 328
International Society for Contemporary Music (ISCM), 309
Interpretative ability, xiii, 206, 210, 212, 240; sexual aesthetics in criticism, 226–227

Jacobsen, Sascha, 270
Japan, women composers in, 329
Jerusalem, around A.D. 400, 4–5
Jeux à l'honneur de la victoire, Les (La Guerre), 62
Joachim, Amalie, 103n, 105
Joachim, Joseph, 100, 101, *102*, 103, 105, 114, 115, 159, 281, 285
Jones, Dick, 136
Jones, Sissieretta (Mathilde S. Joyner, the "Black Patti"), 135–136, *137*, 138–142; as concert artist, 135–141; in vaudeville and opera, 135, 141–142; at White House, 138
Jongleresse, 28, *30*
Jongleur (joglar), 26n, 28
Journal de Paris, 88
Joyner, Mathilde S. *See* Jones, Sissieretta
Juilliard School of Music, 250, 260, 262

Kalischer, Alfred, 171
Kansas City Symphony Orchestra, 272
Karsavina, Tamara, 318
Kelly-Gadol, Joan, 37
Kerker, Gustav, 202–203
Keyboard players, female, xiii, xiv
Keynes, Maynard, 317
King, W. Owens, 136
Klingemann, Carl, 147
Kobialka, Daniel, 327
Kolb, Barbara, 324
Kolisch Quartet, 35
Kortschak, Hugo, 232–233, 234
Kovar, Eleanor, 263
Kozeluch, Leopold, 85, 86

Kreisler, Fritz, 234
Kroll, Lily, 270
Kullak, Theodore, 109

Lady at the Positive Organ, The (Unicorn Tapestries), 32
Lady Folkstone's String Band, 282
Lady orchestras, 192–197, 253, 282n
Lady Playing the Virginals (Holler), 57
Lady with a Harp (Sully), 76
La Guerre, Elisabeth-Claude Jacquet de, xiv, 62–64
La Guerre, Marin de, 64
Lambert, Constant, 316, 317–318
Lamond, Felix, 235
La Motte, Antoine Houdar de, 64
Lang, Josephine, 165, 165n
Latilla, Gaetan, 66
Laurent, Georges, 235
Lavoie-Herz, Djane, 304
League of Women Composers, 323, 325, 326–329
Le Beau, Luise Adolpha, 167–174, 206
Leginska, Ethel, 249
Leipzig Conservatory, 156, 162
Leipzig Gewandhaus, 91
Leitert, Johann Georg, 116, 117
Lenox Quartet, 235
Leonardo Ensemble, 321
Leschetizky, Theodor, 314
Letz Quartet, 235
Leventritt, Edgar, 270, 272
Levi, Hermann, 292–293
Levy's American Band, 138, 139
Lewes, George Henry, 159
Liberazione di Ruggerio dall'isola d'Alcina, La (Caccini), 55
Lieder, 87. *See also* Songs
Liederbuch (Lang), 165n
Lieder und Balladen, op. 3 (Smyth), 163n
Life of Saint Macrina, The (St. Gregory of Nyssa), 6
Limberg-Dengel, Eugenie, 263
List, Emilie, 97
Liszt, Franz, 91, 109, 116–121, 175
Litchfield County Festivals, 233
Littlehales, Lillian, 235

Liturgical music, Hildegard von Bingen on, 17–20
Liturgical singing, 11, 14
Liturgical songs: Caccini, 55; Hildegard von Bingen, 14, 16–17
Loeffler, Charles Martin, 235
Lombardini-Sirmen, Maddalena, 65, 69, 69n, 199, 199n
London, 214; Promenade Concerts, 315
London Philharmonic, 285
London String Quartet, 235
London Symphony Orchestra, 285
Long Beach Woman's Orchestra, 248
Longy, Georges, 234
Lopokova, Lydia, 317, 318
Louis XIV, King of France, 62–63
Lucuvich, Antonia, 68
Ludwig II, King of Bavaria, 175, 177n
Lute, xiii, 40–41, 43, 58–59, 199n
Lutyens, Sir Edwin, 312, 317
Lutyens, Elisabeth, 312–322; on mode of composing, 321–322
Luzzaschi, Luzzasco, 47, 49, 50, 52
Lyra-viol, 43
Lyre, 28–29
Lytton, Lady Edith, 312

Magazin der Musik (periodical), 87
Magnes, Frances, 262
Malipiero, Francesco, 235
Manziarly, Marcelle de, 316
"March of the Women, The" (Smyth), 278
Margherita Gonzaga, Duchess of Ferrara, 45, 50
Marguerite de Navarre, 199, 199n
Maria Theresia, Empress, 85
Marimba, 261
Markevitch, Igor, 246
Martinez, Marianne von, 80–84
Martinů, Bohuslav, 235
Masselos, William, 262
Matthews, C. H., 136
Meadows-White, 214–216
Medici, Francesco de', 52
Medici, Giuliano de', 37
Medici court, Florence, 50, 55
Mehrkens, Adolf, 171
Mendelssohn, Abraham, 143–144

Mendelssohn, Fanny. See Hensel, Fanny
Mendelssohn, Felix, 143, 143n, 144, 147, 148, 156, 163, 177; death, 151; on publication of compositions by his sister, 148–149
Mendelssohn, Rebecca, 143, 147, 150
Menestrelles vs. menstreus, 28
Menotti, Gian Carlo, 261
Menzel, Adolph Friedrich, 102
Mercure galant (monthly), 62
Mesteschkin, Elfrieda Bos, 257, 272
Metastasio, Pietro, 80–81
Metropolitan Opera, New York, 123, 136, 203, 225, 255, 271, 273
Meyerwisch, Johanna, 172, 173
Michelangelo Buonarroti the Younger, 55, 60
Middle Ages, women in music, 3–33; in convents, xiv, 11–20; minstrels, xiii, 28, 29–30; troubadours, 21–27
Milde, Hans Feodor and Rose Agthé von, 162, 162n, 163
Milhaud, Darius, 235, 242–243
Mill, John Stuart, 280, 280n, 289
Minstrels, xiii, 28, 29–30
Mitropoulos, Dimitri, 262–263
Molza, Tarquinia, 50
Moore, Charles, 236
Morini, Erica, 270
Motet, op. 27 (Lutyens), 319
Motto, Marie, 313–314, 315
Movie orchestras, 251, 265
Mozart, Wolfgang Amadeus, 199, 218, 262, 284
Müller, Wilhelm, 114
Munich Conservatory, 219–222
Musical America, 255, 328
Musical Art Quartet, 270
Musical Association of London, 214
Music clubs, xv, 188–191, 324–325
Music criticism, 167, 330; sexual aesthetics in, 223–227
Music education of women, 282, 299–300, 325, 326–327; inequalities in, xiv–xv, 211–213, 215, 220–222, 282–286
Musicians Emergency Fund, 255

Musicians Symphony Orchestra, 256, 271

Musicians' Union, New York, 202, 204, 252, 258

Music patrons, xv, 188, 189, 231–237

Music schools, 80, 85, 87, 184, 186, 252. *See also* Conservatories

Music Study in Germany (Fay), 109

Napier, Mrs. William, 161

National Association for American Composers and Conductors, 308

National Association of Composers, U.S.A., 328

National Endowment for the Arts, 329

National Endowment for the Humanities, 331

National Organization for Women, 327

Neue Zeitschrift für Musik, 95n, 98n, 171n

New England Conservatory, 109, 122, 135, 219

New Jersey Symphony Orchestra, 272

New Orleans Symphony Orchestra, 272

New York Age, 135, 136

New York City, 194, 251, 264, 270–272; "Black Patti" in, 138–139; Civic Orchestra, 271; Musicians Symphony Orchestra, 256, 271; Musicians Union of, 202, 204, 252, 258; Vienna Damen Orchester in, 192–193; women music teachers in, 185–187. *See also* Carnegie Hall; Metropolitan Opera

New York Herald, 138

New York Philharmonic, 259–260, 261, 262, 273

New York School of serial composition, 331

New York Sun, 249

New York Times, The, 140, 193, 251

New York University, 259

New York Women's Chamber Orchestra, 271

New York Women's Symphony Orchestra, 252, 253, 254, 256–257, 271

Nichols, Caroline B., 194, 195–197, 253

Nordica, Lillian (L. Norton), 122–130; as Elsa in *Lohengrin*, 124; opera debut of, 128–129

Norman-Neruda, Wilma, 281

Norris, Wesley, 136

North, Gladys, 235

Norton, Amanda Allen, 122; letters of, 123, 125–130

Nunnery Officials and Procession, *12*

Oboe, 66, 68, 257, 263

Ochs, Siegfried, 170

O'Day, Caroline, 276

Ode to the Passions (Smith), 214

O'Neill, John, 122, 129

Opera, xii, 50, 55; female composers of, 55, 62–63, 64, 167–174, 225; viewed as "masculine" music, 223

Opera orchestras, 203–205, 251

Opera singers, xii, 55, 122; Anderson, 273; castrati, xii; Jones, the "Black Patti," 141–142; Nordica, 122–130

Orchestras: all-female, xiii–xiv, 66, *67*, 68, 192–197, 247–249, 251, 253, 254, 256–257, 260–264, 271–272; blind auditions, 329; chamber, 253, 271–272; concert vs. opera, 205; exclusion of women from, xiii, 192, 202–204, 205, 247, 251–252, 261, 263, 267, 270, 282–285, 291, 325, 328; mixed, xv, 200–201, 203–205, 247–248, 249–250, 251–252, 254, 257, 261, 264, 266, 272; opera, 203–205, 251. *See also* Symphony orchestras

Orchestrette of New York, 260–264; Petrides with, *260*

Ordo virtutum (Hildegard von Bingen), 14

Organ, 64, 66; women players, *32–33*

Orlando (Woolf), 284, 284n

Ormandy, Eugene, 262

Our Singing Country (Lomax), 310

Pactrez, Iris, 255

Paderewski, Ignace Jan, 304

Paine, John Knowles, 109

Pankhurst, Emmeline, 284, 284n

Paradis, Maria Theresia von, 85–86

Paris, 239, 307, 316; Concert Spirituel series, 85; Trocadero, 127
Paris Conservatory, 198, 199, 204, 239
Paris Opéra, 66, 129, 202, 204
Parnasse français (Tillet), 63
Passmore, Dorothy, 267n
Passmore, Mary, 267, 267n, 268
Patrons, xv, 188, 189, 231–237
Patti, Adelina, 135, 139
Percussion instruments, exclusion of women from, xiii
Pergolesi, Giovanni, 65
Peri, Jacopo, 55
Persinger, Louis, 260
Petrides, Frederique, 253, 259–264; with Orchestrette, 260; *Women in Music* newsletter, 247–248, 264
Peverara, Laura (La Turcha), 50, 52
Philadelphia Orchestra, 258n, 262
Philo, Judaeus, 3
Philomena (Chrétien de Troyes), 29
Pia, Lodovico, 37
Pianists, xv, 85, 88, 167; Carreño, 226–227; Epstein, 262; Fay, 109; Paradis, 85–86; Schumann, 91, 96, 98–103, 106–107, 114–115
Piano: a "feminine" instrument, xiii, 192; playing for social accomplishment, 73, 179–183
Piano concerto in A minor, op. 7 (Clara Schumann), 92, 96, 153
Piano concertos, Martinez, 80
Piano teachers, women as, 107, 110, 184. *See also* Teachers, women as
Piano trio in D minor, op. 11 (Hensel), 151
Piano trio in G minor, op. 17 (Clara Schumann), 154–155
Pieces for the Harpsichord (La Guerre), 64
Pierce, Melusina Fay, 109
Pierce, Will H., 136
Pistocchi, Francesco, 81n
Piston, Walter, 246
Pittsburgh Gazette Times, 194
Pittsfield, Mass., 232–235, 236, 237
Pius X, Pope, 283n
Pizzetti, Ildebrando, 233, 235
Plotnikoff, Eugene, 271

Pohl, Richard, 172–173
Polyphonic music, 43, 44n. *See also* Counterpoint
Pond, Major James B., 135, 140
Popular music, women composers, 206
Porcairages, Azlais de, 22, 24–26
Porpora, Nicola, 80
Porta, Costanzo, 47
Poulenc, Francis, 243
"Prayers of Steel" (Crawford-Seeger), 307
Pride and Prejudice (Austen), 73–74
Primo libro (Caccini), 55
Prince, Mrs. Sidney, 255–256
Prix de Rome, 239, 242, 324
Processions, women musicians in, 12, 29
Prova, 128, 128n
Providence Academy of Music, 135
Prüwer, Julius, 269
Psalms, 4, 4n, 9–10, 14
Psaltery, 19, 28–29
Publication of compositions, obstacles to, 167–168, 169–170, 288–289, 326; for women composers, 87–88, 143, 148–149, 165–166, 167–168, 294–295
Pugno, Raoul, 242, 242n
Putnam, Herbert, 236

Queen's Hall Orchestra, 283, 315, 315n

Radio, 237, 328; orchestras, 249, 251, 254, 268, 284
Randegger, Alberto, Sr., 125
Ravel, Maurice, 240, 242, 315
Rebec, 29
Recorder, *40*, 43
Recordings, 251, 325, 326, 328
Redeker, Louise, 157, 159, 164
Reinthaler, Karl, 105, 106
Reis, Claire, 297
Renaissance, women in music, xiii, 37–52; in convents, xiii, xiv, 43–49, 192; at court, 37–39
René II, Duke of Lorraine, court, *33*
Respighi, Ottorino, 235
Rheinberger, Joseph, 219, 220
Richter, Alfred, 268

Ridge String Quartet, 327

Rieter-Biedermann, J. Melchior, 106

Risegari, Laura, 68

Rissolty-Rossoltry (Crawford-Seeger), 309

Ritter, Fanny Raymond, 188–190

Robischeck, Robert, 269

Rochberg, George, 331

Roemaet-Rosanoff, Maria, 270

Romantic period, xiii, 192

Rome, 50, 234–235; American Academy, 235–236

Roosevelt, Eleanor, 273

Rossi, Francesca, 68

Roth Quartet, 235

Roussel, Albert, 235, 242

Royal College of Music, 282n, 314, 316

Royal Conservatory of Munich, 219–222

Rubinstein, Anton, 91, 163–164

Rübner, Cornelius, 171

Rudhyar, Dane, 304

Ruskin, John, 217

Sackville-West, Vita, 284, 284n

St. Basil, 6, 7

St. Cecilia, 199

St. Gregory of Nyssa, 6–10

St. Macrina, 6–7; funeral of, 8–10

Saint-Saëns, Camille, 224

St. Ursula, 14

Salieri, Antonio, 85

Sand, George, 194n

San Francisco Symphony Orchestra, 267n, 327

Sangiovanni, Antonio, 123, 126, 127, 128, 129

Santley, Charles, 164

San Vito, Convent of, Ferrara, 43–44; concert described, 44–49

Sappho with a Harp, Boccaccio manuscript, *31*

Sargent, John Singer, 158

Scheerer, Jeannette, 253, 265–272

Scheffel, Victor von, 168

Schindler, Kurt, 235

Schneider, Jean, 252, 272

Schoeffel, John B., 136

Schönberg, Arnold, 235, 304, 312

"Schön Rohtraut" (Smyth), 163, 163n

School of Musical Art, Jacksonville, Florida, 304

Schreurs, Joseph, 265–266

Schröter, Corona, 87, 88

Schubert, Franz, 159, 208

Schumann, Clara, 91–108, 153–155, 156–157; as composer, 92, 96, 153–155, 165; as concert pianist, 91, 96, 98–101, *102*, 103, 106–107, 114–115; correspondence with Brahms, 104–105, 106–107; diary, 101, 103, 105–106, 154–155; letters to Robert, 92–93, 94–97, 101, 153–154; as teacher, 107; mentioned, 109, 314

Schumann, Robert, 91, 97–107 *passim*, 153, 154, 155, 163, 208, 224; diary, 98–99, 154; illness and death, 99, 100; letter to Clara, 93–94

Schwabe, Mary, 156, 160–161

Scriabin, Alexander, 304

Seashore, Carl E., 297–302

Sebastiani, Fanny, 144

Seeger, Charles, 303, 305, 309–311

Selika, Maria, 141, 141n

Sense of Hearing, The (Bosse), *58*

Sermissy, Claudin de, 41

Sex discrimination, 278–296; in music education, xiv–xv, 211–213, 215, 220–222, 282–286; in musicians' employment, 251–252, 258, 261, 265, 267, 282–286; in teaching jobs, 186, 221, 325–326; unequal pay, 184, 202

Sexual aesthetics in criticism, 223–227

Sexual prejudice, xii–xv, 37, 157, 159–161, 186, 191, 217, 278–302; creative powers doubted, xiv, 153, 206–213, 242, 291–292, 297–302; against female composers, 87–88, 144, 146–147, 167–168, 170, 206–218, 223–226, 242, 278, 286–288, 291–296, 323–330; against female conductors, 253, 254, 256, 258; as source of doubt and timidity in women, xiv, 87, 153, 163, 166, 187, 213; in teacher acceptance, 186–187; against women in mixed orchestras, xiii, 192, 200–

Sexual prejudice (*cont.*)
201, 202–204, 205, 247, 251–252,
261, 263, 265, 267, 270, 282–285
Sexual stereotyping: of instruments,
xiii, 37, 39, 192, 200, 202–203, 204;
of music forms, 223; of women as
amateurs, 206, 323–324
Seyffardt, E. H., 171
Shapero, Harold, 246
Shawm, *33*
Signorini, Giovannibattista, 60
Silverstein, Ernest, 270
Simon, Paul, 171
Simrock (music publisher), 164
Singers: Anderson, 273–277; Candeille,
88; castrati, xii, 283n; concert, 123,
125, 135–141, 273; debuts, 128;
Favart, *82*; Jones ("Black Patti"),
135–142, 173; Martinez, 80–84;
Nordica, 122, 130; Schröter, 87;
professional, emergence of, 50–52;
secular, xii, xiv, xv, 50; women
barred in church, xii–xiii, 3, 6;
women in church choirs and
choruses, xii–xiii, 3–5. *See also*
Opera Singers
Slonimsky, Nicolas, 303
Smith, Alice-Mary, 214, 215
Smith, Fanny Morris, 188, 190–191
Smith, James R., 136
Smith, Julia, 260, 261
Smyth, Dame Ethel, 156–157, *158*,
159–166, 318–319; as composer, 156,
162–165, 206, 225–226; *Female
Pipings in Eden*, 278–296, 297;
Lieder und Balladen, 163n; *Der
Wald*, 225–226
Society of American Women
Composers, 247
Sonatas (La Guerre), 64
Song, The (Bartolozzi), 75
Songs, composed by women, 21–22, 54,
85, 87; Hensel, 143, 143n, 148, 151;
Hildegard von Bingen, 14, 16–17;
Lang, 165, 165n; Schumann (Clara),
153, 165; Smyth, 163, 163n, 165
Southeastern Composers' League, 327–
328
Sowerby, Leo, 235

Spencer, Penelope, 316
Spiering, Theodore, 267
Stavenhagen, Bernhard, 220–222
Stein, Gertrude, 243
Steinbach, Friz, 171
Stimmer, Tobias, 41
Stock, Frederick, 233–234, 266, 267,
268
Stockhausen, Julius, 106, 172
Stoeber, Emmeran, 234
Stoeckel, Carl and Ellen, 233–234
Stojowski, Sigismund, 254, 256
Stone, Ellen, 272
Stravinsky, Igor, 235, 242, 246, 304
Striggio, Alessandro, 52
Strinasacchi, Regina, 65, 199, 199n
String Quartet (1931, Crawford-
Seeger), 303, 307, 309, 310
Strings, 192, 199, 282, 284; large,
women excluded from, xiii, 192, 193
Strozzi, Barbara, xiv
Stuber, Ruth, 261
Suffrage movement, 278
Suite for Wind Quintet (Crawford-
Seeger), 308
Sully, Thomas, 76
Sundstrom, Ebba, 248–249
Swynnerton, Annie Louisa, 292
Symphonies: composed by women, 80,
223; viewed as "masculine" music,
223
Symphony for Organ and Orchestra
(Copland), 244–245
Symphony News, 328
Symphony orchestras, 247–250, 252;
all-female, 247–249, 251, 253, 254,
256–257, 260–264, 271; female
conductors, 253–264; mixed, 247–
250, 251, 254, 257, 261, 264, 266,
272; obstacles for women
instrumentalists, 251–252, 261, 263,
267, 270

Taffanel, Paul, 204
Tartini, Giuseppi, 199
Tausig, Carl, 109, 111, 112, 114, 120,
121
Teachers, women as, xv, 85, 167, 184–
187, 261; Boulanger, 239–246;

Teachers (*cont.*)
  census statistics, 184; college level,
    325–326; Crawford-Seeger, 304, 308;
    Etude article, 184, 184n, 185–187;
    Fay, 110, 184–187; job
    discrimination, 186, 221, 325–326;
    Martinez, 80; Paradis, 85; pay
    discrimination, 184, 186; Schumann,
    107; Van de Vate, 323
Te Deum (La Guerre), 64
Tennessee Concert Company, 136
Terry, Ellen, 286, 286n
Tertis, Lionel, 235
Thalberg, Sigismond, 91, 182
Therapeutae, 3–4
Thomas, Dylan, 319, 320
Thomas, Emma A., 184
Thomas, John Charles, 256
Thomas, Theodore, 232
Thompson, Randall, 235
Thomson, Virgil, 246
Three Songs for Contralto and
    Orchestra (Crawford-Seeger), 309
Thuile, Ludwig, 219
Thygeson, Charlotte, 151
Tillet, Titon du, 63
Timpani, 250, 257, 261, 272
Tomj, Francesca, 68
Toscanini, Arturo, 261, 276
Tovey, Donald, 296
Toye, Wendy, 318
Trobaritz vs. *trobador*, 21, 28
Trombone, 43, 48, 203, 257
Troubadours, women as, 21–27
Tuba, 250
Twelve-tone system (dodecaphony),
    246, 312, 331
Twentieth Century Composers
    (Ewen), 297

Upton, George, 206–210
Urbani, Orazio, 51
Urso, Camilla, 198
Urspruch, Anton, 116–117
U.S. Library of Congress, 236–237, 311

Valediction, op. 28 (Lutyens), 320
Van de Vate, Nancy, 323–332
Varèse, Edgard, 308, 331

Vaudeville, 135, 141–142, 194
Vaughan Williams, Ralph, 261
Vehanen, Kosti, 276, 276n
Venetian conservatories, xiii, 65–69,
    192, 199n
Vermeer, Johannes, 59
Vienna, 80, 85, 91, 104, 305
Vienna Damen Orchester, 192–193
Vierling, Georg, 170
Viol, xiii, *42*, 43, 199
Viola, 263; da gamba, *58*
Viole bastarde, 43
Violin, 43, 192; women excluded from,
    xiii, 192, 198–200, 204
Violinists, xiii, xiv, xv, 65, 68, 192, 198,
    257, 259, 262, 272, 281;
    concertmistresses, 263, 266, 272;
    Urso, 198; Urso quoted on, 198–201
Virginal, *57*, 199n
Vivaldi, Antonio, 65
Vocal music: earliest Christianity, 3–5,
    9–10; medieval convent, 11, 14, 17;
    Renaissance convent, 43; rise of
    professional singers, 50–52. *See also*
    Singers
Vogler, Abbé, 85
Voice teachers, women as, 80, 131, 184

Wagner, Cosima, 124, 175–178
Wagner, Richard, 101, 101n, 123, 175–
    176, 177n, 178, 208, 218, 219
Wald, Der (Smyth), 225–226
Walter-Chionanus, Iduna, 173
Walton, Blanche, 305
Wann, Lois, 257, 263
Washington, D.C., 237; Anderson
    concert, 273–274, 275–276; Grand
    Opera House, 142
Washington Post, 138
Watson, Muriel, 257
Webern, Anton, 246, 312
Weidig, Adolf, 304
Weingartner, Felix, 259
Wellesz, Egon, 305
Weston, Horace, 136
West Side Orchestral Concerts, 264
Whistler, Rex, 317, 318
White, Walter, 277

"Why No Great Women Composers?"
    (Seashore), 297–302
Wieck, Friedrich, 91, 97
Wielich, Ludwig, 255
Wilson, Billy, 136
Wilson, Ruth, 252
Wind instruments, 43, 47–48, 192,
    282; women excluded from, xiii, 192,
    203, 204
Wind Quintet, op. 45 (Lutyens), 320–
    321
"Woman composer question," xv, 206,
    214, 223, 278, 297; defense of
    women, 211–222; literary career
    analogy discounted, 287–289;
    Seashore on, 297–302; Smyth on,
    279–296; Upton on, 206–210
Woman in Music (Upton), 206–210
Woman Playing a Viol (Stimmer),
    42
Woman's Musical Congress (Chicago,
    1893), 198

"Woman Teacher in a Large City" (Fay,
    in Etude), 185–187
Woman with a Lute (Vermeer), 59
Woman with the Unicorn, The
    (tapestries), 32
Women in Music (newsletter), 247,
    247n, 248–250, 264
Women's movement, 278, 325, 327
Women's Symphony Orchestra of
    Chicago, 249
Women's Symphony Orchestra of New
    York, 252, 253, 254, 256–257, 271
Wood, Henry, 283, 283n, 315n
Woolf, Virginia, 278, 284n
World War II, 251, 252, 254, 263
WPA (Works Progress Administration),
    256, 270–271

Ysaÿe, Eugène, 259

Zelter, Carl Friedrich, 151
Zerr, Ferdinand, 173
Zimbalist, Efrem, 235

DATE DUE
